AMERICAN ICONOCLAST

The Life and Times of Eric Hoffer

Books by Tom Shachtman

Nonfiction

Airlift to America
Rumspringa: To Be or Not To Be Amish
Terrors and Marvels
Absolute Zero and the Conquest of Cold
"I Seek My Brethren"
Around the Block
The Most Beautiful Villages of New England
The Inarticulate Society
Skyscraper Dreams
Decade of Shocks, 1963-1974
The Phony War, 1939-1940
Edith and Woodrow
The Day America Crashed

For Children

Driftwhistler
Wavebender
Beachmaster
Video Power (with Harriet Shelare)
The President Builds A House
The Birdman of St. Petersburg
Parade!
America's Birthday
Growing Up Masai

AMERICAN ICONOCLAST
The Life and Times of Eric Hoffer

TOM SHACHTMAN

Hopewell Publications

Published by Hopewell
Publications, LLC
PO Box 11, Titusville, NJ
08560-0011 (609) 818-1049

info@HopePubs.com
www.HopePubs.com

Material from the unpublished papers of Eric Hoffer,
used by permission of Eric Osborne.

Excerpts from THE TRUE BELIEVER by Eric Hoffer
Copyright 1951 by Eric Hoffer, copyright renewed 1979.
Reprinted by permission of HarperCollins Publishers.

Material from Calvin Tomkins Papers, Museum of Modern Art,
used by permission of Calvin Tomkins.

Cover photo of Eric Hoffer in the old San Francisco Library by
George Knight and used by permission of the Bancroft Library.

International Standard Book Number: 9781933435381

Library of Congress Control Number: 2011933312

First Edition

Printed in the United States of America

To Lili Fabilli,
whose zeal for Eric Hoffer's work
and care for his papers
assured that his legacy would survive.

"Don't they know how badly we need
men of mystery—honorable mystery?"
-John Ford Noonan,
The Year Boston Won the Pennant.

Table of Contents

Prologue: The Interview 1
Chapter One: The Tourist 13
Chapter Two: Through Fiction to Non-Fiction 31
Chapter Three: On the Docks 50
Chapter Four: The True Believer 71
Chapter Five: Between Big Books 86
Chapter Six: Change and *The Ordeal of Change* 109
Chapter Seven: Becoming Controversial 127
Chapter Eight: "A Savage Heart" 149
Chapter Nine: Voice of the Silent Majority 172
Chapter Ten: "Old Age is Not a Rumor" 191
Epilogue: The Dedication 214
Source Notes 221
Selected Bibliography 231
Acknowledgements 234

Prologue:
The Interview

Late May of 1967 was a time of restlessness and social upheaval in the United States of America. The war in Vietnam, involving a half-million American troops, was at its height and in danger of being lost. Some Americans were chagrined at that possibility while others were not at all dismayed. Headlines in San Francisco's newspapers reported protests at the Berkeley campus of the University of California against continued American involvement in that war, and Reverend Martin Luther King Jr. had come out in favor of an American withdrawal. Inflation had begun to take its toll on the economy. There were occasional riots in the ghettoes of large cities, partly in reaction to African-American rage at chronic unemployment, partly at the slow pace of civil rights progress. In San Francisco's Haight-Ashbury district, the "summer of love" had begun, an anarchic cultural gathering of youth in rebellion whose rejection of traditional values was stoking the fires of an intergenerational clash.

A shooting war loomed in the Middle East and would likely draw the U.S. into it on the side of Israel and bring in the Soviet Union on the side of some Arab countries. Soviet aircraft tested American and British airspace while Red China threatened the integrity of America's ally, Taiwan. President Lyndon B. Johnson's popularity was declining so rapidly as to raise the question of whether he could be re-elected in 1968. Increasing polarization between blacks and whites, hawks and doves, haves and have-nots seemed to be leaching away American civilization and democracy.

It was also an era in which Americans turned increasingly to newspapers, magazines, and especially to television to keep track of

1

and attempt to understand the seismic changes going on around them.

For several months, emissaries from the leading network news organization, CBS News, had been shuttling from the East Coast to San Francisco to entreat Eric Hoffer, the aging dockworker, former agricultural migrant, Berkeley lecturer, and author of books on mass movements and drastic change, to grant a long interview to the network's chief commentator, Eric Sevareid. Hoffer, known as an astute social observer, was suddenly hot: in January he had been profiled in *The New Yorker*, and in March was the subject of a *Life* photo-essay, "Docker of Philosophy," articles themselves stimulated by a series of public television conversations with Hoffer conducted by James Day of KQED.

Perhaps a quarter-million people had seen Hoffer on the then-new public television network; a CBS prime-time interview could expose him to an audience a hundred times that size, 25 million people. The major networks' half-hour early evening newscasts had surpassed the daily newspapers as Americans' main source of information. Polls regularly chose *CBS Evening News* anchor Walter Cronkite as "the most trusted man in America," and ranked Sevareid not far behind.

Many writers might have jumped at the opportunity to voice their opinions to 25 million people, but CBS had not found it easy to secure Hoffer's agreement. The "longshoreman philosopher," as his publisher had christened him, still worked on the docks and adhered to an ascetic lifestyle, residing alone in a small, Spartan walk-up in a rooming-house atop one of Chinatown's steep hills, with no car, no telephone, and no television. Sometimes he did not even respond to telegrams delivered to his door.

Sevareid wanted to interview Hoffer because of his keen understandings of human behavior: Hoffer's insight that the ranks of Nazism and Communism were filled by similar "true believers" although they espoused opposite ideologies had become the way many Americans now understood America's World War II and Cold

War enemies. President Dwight Eisenhower had touted Hoffer's first and most successful book, *The True Believer*, as had philosopher Bertrand Russell. "Blind faith is to a considerable extent a substitute for the lost faith in ourselves; insatiable desire a substitute for hope; accumulation a substitute for growth; fervent hustling a substitute for purposeful action; and pride a substitute for unattainable self-respect," Hoffer had written in his second big book, *The Ordeal of Change*. In recent years, with clarity and wit Hoffer had gone beyond analysis of mass movements to dissect the roles of intellectuals and misfits in various historical eras, the fault-line in individuals' minds that gave rise both to creativity and to blind obedience, the relationship between human progress and nature, and other grand subjects, as well as addressing current issues such as student anti-war protests and civil rights aspirations. But although a half-million copies of his books had been sold, the vast majority of America's 200 million people still were not aware of Eric Hoffer.

Tens of millions of viewers recognized Eric Sevareid. The distinguished gray eminence of television commentators, with the air of a patrician intellectual, Sevareid had been broadcasting for CBS since the onset of World War II. Presidents, cabinet secretaries, and congressional leaders regularly telephoned him for advice. Urbane and sophisticated, he kept alive as a touchstone for his viewpoint his rural roots in Minnesota and the difficult Depression years. In 1967 he was interviewing his way through his dream list of thirteen important thinkers who were nonetheless "just below the surface of the news," as he put it in a memo to his bosses. That list featured his Washington inner-circle friends, senior political columnist Walter Lippmann and Supreme Court Justice William O. Douglas, as well as author Anne Morrow Lindbergh and Daniel Patrick Moynihan, creator of President Lyndon B. Johnson's war on poverty.

Sevareid also wanted to interview Hoffer because the liberal political agenda was in trouble and Hoffer could provide a workingman's perspective on that. Set in motion by President John F. Kennedy and expanded after his death by President Johnson, the

Sixties liberal agenda was faltering as the war in Vietnam leached away resources that had initially been destined for domestic initiatives. The Vietnam war also provided to the hoped-for interview a decidedly personal context: for decades Sevareid had supported liberal policies but was now beginning to question his support as he became disturbed by what seemed to be some bad consequences of liberality—student rebellion and African-American rage. Sevareid had once "shied away" from Hoffer's books, he later confessed, simply because he knew they had been favorites of President Eisenhower, whom Sevareid had disliked; but recently, upon reading the books the newsman had come to respect Hoffer's viewpoint and found himself in basic agreement with Hoffer's hardheaded opinions on student protesters and ghetto rioters—positions that other liberals decried as conservative bordering on reactionary.

Sevareid not only had to convince Hoffer to do the interview; he also had to sway his skeptical bosses at CBS News, who were concerned at what Hoffer might say. The newsman argued that although Hoffer's opinions might be unpalatable to liberal sensitivities, they would be provocative and not unreasonable. The executives allowed Sevareid to proceed with the filming, but reserved decision on airing the results.

To Hoffer, Sevareid was a representative of several groups in American society that he had often chastised as inimical to the country's well-being: the newsman was an intellectual who seemed to disdain the masses, a Washington insider, a member of the media elite, and a powerful man whose support for the war in Vietnam was wavering. He was not sure what would happen when, the night before the filming, the CBS crew picked him up at his Clay Street apartment and drove him downtown to the bar of the elegant Fairmont Hotel, where for the first time he met Sevareid.

Eric Hoffer was a nearly bald six-footer with a large head, burly physique, barrel chest, and scarred workmen's hands, wearing green work pants and shirt, boots, jacket, and a leather cap. Eric Sevareid— taller, slimmer, nearly ten years younger and with a full head of swept back silver-gray hair—wore tailored clothing. As they began to chat, Hoffer twisted his cap in his hands and, as Sevareid later put it, they quickly "got into an argument about the psychological reasons for the lack of organized charity and the cooperative instinct among Latin Americans." Hoffer considered backing out of the interview but, Sevareid later guessed, decided to continue because Hoffer sensed that "we were on the same wavelength" about many contemporary matters.

Beyond that, the men found a shared, bedrock experience: Sevareid, like Hoffer, had done itinerant labor and had ridden the rails in the 1930s, experiences the newsman had recalled in an auto-biography, *Not So Wild A Dream*, in words that echoed Hoffer's own about his migrant years. For instance, Sevareid wrote that he had worked and traveled alone, because "It is the right and only way. You do not have to talk if you would rather be silent; you can stop where you will, doze when you wish, and think your own thoughts. All that the eye sees, the mind registers, and the heart envelops is filtered by the screen of Yourself, untreated, unmodified by the conditioning presence of another human being." Other writers who had ridden the rails in those years had seen things differently, but Sevareid's sentiments matched Hoffer's. Both had come to understand the migrant life as what Sevareid called "a relentless, never-ending struggle" in which migrants traveled constantly but never arrived, fought and stole from one another, and were "happy only when the wheels [were] clicking under them, the telephone poles slipping by." Like Hoffer, Sevareid had mined for gold and judged the miners as natural artisans, able to handle anything and prevail over abysmal conditions: "None of them ever read a book of directions, studied a blueprint, or consulted with a colleague. They just did it ... and it stayed done."

Admirers of the independent spirit, of what the immigrants had accomplished, and of America's fights against Nazism and Commun-ism, Sevareid and Hoffer were deeply worried about the future prospects of the country they loved. "Within ten minutes of our first meeting," Sevareid would later recall, "I felt he knew me through and through and I had glimpsed his dimensions if not his complexities." Hoffer, for his part, after the introductory chat went to a pay telephone and called his closest friend, Lili Osborne, to say the Sevareid interview was going to go all right.

Next morning, Hoffer sat in an empty suite at the Fairmont, in front of two cameras and klieg lights, and for two-and-a-half hours answered Sevareid's questions. He did it so appealingly that at the conclusion of filming the camera crews applauded, which they seldom did for interviews; their enthusiasm was a reflection of Hoffer's directness in his answers as well as of his ability to speak for and to the average workingman and union member. Sevareid flew back to Washington, "absolutely certain that we had in those cans the greatest filmed monologue I had ever had anything to do with in all my years in television." Accordingly, he "did something I had never done before," threatened his CBS bosses with "all manner of dreadful things" should the Hoffer interview not air in prime time and at an hour's length. They agreed to the hour, and to a prime time broadcast in September.

In the several months before the broadcast, Hoffer reached the mandatory dockworker retirement age, and, as he later put it, was persuaded to accept a $297 a month union pension and to start receiving $135 a month from Social Security. As he told Mitchell Gordon of the *Wall Street Journal*, his retirement income was supplemented by royalties of $4,000 a year, and a $12,000 salary from Berkeley. He was making more money than about two-thirds of the households in the United States. Nonetheless, he continued to live in his $80 a month walk-up, and although no longer working on the docks, to frequently dream at night that he was unloading ships, and in the mornings to wake up exhausted.

With reporter Jack Fincher of the Los Angeles *Times*, that summer of 1967, Hoffer took his favorite stroll, through Golden Gate

Park, feeding Lifesavers to the squirrels, identifying plants with a botanist's surety, and consulting his gold fob pocket watch to give passersby the correct time:

> His blocky body seems to float on a torrent of words. The big, breathless, guttural voice—as unreconstructedly Teutonic as the first-generation immigrant he most resembles—rises and falls with the excitement of his ideas, ideas that erupt and flow from the surface of his volcanic mind like lava. Now and then, to stress a point, he tattoos the pavement with the tip of his walking stick. Occasionally he stops stock-still and, as passersby gape at such unseemly behavior, spreads his arms in a declamatory stance and bawls a particularly infectious thought against the cool morning air, or smacks one hammy palm with the other fist for emphasis. Rumbles of rough Jovian laughter issue often and easily from his heavy, windburned face.

In the interim between filming and broadcast, Sevareid published an article in *Look*, "Dissent or Destruction," that, his biographer would write, "summed up with extraordinary precision his interpretation of the Sixties." Sevareid quoted Hoffer in it and also paraphrased Hoffer sentiments about campus rebels and African-American rioters that Hoffer had voiced during their interview, labeling the protests and desecrations "outrageous and unsup-portable." As the newsman would later write to Hoffer, "I continue to plagiarize you in speeches and writings, to excellent effect."

On Tuesday evening, September 19, 1967, CBS News aired "The Passionate State of Mind." Sevareid's brief introduction set out Hoffer's background—blind for seven years as a child, never schooled, orphaned at 20, worked odd jobs, then as a migrant, and since early in World War II as a dockworker—and asked where his ideas came from.

I think some of the most original ideas I had, Mr. Sevareid, came to me while I was working. And you know, what a glorious feeling it is! Here you work, you talk with your partner ... and in the back of your head, you compose sentences. That's when life is glorious. ... And then you come home in the evening and before you even wash your hands, you sit down and it's all there, see. It's a glorious feeling.

Hoffer's tone was colloquial, and at a seeming distance from that of the writer whose thoughts were often described as icily precise and pessimistic. And Hoffer was a man continually at odds with himself, caught between what he had said was the "terrible gloom ... oozing out" of his notebooks, and his joyous, celebratory sentiments about America and the common man, which emerged more in his interviews than in his writing. Sevareid, perplexed and intrigued by this split, tried to approach it by characterizing *The True Believer* to Hoffer as "cold."

Although he rejected the "cold" label, Hoffer then recited the equally-frosty first sentence of one of his most celebrated articles, on brotherhood: "It is much easier to love humanity as a whole than to love one's neighbor." He confided that one day he had shared that first sentence with co-workers, who had mostly agreed with it and then had spent the rest of the day with him, hashing over the subject, "on the company's time, under the hook, on the stringer, see—and *they* wrote [the article]."

Hoffer insisted that he was the common man, the working stiff who did most of America's manual labor. "If you want to know how the average longshoreman's going to vote on anything, you ask me," Hoffer boasted, but added, "You could be a Michelangelo and still be a plain workingman. ... America is for the poor, Mr. Sevareid. Only we have a good time in this country. The rich have it much better elsewhere—better service, more deference."

Asked how America had changed in recent years, Hoffer launched into one of his set pieces, about how the reaction to the Soviet Union's launch of Sputnik in 1957 had rapidly tilted the country from business to intellectual pursuits, "And right now the kids on the campus at Berkeley would be ashamed to admit that their father was a businessman, just a grubbing businessman. They wouldn't be proud." At Berkeley, "two-bit intellectuals" spoke of the masses as "Pavlovian dogs," which "made me furious. What the hell do these people know about us?" Hoffer's anger at campus rebels and professors was part of his long battle against "intellectuals," who were "more corrupted by power than any other human type." The intellectual, he charged, "doesn't want [you] just to obey. He wants you to get down on the knees and praise the one who makes you love what you hate and hate what you love." "Soul-raping," Hoffer said.

Hoffer's solidly populist opinions reflected the sentiments of that majority of adult Americans who had never been to college and who resented being looked down upon. Few people in public life, however, dared, as Hoffer so often did, to insist that the prevailing wisdom was in error:

> The vigor of a society should be gauged by its ability to get along without outstanding leaders. When I said that at the University of Stanford, all the young intellectuals were up in arms. They ran after me after I finished and said, "Mr. Hoffer, the vigor of a society should be gauged by its ability to produce great leaders." And then I stood there and I said, "Brother, this is just what happened. Precisely a society that can get along without leaders is the one that's producing leaders."

He recalled another argument, with Southeast Asian reporters, about Communism: he had contended that in the U.S., those who had been Stalinists at age 20 would at 40 be successful real estate dealers, those who had been Trotskyites at 20 would be professors, while young Maoists would go "from brainwashing to laundry washing."

That *bon mot* was the cue for Sevareid to announce a commercial break.

When the program resumed, Hoffer unabashedly celebrated America, telling a favorite story, of how he and a hundred other Skid Row denizens had been randomly plucked from Los Angeles, dumped at a remote location in the San Bernardino Mountains, and given the task of building an intricate section of a highway. With few drawings and little supervision, they had managed to organize themselves, marshal the various skills necessary, and get the job done in "the most glorious experience I ever had." Had the group needed to, he asserted, they could have written a Constitution, and he went on to insist that you could pick anyone on a street and make him president and he would turn out to be a Harry Truman. That was partly why, Hoffer announced, he was very high on President Lyndon Johnson—by then further down in the polls because of frustration with the war in Vietnam and lack of progress on domestic problems. Hoffer said he had worked with Johnsons all his life, that "he is one of us," and predicted that Johnson would be the "foremost president of the twentieth century." He lauded other "everymen" who turned out much better than expected—Earl Warren, the machine politician who became a great chief justice of the Supreme Court, and Warren's colleague Hugo Black, a member of the Ku Klux Klan early in life who became a great champion of equal justice under the law. He dismissed the assassinated President Kennedy as a patrician more European than American in his orientation, and Governor Ronald Reagan as a "B" movie actor attempting to turn California into a "B" picture state. He lauded the Jews for birthing the basic ideas of Western civilization, and Israel for persevering against enormous odds. "Don't forget, Mr. Sevareid, the whole of the Occident was involved with the persecution, the humiliation, and the final annihilation of six million Jews."

Hoffer's arms pumped, his fists thumped into one another, he leaned far forward and far back in his chair, his voice rose to a roar and subsided to a whisper as he poured out pithy sayings on hot-button subjects. The student protesters had no clue to what this country was about; "the Negro Revolution" was "a fraud," with "phony" leaders such as Black Panther Stokely Carmichael, whose preaching was nothing but "sound."

"But its race hatred they're preaching," Sevareid put in.

"Yeah, but who's going to listen to them? Maybe a few. ... They do not realize that it's the long-term projects, things that you go about patiently and quietly, that will achieve results." Hoffer had much more to say on the subject of "the Negro Revolution," and some of it had been branded racist, so in this interview he did not elaborate. Rather, he told another totemic story, of picking peas and not having enough at the end of an exhausting day to make his quota, and of an unknown man who emptied his hat-full of peas into Eric's hamper and told him he now owed a hat-full of peas to someone else.

"This is a fantastic country and a good country for me," he summed up. "Death will come tomorrow. Death will come this evening. It matters not, see. I have no grievance against anybody. I always got more than I deserved."

Critics were unanimous in their praise. Reese Cleghorn in the Atlanta *Constitution* pronounced Hoffer "a refreshing change on television" because "he is real. He is not playing a game or defying conventions: his whole life is a defiance of conventions, chief among them ... that a man 'rises' in status and outer trappings as he becomes more 'successful.'" Jack Gould in *The New York Times* called the interview "fascinating [and] pragmatic. ... Amid the predictable humbug of so many authorities, [Hoffer's] down-to-earth philosophy was a provocative breeze that challenged the thinking mind." *Seattle Times* reviewer Rick Du Brow celebrated "a man full of happy angers and gorgeously confident bluster [who] denies he is an intellectual." Viewer response astonished Sevareid: the switchboards at every CBS affiliate around the country "lit up like a Christmas tree" with calls wanting the program rebroadcast or seeking information on Hoffer's books, calls echoed by the next day's flood of telegrams and viewer mail. CBS executives scrambled to schedule a rebroadcast for November, and planned an annual chat with Hoffer. Sevareid would write that in the broadcast, Hoffer "made millions of confused and troubled Americans feel very much better about their country [by showing] them again the old truths about America and why they remain alive and valid."

Hoffer's books soon sold out from every bookstore. Offers for him began arriving: to write a syndicated weekly newspaper column, to speak at various universities, to visit the White House for a private chat with President Johnson. Learning of these, Sevareid telephoned Hoffer at the Berkeley office on the one afternoon a week that he could be found there, and proclaimed his fear of having ruined Hoffer's life because now Hoffer was "a celebrity, God help him."

Eric Hoffer roared with laughter. "Ruin my life, at the age of sixty-five? Nobody could ruin my life!"

Chapter One:
The Tourist

Eric Hoffer's persona as the enigmatic, reclusive, working-class philosopher was an inextricable part of his appeal as a writer. Critical to an understanding of that identity, as well as of his writings, are the four decades of life prior to his settling in San Francisco to work on the docks and write *The True Believer*. Material about those days is sparse. Hoffer offered a few memories in his posthumously published, autobiographical *Truth Imagined,* and before that he broached the subject in various interviews. But the fragments that he provided seem almost deliberately chosen as building blocks of a legend: of the part feral child, part *tabula rasa*, part blind seer, never schooled, orphaned and expelled into the world to experience the hardships and rapture that brought him to his unique viewpoint and insights.

Factual ambiguities begin with Hoffer's date and place of birth; as Lili Osborne would later exclaim, "Who knows when and where Eric was born!" In Hoffer's public utterances, and in his notebooks—most of the notebooks, not intended for publication—Hoffer asserted repeatedly that he was born in the Bronx on July 25, 1902. But twenty years after his death, when his papers were opened for research, they revealed a 1937 application to enter the Social Security system that listed his year of birth as 1898. He later told Lili that he preferred a twentieth-century birth, perhaps in the belief that in the 1950s, to have been born in the nineteenth-century made him appear too old.

The New York City and Ellis Island archives have yielded neither records of his birth nor arrival dates for Knut Hoffer, his wife Elsa, née Goebel, or the woman who would serve as Eric's nurse, Martha Bauer, whose origin Hoffer sometimes gave as the Hoffers' Alsatian village (whose name he claimed not to know), sometimes as Bavaria. It is unclear whether any of them ever became naturalized citizens.

In 1941, in a letter written in response to queries from his literary discoverer, Margaret Anderson, Hoffer began his controlled revelations about his early years; in that letter and ever afterwards, Hoffer cited his birth date as 1902. By 1941 he had come to prefer the 1902 date, in part because since the longshoremen's union mandated retirement from the docks at age 65, an 1898 birth date would have forced him to retire earlier than he might want to. The deception may have begun earlier, perhaps as early as Hoffer's childhood. His family might have claimed a 1902 birth date and a New York birthplace because of the rampant anti-German bias in the U. S. during The Great War, which caused many German immigrants to alter names and backgrounds. An 1898 birth date would have raised the possibility that Eric had been born in Alsace, which was then part of the German Empire, prior to his parents' emigration.

Knut Hoffer was a cabinet-maker, and in the Bronx became a member of a *Bruderschaft*, probably the German Cabinet Makers Union of New York City, a group distinct from the larger carpenters and joiners unions. Hoffer remembered him as "methodical [and] serious," "a silent, slight man with red hair" who never laughed, "a small town atheist ... to whom the Bible was a dirty word." But, Hoffer later opined, in small-town Germany to be an atheist was to be an intellectual, which was perhaps why his father had in the apartment a library of 100 books in German and English, including encyclopedias, dictionaries, and tomes on philosophy, botany, and travel. Hoffer remembered himself at five as "brilliant," able to read the books' titles and to sort them by content. He also inculcated his father's obvious reverence for books.

He recalled his mother, a housewife, as small and continually afraid. What her fears were, he did not say. When he was five, she fell down an entire flight of stairs while carrying him, and his life irrevocably changed. Mother and son were both injured seriously— throughout the rest of his life, Hoffer bore a deep cleft in his forehead

—and "almost immediately my eyes began to go bad." He was seven when his mother died, likely from the repercussions of the fall, and he became blind, a condition accompanied by searing headaches and the loss of short-term memory. Medical research suggests that loss of short-term memory often accompanies the onset of blindness, but also that short-term memory usually recovers after a while, as Hoffer's did.

During his diminished-memory period, Knut referred to him as an "idiot child," an epithet Hoffer never forgot. Even so, Knut took his blind son at age nine to a performance of Beethoven's Ninth Symphony. His father knew the music, Hoffer recalled, and was "strangely excited." When the orchestra reached the third movement, touted by Knut as "sublime," his father gripped his arm "and I soared as if I had wings." Later, whenever Hoffer felt "alone and abandoned," he hummed the third movement.

During his years of blindness—variously reported later as seven, eight, or nine years—Martha Bauer cared for him with great affection. The two were continually together, even sleeping in the same bed. In Hoffer's final notebook, penned in 1981-82, a year before his death, he confessed to thinking of her quite a bit in his old age, and recalled her aroma and her "large body [with] small hard breasts with nipples like fingers," a body she had encouraged him to touch. Had there been sexual congress between the mature woman and the under-aged Eric Hoffer? He never said.

So that Eric would become fluent in English, she learned the language and spoke and read to him only in English; but she also sang, German ditties from her "hellion" days in company of students and military men, that Hoffer would later repeat with gusto. He told James D. Koerner, author of *Hoffer's America*, a 1973 book of conversations with him, that during his blind years, "I was talking my head off all the time, making up stories and asking questions. ... I must have been a very interesting child. ... Martha remembered everything I said, and she brought me up to think anything I said was worth remembering." Her care was "as though I had returned to the womb," and as an adult he would unfavorably compare other women's attentions to "Martha's total awareness of me." Elsewhere, however, he characterized his childhood as a "nightmare" whose shadow never left him.

Another mystery is why Hoffer never attended school. He contended it was due to his blindness during his prime school years; but New York had schools for the blind, and tuition for poor students was underwritten by wealthy donors. In later life Hoffer attributed his "savage heart" to never having been "gentled by school marms." Lili Osborne also suggested that an important element in his personality derived from his lack of religious education or orientation; he was, she observed, as "free" of religion as he was of formal education. The absence of schooling and religion combined to render him unso-cialized in a society that stressed the ability to get along with, learn from, and have intimate relationships with other people.

At fifteen, Hoffer gradually regained his sight, though precisely how he did so, and over what length of time, is not known. Many people who later knew him observed that in adulthood Hoffer retained several behavioral traits of long-blind people: closing his eyes and sitting motionless and lost in thought, minutely organizing possessions so they could be found by touch, and sleeping only in places from which he could see the stars and the night sky. His greatest fear was that his sight would again vanish.

In the years immediately after recovering his sight Hoffer did not seek the cause of his blindness, but did later acknowledge that it must have had a mental component, although he was reluctant to guess what that might have been. It likely involved his granting himself forgiveness for his mother's death. What he was quite certain of, however, was that the return of his sight brought to a close his period of "enormous intimacy" with Martha. Shortly, she decamped for Germany. Did she do so as a spurned lover? Or simply because she was no longer needed in the Hoffer household and wanted to return to her roots? Hoffer did not speculate; rather, he later chastised himself for being callous when she left.

He wrote that the loss of Martha was "mitigated by a plunge into reading." Earlier, she had drummed into him that the Hoffers and Goebels were short-lived, and that he would likely die by the age of forty; he would claim that this idea freed him—since he would die soon, it did not matter what he might accomplish, and so he became a "tourist" in life. To be a tourist is not merely to be acutely aware of passing through places without the intent to remain; it is also to exist without seeking to develop close relationships with anyone met along the way.

In a second-hand bookstore not far from the Bronx apartment, Hoffer reported, his teenaged eye was caught by *The Idiot*, a novel by Fyodor Dostoevsky. Although written in 1869, *The Idiot* had only been translated, by Constance Garnett, in 1913. He bought the book and began to read. *The Idiot* became so important to him that he reread it, annually, during the remainder of his life.

Prince Lev Nikolayevich Myshkin, the "idiot" of Dostoevsky's novel, is not an imbecile but an outsider, an anti-hero, a detached but perceptive observer who refuses until the last moments of the novel to initiate action. "They found it impossible to educate me systematically because of my illness," Myshkin tells his companions. He speaks of being awakened from mental darkness, of his chaste happiness with a woman from his past, of money as the most ambiguous of values. Hoffer's life as a child and teenager echoed those points. In *Truth Imagined*, Hoffer wrote that Dostoevsky's characters were, in general,

> ... strange, extravagant beings ... made up of the essence of humanness, and however eccentric and outlandish, they are close to our heart and understanding. There is a grandeur in Dostoevsky's extremes. They give us a glimpse of an explosive at the core of the human entity, of the enormous distance between the unknown depths and the familiar surface of our daily existence.

In 1919, closer to the time that Hoffer first read *The Idiot,* the German novelist Herman Hesse wrote an essay about the novel. He wondered,

> Why does no one understand [the idiot], even though almost all love him in some fashion, almost everyone finds his gentleness sympathetic, indeed often exemplary? What distinguishes him, the man of magic, from the others, the ordinary people? Why are they right in rejecting him? Why must they do it, inevitably? ... It is because the "idiot's" way of thinking is different from that of the others. ... This gentle "idiot" completely denies the life, the way of thought and feeling, the world and the reality of other people. His reality is something quite different from theirs.

Hesse's queries were also Hoffer's, and Hesse's conclusions about Myshkin were similar to Hoffer's own as he faced the world upon emerging from blindness. Hoffer might also have agreed with the contentions of a latter-day reader, novelist A. S Byatt, who suggests, "The Prince is in some absolute moral world in which he can instinctively gauge who is being cruel to whom, who is in need, and who is tormenting or tormented. ... He isn't really in [the other characters'] world, and neither they nor he quite understands this."

"The chief thing is that [all the other people in the novel] need him," Dostoevsky wrote in his notebook about Prince Myshkin; "In his most *tragic,* most *personal* moments," the notebook continues, "the Prince is concerned with solving general problems." Throughout Hoffer's adulthood he sought to create a similar persona for himself: the detached and brilliant outsider who addresses his mind to the larger problems of mankind. A first instance of his detachment was not being terribly affected when Martha left him and returned to Germany after the War. Later he would tell Koerner of having insomnia and nightmares that he traced to guilt over his callous indifference to Martha after he regained his sight.

The next seminal event in Hoffer's life was his moving to California. This occurred after Knut's death in 1920—at an age that Hoffer put sometimes at 42, at other times just short of 50—and after living with his aunt for a year. In 1941 he told Anderson that he had "scraped together a few dollars" to reach California. To later interviewers he provided a slightly different story: the Bruderschaft asked what he wanted to do, perhaps to arrange an apprenticeship, which they owed him as the son of a member, and when he wanted to go to California, gave him $300 and a one-way train ticket. He set out for a climate that he expected to be sunnier and more hospitable, a paradise where you could sleep out of doors at night and, if hungry, "you just leaned over the road somewhere and picked an orange."

In April 1922, Hoffer rented an inexpensive room near the Los Angeles public library and settled down to read, giving no thought to earning a living or what might happen once his money ran out (or his sight vanished again). "Reading was my only occupation and pastime. I was not a normal American youth—no friends, no games, no interest in machines, no plans and ambitions, no sense of money, no grasp of the practical."

Many of the dozen tales Hoffer later offered about Los Angeles in the 1920s and as a migrant in the 1930s were Aesopian. His years "on the bum and ... one step ahead of hunger," he wrote in a late diary, became "a procession of stories in which truth and fiction are so interwoven that I cannot tell them apart." This was a confession, of sorts, that he had exaggerated, combined, and otherwise shaped the experiences of those years "into fabulous hilarious tales."

One such Aesopian tale was a yarn about not wanting to be a salesman but being maneuvered into selling oranges door-to-door, and discovering to his horror not only that he was very good at it but also able to lie easily to customers—and, therefore, had been impelled to quit at day's end to preserve his integrity and poverty. Another Hoffer tale told of being picked up as a hitchhiker by a German-speaking driver who quoted a Goethe adage about a mental quality that, if lost, meant doom. The driver cited it as *hoffen*—

hope—but Hoffer, researching it in the Anaheim library, found that Goethe had used the word *mut*—courage. The morals of Hoffer's story, which he told repeatedly, were that hope was an illusion, and that courage rather than hope was the essential quality.

That, too, was the lesson he took from his blindness, which, in a complex way, had prepared him for life as a day laborer and migrant worker, tough existences in which self-reliance and courage were vital in helping him to maintain his dignity, identity, and curiosity about the world.

In Los Angeles, when Hoffer had exhausted the money he had brought with him, along with that obtained from selling his books and clothes, he went hungry. Starving, he discovered that he was able to push hunger's pangs out of consciousness as he became fascinated with pigeons courting and mating in a pet-store window. Emboldened by this evidence that ideas could trump physical sensations, he walked into an eatery, offered to wash dishes in exchange for a meal, and began a hand-to-mouth existence as a day laborer. His encounters with starvation and homelessness birthed what he recalled as his first insight: "Men are truly alive only when they suffer." As he would write to Anderson in 1941, "My mind was wholly preoccupied with the question of suffering. ... The extreme sensitivity to outside impressions during the days of hunger, and the fact that even the most trivial of these impressions burnt themselves into my mind suggested that suffering is a sensitizer. I also developed a contempt for imagination. There was no substitute for experience." He would retain only one Dostoevskyan, romantic sentence from his early scribbling: "It is through our bleeding wounds that we grow into the tree of life."

Hoffer's reports of his reactions to his Bronx childhood and his early days in Los Angeles were relatively straightforward. But on Los Angeles' Skid Row, his environment changed, and his reactions to it— at least, from his 1941 retelling of it onward—were more analytic and much less ordinary. When he began to think in aphoristic terms, he quipped that he had gone directly from the nursery to the gutter. The statement seemed to have contained no trace of suffering or self-pity;

it was exaggerated, as with much of the Hoffer discourse, but it was nonetheless descriptive. But the ways in which he construed his time in the gutter were anything but descriptive. For instance, where-as most people precipitated into a hand-to-mouth existence claimed resulting stress and fright, Hoffer characterized existence in the gutter as emancipation. Once he had understood how to find enough day-labor work to survive, and how to deal with bouts of privation, he wrote, he was able to configure a life dependent upon no one other than himself for his livelihood, and in which he had no obligation to care for others nor even to better his own lot, and, therefore, was more able to subsume his existence to reading, learning, and thinking.

This was when Hoffer, along with a hundred other Skid Row men, was swept up and taken into the San Bernardino mountains to build part of a road; this seminal collaborative experience certified in him not only his own competence as a laborer but also his confidence in the abilities of his fellow social cast-offs, whom he thereafter envisioned less as downtrodden victims of society than as bearers of unrealized potential. This romanticized assessment fed into Hoffer's burgeoning sense that everyone had the capacity to endure, but that a survival-of-the-fittest ethos controlled who among them would prevail.

Between 1922 and 1930 Hoffer worked mostly at odd jobs, interspersed with two lengthy stints with single employers, each for two years. The second was with a Jewish-named owner of a pipeyard; to Anderson, Hoffer dubbed him Farbstein but in *Truth Imagined* called him Shapiro. The pipeyard provided Hoffer with stability that he was not sure he wanted, as well as introducing him to the works of French religious historian Ernest Renan. Farbstein owned Renan's five-volume *History of the People of Israel Till the Time of King David*, published in the 1890s and forgotten by the 1920s. Renan would influence Hoffer's thoughts about mass movements and their fanatical components, and motivate Hoffer for the first time to read the Old Testament.

The Pentateuch was a revelation, though not a religious one. "What grandeur, vividness, and freshness of perception," he later wrote, using terms he also employed to praise Dostoevsky. The Old Testament's pages reflected "a primitive mentality, naïve, clumsy, yet bold and all-embracing," and a Jewish people that imagined a lone God who made mankind in His image—a God that gave man the tasks of acting as He had, to create, to subdue nature, to build cities, and to live fully in the present.

Hoffer was impressed that ancient Jews had been so involved with the present that they did not bother to imagine a hereafter; and that several thousand years since the Old Testament had been written, its characters still came across as very "real": King David, a "fascinating mixture of manliness and feminine waywardness ... equally ready with his sword, his harp, and his tears"; King Saul, "a big clumsy plowman forced into kingship, weighed down by his melancholy"; Esau, a "red-haired roughneck [with] a ravenous appetite" that caused him to sell his soul for a meal. Hoffer thrilled to the Old Testament's acceptance of the bad with the good, with "no touching-up to lend a false appearance of perfection." "The imagined truth" of the Jews, Hoffer concluded, was "more alive, more true, than truth." After his reading of the Old Testament, Hoffer later confided, there was "probably a faint echo of the Bible" in all that he wrote, even as he continued to be profoundly agnostic and unaffiliated with organized religion.

In 1930, when Farbstein died, Hoffer felt liberated from a job that had been too safe. Thus far, in his assessment, he had been liberated from schooling by his blindness, liberated from New York by moving to California, liberated by being in the gutter, and now from a confining job. He also applied the term to what he told Anderson happened to him next. "I had some money saved up," he recalled, "and I decided to spend a few months of leisure, and then [to] commit suicide. Just like that!" The months with no work obligations enabled him to go around "probing and sniffing everything within reach," learning to experience the world. He tried to commit suicide by means of a poison, but threw it up before it had damaged him; and then he walked it off, and felt, once again, liberated, perhaps from the obligation to rid himself of life. He became ready for a rebirth that would center upon his increasing appreciation of the world.

He began that phase by walking out of town. Since there were fewer day-labor jobs to be had in Los Angeles—the Great Depression had begun, though he and the country had not yet begun to label it as such—Hoffer walked and hitched south to San Diego, in search of a job, any job. On reaching that city, he soon found work as an itinerant agricultural hand.

"**Crops changed and scenery; but not the routine,** the strangeness, and the harassment. Grapes, olives, oranges, grapefruit, peas, spinach, beet-thinning, fruit-thinning, cherries, apricots, haying, peaches, apples, pears, hops, prunes, and then tomatoes again. ... Always on the run; always with the crowd; and always utterly alone."

The paragraph is from an unpublished Hoffer novel. All novel writing is to some degree autobiographical, but stories specifically based on the writer's experience are likely to be even more so, as this one was. In later years, Hoffer would be of two minds about his migrant decade. He would write that he enjoyed the physically arduous and relatively mindless migrant labor, but he would also claim just the opposite, recalling to a 1969 diary that sometimes when working in the fields he had "cried for weeks."

According to a letter that he wrote to Anderson while he was still a migrant, he had continued such work out of a belief that "to retain my tolerance, love of humanity and the awareness of the marvel of life on this earth ... I must lead an insecure existence, to guard against fear, self-righteousness, and wishful thinking, for these blunt the mind and the senses."

But every so often, during his migrant years, he settled in a town, took a room halfway between the library and the brothel, and frequented both depots. When his money ran out, he hit the road again.

Making money as a migrant became more difficult in the fall of 1931, when the competition for migrant jobs intensified as the tide of would-be migrants (and their families) arriving in the state of California swelled to 1,200 - 1,500 a day; competition became even more cut-throat in 1934, when the Dustbowl brought in more Okies and Arkies. Farm owners used the excess of available labor to suppress wages. The glut of migrants also occasioned the enactment of vagrancy laws; migrants were then frequently and arbitrarily arrested, convicted, and loaned to farmers to work off their fines.

Okies, Arkies, and other migrants from the east changed the character of the throngs who were "on the bum" and looking for work, making them into a mass migration—what Hoffer would later label a "mass vagabondage"—that included many people who had previously held steady jobs, or owned farms and small businesses, or had been to college.

Hoffer acknowledged this new type of migrant in a story that survives in a notebook from the 1930s. During that decade he wrote many such notebooks; most are undated but contain quotations from then-current magazines that places the majority of them in the second half of the decade, although some contain fiction that reflects earlier Hoffer experiences. These include the one quoted above, and a shorter story that began, "They were waiting for the Tracy-bound freight out of Stockton ... about twenty of them, greasy with dirt. ... A dazed-looking young man of about 25 sat slightly apart from the crowd. He had no food or sleep for two days and his mind was whirling and twisting like a flea-bitten dog, scratching up now one memory, now another."

The ability to write is comprised of equal measures of one's powers of observation, unique viewpoint, word-sense, and curiosity. Hoffer's notebooks show these qualities developing. In 1941 he would tell Anderson that when his mind was working at its best, "You seem to catch glimpses of the inner working of things." Such a realization of the world behind and beyond the obvious could have led him either to poetry or to deep analytic prose. Those tough times made novelists of many aspiring writers, but Hoffer's experience as a long-term migrant worker—not just for a season, but for years on end—pushed him toward analysis rather than toward extended description.

From his experiences, as well, he developed his viewpoint, a version of "social Darwinism." Irreligious from childhood, and immersed in a lifestyle that reinforced at every turn the need for toughness and resilience, Hoffer evolved the view that human existence was governed, if at all, by the imperative to survive, and the concurrent belief that only the fittest survived. It was a viewpoint that he could not have embraced had he not attempted suicide and been lucky enough not only to come out of it relatively unscathed, but with the presence of mind to learn from the experience.

His version of social Darwinism also differs from that of others in that Hoffer's never included the usual, concomitant belief that an individual either fights his or her way up the ladder of success or is consigned to failure. Hoffer's experience in work gave the lie to the idea that ambition was part of human natural selection. His smart and resourceful attributes had now and then become obvious to various employers—such as Farbstein—and they had offered him managerial opportunities. He had steadfastly rejected them, unwilling to leave the working class for the dubious perquisites of the supervisory or academic class.

His refusal to rise was tied to his belief that survival was a relative concept, not an absolute, and that its degrees must be measured not alone by toting up of material comforts, but must also factor in the individual's assessment of himself—his own view of what he needed and wanted.

Furthermore, although Hoffer was not an entrepreneur, he had the entrepreneur's insistence that society was under no obligation to help any individual survive and, similarly, that governments ought not to do any large-scale tinkering with society. All that was required by individuals to prevail in a reasonable society, Hoffer was certain, was good availability of opportunities.

In Depression America, Hoffer's view of what government should refrain from doing was a contrarian one; jobs were so scarce that even many so-called rugged individualists conceded that the government must step in, at least temporarily, to assist people in finding work, food, and shelter. Hoffer disagreed because his experience taught him otherwise: despite coming from a terrible background, from "the gutter" in Los Angeles, and completely without schooling, he had always managed to find paying work— therefore, he concluded, everyone else could and should be able to bootstrap themselves to survival without governmental assistance, interference, or coddling.

Decades later, Lili Osborne would contend that Hoffer's worldview—the belief in social Darwinism, the fierce insistence on the need to make one's own way, the lack of feelings of entitlement, and the expectation that one's efforts would result in adequate rewards and would not be unreasonably swept away—were common to that of a first-generation immigrant to the United States, rather than to that of a native-born American. Yet Hoffer thought of himself as quintessentially American.

Hoffer's self-confidence, at around age 30, allowed him to give greater rein to his burgeoning curiosity. In 1932, while working in a seedling nursery, he was seized with a wonder as to why plants grew upwards above the ground, while below the ground their roots grew downward. So urgent was this sensation that he immediately quit his job and moved to a nearby larger city to peruse books about botany. The reference volumes he found were so tough to digest that he had to take precise notes and to also acquire knowledge of organic and inorganic chemistry to properly understand them.

The botany served him well during an episode whose exact date, circumstances, and validity have been difficult to verify. During the winters, when there was no harvesting to be done, Hoffer took other positions, including that of a busboy near the university at Berkeley. There, because he could read German and speak English, an agriculture professor hired him to translate some German texts.

Several versions of this episode exist, in *Truth Imagined*, in an unpublished novel, and in other fragments. The gist of the tale was that Hoffer became involved in the research of the "head of the citrus department," Professor Andrew T. Stilton, to find a way to reduce the terrible effects of chlorosis, a recently discovered blight on lime trees. Hoffer figured out that the disease was not, as had been theorized, a matter of the lime trees not getting enough water, but rather involved the chemical make-up of the fertilizer. Substituting a calcium nitrate for the sodium nitrate fertilizer prevented the lime trees from absorbing minute traces of boron, an action that prevented the blight. In the unpublished novel, Hoffer devoted twenty pages to this episode, and had Stilton awarding to his main character, George Anseley, co-authorship of the scientific article on chlorosis. In *Truth Imagined*, Hoffer credited himself with the discovery.

There is no record of a Hoffer, a Stilton, or an Anseley ever publishing an article about a treatment for chlorosis, but a professional journal article in 1928 on the subject of citrus chlorosis asserted that the general problem of chlorosis and its causes had been known in the nineteenth century, and that the citrus chlorosis instance had recently been solved. "Citrus chlorosis as affected by irrigation and fertilizer treatments," by P. A. Burgess and G. G. Pohlman, is in issue 124 of the *Arizona Agricultural Experiment Station Bulletin*. However, in Hoffer's later writings he routinely used metaphors and similes from chemistry and botany, and conveyed more knowledge about those subjects than could have been gained from cursory acquaintance. His chemistry, he later said, derived from his study of Joel Hildebrand's *Principles of Chemistry*. James Koerner, who later did the book of conversations with him, was a program officer at the Alfred P. Sloan Foundation, which underwrote scientific research; Koerner knew Hildebrand, and in the 1970s introduced him to Hoffer, who, Koerner reported, was "giddy as a child" to meet him and inscribed a book to "my hero, Joel Hildebrand."

During one of the town-based intervals in his migrant period, Hoffer became fascinated at a college by a very beautiful young woman, possibly a law student. She wanted him to remain with her and to pursue the academic career that she knew he was capable of achieving, but he ran away from that vocational possibility and from her; and ever after, as he wrote in *Truth Imagined*, he regretted losing her. Was he describing a particular woman? Probably, since Hoffer's attempts to tell her story troubled him for decades. He began to do so in his novel, "Four Years in Young Hank's Life," and later on he returned to it and sought help from friends in telling the story, which appeared in truncated form in the *Truth Imagined*. In that book, he stated that not staying with "Helen" was a major regret of his life.

In early 1934, destitute and starving in San Diego, Hoffer helped unload a truck full of cabbages, and then had cadged a ride to the El Centro area, where he expected to be able to obtain migrant work. There was a glut of migrants in the vicinity, and the authorities swept many of them up and insisted they become residents of a federal camp, rather than remaining on the loose—for their own good, and for that of the surrounding farms and towns.

Being in the El Centro camp, one of a dozen recently taken over by the federal government to deal with the large number of migrants, was a life-altering experience for Hoffer. His month-long stay there was so different from all that he had previously known, that for the first time, he was moved to write in order to record and preserve his impressions of the place.

On first glance, the camp seemed to him a cross between a factory and a prison—the sort of places he loathed, though he had never been a factory hand or a prisoner—but the inside of the El Centro camp was better: clean sleeping facilities, a kitchen capable of making hundreds of meals at a time, indoor toilets, a well-equipped recreation hall, and a small library. "It was my first experience of life in close contact with a crowd. To eat, sleep, and spend the greater part of the day with two hundred strange human beings was something new."

The camp residents—strangers—were an odd bunch of misfits, drunks, the lamed and the physically and mentally maimed. They made him realize two things: that in some ways he was quite different from them, for instance in being quite hale, intelligent, and sane, but conversely, that he too was a misfit, an outcast, an "undesirable." Prior to landing in the camp he had considered himself "just a human being—neither good nor bad, and on the whole, harmless." But during the month's stay in the El Centro facility, he realized he belonged to a "certain type of humanity, the undesirables."

A second jarring thought came to him when he and many others were taken from the camp into the desert. On the ride, he remembered having passed through many other beautiful and productive towns carved out of the desert, and was moved. As he later recalled for an interviewer, the thought was, "If we—I mean, the transient workers—were to transform this [desert] into orchard, we would be pioneers. And it hit me, it was just like a revelation: the connection between tramps and pioneers. I started to ask myself, who were those pioneers?"

Very quickly he decided that the pioneers had not been the best or the fittest of men but, rather, "men who went broke or never amounted to much; men who though possessed of abilities were too impulsive to stand the daily grind; men who were the slaves of their appetites—drunkards, gamblers, and women chasers; outcasts." In other words, men very much like the migrants in El Centro.

Hoffer recognized his new hypothesis as more than a good joke. He thought it was an important point, something to ponder and expand upon. He may also have seen in it the seeds of a fundamental adjustment to his social-Darwinist philosophy. But how could he ascertain whether it was true? Only by collecting facts and testing the hypothesis. And so, he went around the camp doing something else that he had never done before: assess his surroundings with notebook in hand. He tallied up how many people were impaired and how many were "apparently normal." There were more in the first category than in the second; taking this as affirmation of his hypothesis and excited by the idea, he resolved to do further research among the old-timers in other cities, and to write an article. In a flash—he would come to trust such flashes—he also envisioned the grand intellectual territory that could be explored by pursuing this notion of undesirables as the vanguard of history.

Unable while at the camp to complete his research, he diverted his energies into skits. In *Truth Imagined* he remembered them as an entire musical comedy that he wrote and performed, although he told *The New Yorker's* Calvin Tomkins that he had left El Centro without seeing the play mounted. One particular skit, which he later termed "hilarious," survived in an early notebook.

A satire, it purported to be an article about the "outbreak of an epidemic" of a newly named disease, "*transitis ergophoby*," an article written by the German physician who discovered the disease's symptoms. These were a "stiffening of the muscles" that caused sufferers to avoid work, to "make as few movements as possible in the conveyance of food to the mouth"—Hoffer provided a diagram—and to learn how to "mooch." The underlying cause was "*bacillus transiti sacharivori*," a yen for sugar; and so, "By offering transients large quantities of candies ... we could actually persuade them to dig a sewer-ditch." The German doctor quoted a patient who claimed that in the transient camp, "I eat all I want, sleep all I want, read all I want, and not a single <u>worry</u>." The cure for the patient's disease, the doctor confessed, had yet to be found.

"My stay in a transient camp, " Hoffer told Anderson in 1941, "gave direction to my thinking; induced me to go on scribbling and under conditions which are far from optimal for composition; and it supplied me with a working hypothesis to integrate much that I see, experience, and read." He would reach that integration gradually, working things out in short stories and novels until he was ready to state them in essays. And in the process, he would transform himself from a man who saw himself as "on the whole, harmless," to one who would be characterized as "dangerous" because of the provocative and challenging nature of what he wrote and said.

Chapter Two:
Through Fiction to Non-Fiction

Leaving the El Centro camp, the fruit-tramp Eric Hoffer had little intention of changing his "tourist" attitude toward life. In the next half-dozen years, without altering how he earned money to stay alive, and without shedding the belief that he would die within the decade, he would reinvent himself. Seizing on the idea of tramps as pioneers, he pursued it with an iron will and an unconstrained intellect, and it led him to become a social critic, interpreter of history, and deep biographer of mass movements and their leaders and followers.

This rather complete transformation began during the winter of 1936. In some years, when fruit-and-vegetable harvesting seasons came to a close, Hoffer placer-mined for gold in the Sierra Nevada Mountains, and occasionally became snowbound. Anticipating that for 1936, he purchased the thickest book he could find. During that winter he read the 1,200 pages of Michel de Montaigne's *Essays* twice and skimmed them a third time, discovering in them the master to unlock his potential and influence his writing style and attitude toward life. Placer mining during the day—a process that required lots of patience to find flakes of value—and reading through the many pages of Montaigne at night and when snowbound, which also needed patience in sifting for value, Hoffer found the seed of many later thoughts on which he would later expound. As had Blaise Pascal, Aldous Huxley, Ralph Waldo Emerson, and Virginia Woolf, Hoffer was amazed to find himself limned in this sixteenth century French aristocrat's self-examinations. "He knew my innermost thoughts," Hoffer wrote. For Montaigne, too, detested schoolteachers, was intensely patriotic, wanted no undue ties to employers, dealt stoically with chronic illness, kept his women at a distance, and yielded to desires more than he wanted to but was tough on his other foibles. Montaigne's assertion that one's preferences, prejudices, and patterns—many of which Hoffer shared—were fundamental to one's ability to make good social analyses, encouraged Hoffer to feel the same way, to utilize rather than mask his biases in his writings.

The aristocrat wrote of being aware of the need to moderate only one particular tendency, that "combative arrogance which has complete faith and trust in itself: it is a mortal enemy of finding out the truth." But he admitted that he enjoyed "bashing people's ears with that word which runs so strongly counter to their minds." Montaigne asserted that the only thing a writer of non-fiction could and should do was to seek truth and virtue, goals he judged as not fully attainable but as approachable through rigorous endeavor; and he identified as "one of virtue's main gifts ... a contempt for death, which is the means of furnishing our life with easy tranquility, of giving us a pure and friendly taste for it; without it, every other pleasure is snuffed out." Montaigne tried to live as the Stoics and Epicureans had, maintaining emotional distance in order to assay life with proper detachment. Compiling his book took twenty years, and Montaigne continued to revise and refine its thoughts in later editions. As Sarah Bakewell writes in a recent biography, Montaigne's essays

> ... rarely offer to explain or teach anything. Montaigne presents himself as someone who jotted down whatever was going through his mind when he picked up his pen [and] used these experiences as the basis for asking himself questions, above all the big question that fascinated him as it did many of his contemporaries. ... "How to live?" This is not the same as the ethical question, "How *should* one live?" ... [He] was less interested in what people ought to do than in what they actually did [and was] curious about all human lives, past and present. He wondered constantly about the emotions and motives behind what people did.

Bakewell identified twenty Montaigne answers to the question of "how to live." Many of them, such as "Don't worry about death," "Pay attention," "Read a lot, forget most of what you read, and be slow-witted," "Live temperately," "Reflect on everything; regret nothing," and others, could as well be said of Hoffer's answers to that big question.

Huxley described the three "poles"—three axes—on which Montaigne's essays hinged: "from the personal to the universal, from the abstract back to the concrete, from the objective datum to the inner experience." Charles A. Foster, a modern critic, added,

> In their freshness of sudden discovery, the essays everywhere give the impression that they must have grown spontaneously ... surprising him quite as much as they surprise us. But the sentences are too precise, beautiful, and economical ... and the way in which topic yields effortlessly to topic cannot be always accidental. Montaigne must have written at the crossroads of the conscious and the unconscious where creativity and criticism joined forces in a single effort so artfully that we cannot tell what is spontaneous from what is created consciously to seem spontaneous.

At Hoffer's best, his essays resemble Montaigne's in these specific ways. Hoffer would always assert that from Montaigne he learned the value of a good sentence. But what the attentive student learns from such a master far exceeds grammar and technique.

Hoffer's encounters with the El Centro camp and with Montaigne, in the 1934-36 period, shifted his life dramatically toward keener observation, more reflective thought, and greater articulation of ideas.

Notable thinkers throughout history have taught themselves to write; few had such a complete absence of schooling as Hoffer, and almost none has left us such a step-by-step record of their progress toward proficiency as is detailed in the several dozen surviving Hoffer notebooks from the 1930s. These reveal the steady increases in his vocabulary, in the sophistication and range of his word usage, in the accuracy of his images, in the aptness of his metaphors, and the sharpness of his social criticism. The growth came through his attempts at fiction and non-fiction, accompanied in the "daybooks" by quotations from books that he read, all inscribed in a legible, highly controlled hand.

Evidence that the notebooks were central to Hoffer is that they survived at all. Wherever he moved in the 1930s, as a member of the "mass vagabondage," he carried them with him. For the most part they did not contain observations of migrant life; rather, they were his attempts to transmute his experience into a few poems and ditties, stories, paragraph-length essays, and letters.

An early "daybook," with a severely worn, orange-brown cover, began with notes for a short story, "Male & Female."

> Phil Hartwick. A lecher, a miser, persued by the devil. The wife—Verona or ideal woman. Their meeting on a Sunday. Phil's first impression. A lunch of fresh green grapes—firm with the bloom on juicy fragrant. Talk in the room. Her eternal virginity! Passion. Second meeting. Verona's love. Phil's inherent loneliness, awkward, his ignorance of the technique of companionship .... Having visions of her former customers in Ideal rooms including drunks, old tobacco chewers, their fingers .... How he was never affected by the obesity the ugliness the bestial feature of the women he had been with so why should Veronas mind be leprous with memories? The conflict [leads to] a beating. Scene of separation. Getting from Verona. Phil's sensation of freedom of being again by himself.

On the notebook's next page were phrases to remember and perhaps to use in this narrative, some culled from his reading, others that Hoffer generated:

The <u>web</u> and <u>woof</u> of domestic and citizen life.

A quickness to see reason and to <u>trounce</u> nonsense.

His sensitive, highly trained fingers—even wore a pigtail.

railroad yard. They hop down when their accustomed props are removed.

surreptitious done by stalk or fraud

he screwed his head around for a look at the talker

I felt completely <u>cut out</u>.

The <u>methodical confidence</u> of a man born to action.

Universal dominion.

To <u>eshew</u> evil.

If I am proven true let there be acclaim!

To come quick and crowding = to come thick one after the other.

A soul that knows how to <u>stretch</u> and to slacken itself.

Perhaps because he knew German compound nouns, he was astonished, he confided to a second notebook, that *human being* was two words but *footnote* was one, and reminded himself to write *coffee grounds* and *high pitched*. He set out to discover how to spell *foregoing*, and to decide when to use *obstacle to* rather than *obstacle against*. Also in that notebook, a fragment of a second fictional story:

I dreamed that I was standing in front of Benton's house. My hands were in my pockets and the pockets were full of silver. ...I was Old Man Benton. I clucked my tongue and hummed "money like dirt." And there stood Mrs. Benton with outstretched hand demanding money. I said: "Look at your bosom woman! It is full of it. Here let me feel." She unbuttoned her blouse and dropped her skirt and stood there in a one-piece bathing suit. She was Fred[erica]. And there beside her was Ansley. They were looking into each other's eyes in rapt absorption. ... I was barefoot and my feet were stuck in the mud. I reached out for the banister to pull myself out of the mould. ... Ansley's words came in a whisper designed to emphasize It must be a dream. ... Perhaps we died and met again. Was he reciting poetry? I pulled with all my might to get nearer and in the effort I awoke. Ansley's voice was in my ears. This was no dream. He was talking to Fred.

"The Transformation of George Ansley" and "Male & Female" are two of ten story titles that Hoffer listed in another notebook. "Chance & Mr. Kunze," a third story, provides a glimpse of the future essayist in a tale of a wealthy man who chose to work as a migrant to better experience life. Kunze was asked, in front of an audience of migrants, whether money was the root of all evil:

His words came readily. He spoke in fun, yet gave expression to a train of thought he had formulated years ago. "Gentlemen! I take issue with the trite saying that money is the root of all evil. I have no veneration for popular judgment. If the voice of the people is the voice of God, then the bleating of sheep is heavenly music. ... In a society without money there will be no place not only for the idle rich, but also for you and your like—the idle poor. There will be no freedom of choice and no independence. Money is an indispensable step in the development of humanity."

In this passage, Hoffer's social Darwinism is confabulated with the idea of capitalism as a natural outgrowth of human endeavor, leading to social progress.

These were ideas that he would later develop in his essays. Other notebooks contain the germs of thoughts on his touchstone subjects, for instance, on the nature of education. In a fourth notebook, Hoffer mused about the ancient Greek notion that children should only be taught while standing, to avoid them learning useless stuff, and wondered how a future society should be arranged so that "pleasant gifted children would retain [their] vigor and alertness ... into maturity." He imagined a setting: "They will be surrounded on every hand with monuments and magnificent achievements buildings dams aqueducts bridges roads and organizations of large scale production of all of these achieved by their immediate ancestors. ... They will be as familiar with all manner of activity as the child of a nomad Arab tribe with horses and camels."

Hoffer now felt ready to draft "Tramps and Pioneers."

A thirty-page essay in the manner of Montaigne, it began in a light tone, a political observation that there was no "ailment of the social body" that the Roosevelt Administration "has not noticed, probed, and finally proscribed for" in "haphazard, half-hearted, wasteful" experiments. His pages would report on "one attempted cure" of a "minor ailment," the problem of transients. Prior to being called "transients," he noted for the reader, he and his kind had been known as "hoboes, bums, tramps, stiffs, and floaters"—in other words, as "a menace."

The "main attraction" for Hoffer in writing this article, he later noted, "lay in the methodical intellectual effort itself: To fashion a theory, explore its ramifications, test it by facts, adjust and perfect it."

But that was a later comment, written perhaps to justify his having consented to elimination from later drafts of many personal revelations present in the original—for example, the back-story of his desperate existence on the streets of San Diego, having spent his last penny in a peanut slot-machine but unable to beg, "for I had lived so long alone that even a casual contact with strangers was a muddled affair of stuttering and confusion," which made impossible the thought of "soliciting favors, under fear of rebuff."

In the article's first draft, Hoffer recounted his experiences in the camp, his revelation and research, his later talking to old-timers, his chasing down information in libraries about the pioneers of Australia and South Africa, and the extending of his line of thought to larger compasses. By 1937-38, when he wrote that draft, he had reached a startling, world-encompassing extrapolation of his initial thoughts, a classification of mass movements into four distinct categories: "mass migrations to new lands, mass vagabondage, Religious movements and Revolutions." While these types seemingly differed "in their purposes, practices, and particularly the spirit which animates them ... they draw their adherents from essentially the same reservoir of humanity." A dozen years later, this concept would be the basis for *The True Believer*.

His formulation owed as much to the era as it did to Hoffer's powers of thought, for the 1930s were the heyday of mass movements, the coming to full flower of National Socialism under Hitler and Mussolini, of Soviet Communism under Stalin, of religious revival movements such as that led by Aimee Semple McPherson, as well as of the mass migration of the unemployed in which Hoffer himself took part. Keenly aware of this linkage, Hoffer felt fortunate to be addressing his thoughts to a matter so central to the current phase of history.

But he put little research into choosing a magazine that might publish his article before selecting the small-circulation monthly *Common Ground* because he thought it covered immigrants and immigration, and perhaps because its editor, Louis Adamic, a Yugoslavian immigrant, wrote non-fiction books about immigrants and the labor movement in the U.S. Hoffer sent to the magazine a handwritten copy of "Tramps" from a return address of a post office box.

Luck now intervened. Adamic had no use for the article—it was outside of the magazine's purview, the problems and joys of new immigrants assimilating—but its interesting observations and the details of its author's biography attracted the attention of associate editor Margaret Anderson, a single woman in her forties who had spent her working life in the New York literary community. She returned the rejected manuscript to Hoffer, who thought that was the end of it; but she kept a copy and showed it to acquaintances, among them Eugene Saxon of Harper & Brothers, a well-regarded editor of Aldous Huxley, J. B. Priestly, James Thurber, and E. B. White. Based on Saxon's enthusiasm, she sent Hoffer a Christmas card. He answered. Shortly, she conveyed to him Saxon's suggestion that Hoffer write more about himself. Emboldened, Hoffer revised, focused, shortened the article, and prepared to send it in once again.

"It was a real pleasure to read your fine letter," he wrote in his notebook. "You are the first editor I have come in touch with, and if the others are half as fine as you then they must be a good lot. I hate therefore to disappoint with regards to the personal story you suggested. You expected perhaps the story of a regenerated life, of a tramp turned pioneer. But nothing like it happened. I'm still a fruit-tramp and shall probably be one to the end." Her letter made him realize, he said, that his initial submission was an impulse to "show off my wares," so in the new version he was sticking closer to his subject. He enclosed the redraft and another piece, "Oranges," which the notebook described as a set of speeches that he shouted as he walked along the open road. He told Anderson,

> The whole performance though somewhat absurd and affected suited my inclinations. The feeling now and then of being a stranger in this world is ... strongest in me when I'm hungry or tired. But even when nothing is wrong with me I sometimes ... look at the world around me as if I saw it for the first time. After six or eight weeks in the fields picking fruit or in the hills chopping wood a return to town and civilization is like the opening act in a fairy-tale.

> Yet the strangeness which assails the senses is not confusing for as in a fairy tale, it seems to emanate from a simple symmetrical pattern. You seem to catch glimpses of the inner working of things.

Hoffer's description of his path to insights greatly resembled what T. S. Eliot had described in 1922 as the regular procedure of the mind of the poet. The writing process, Eliot wrote, "may partly or exclusively operate upon the experience of the man himself; but, the more perfect the artist, the more completely separate in him will be the man who suffers and the mind which creates; the more perfectly will the mind digest and transmute the passions which are its material." It was this sense of Hoffer-the-artist to which Anderson had responded. He closed his letter to her with an apology: it was the first letter he had written in fifteen years, so if it struck "a discordant note," she must "ascribe it to ignorance rather than to conceit."

Hoffer worked on his fiction as he awaited her response, perhaps believing that his fiction might meet Anderson's request for more "personal" tales. He paid typists to prepare fresh versions of two autobiographical pieces on which he had been working for half-a-dozen years: "Four Years in Young Hank's Life," 170 pages in type-script, and "Chance and Mr. Kunze," 83 pages in typescript.

Neither ever saw publication, but they merit an extended discussion for what they reveal of Hoffer's developing sense as a writer.

Hank, the putative author of "Four Years," informed readers that as a teenager he had run away after his father's death and become a migrant worker, and that that story would demonstrate the truth of Montaigne's statement, "We ask most when we bring least ... and knowing ourselves for what we are, we are less confident and more distrustful; nothing can assure us of being beloved."

After this framing device, the narrative began. Six months or so after Hank's initiation as a migrant, in a cotton field he met George Anseley and restarted his life. He attached himself to this handsome, enigmatic, inscrutable man, some years his senior, "with a tenacity and lack of shame which were alien to my character," and then drifted with Anseley from harvest to harvest. "When I lived by myself I was constantly in the shadow of a vague fear. Restlessness trailed behind me like a petulant child, wanting this or that, pulling me into stores, theatres, gambling joints and pool halls, and there was no end to it until the money was gone."

With Anseley, he banked $100—a lot for a migrant—and encountered individuals who in the novel made statements that Hoffer would later use in *The True Believer*. A stoic Dutch migrant maintained, "Were it not for the habit of nursing the sick we would have had no culture and no civilization. The sensitizing effect of pain is the source of all inquiry and refinement. The incurable invalid was the first cook, doctor, teacher, poet, historian, etc." Hank pronounced himself as impressed by the Dutchman's low opinion of imagination as "the most feeble, the most anemic, the most shallow of all human faculties."

These observations were meant to be provocative and contrary to the prevailing wisdom. They document that from Hoffer's earliest writing, he was a determined provocateur. In his fiction he also regularly assigned facets of his own personality to several different characters in a story—to Hank and to Anseley, and also to young Frederica and Anna, two women whom Anseley befriended during a winter when he and Hank worked as busboys at a northern California university. To Hank, Fred was gorgeous, Anna, "blotched, flabby, sallow," and while he predictably developed a crush on Fred, who was not super-smart but whose "brown eyes were so deep that my heart pounded with fear," he was also attracted, despite revulsion, to the brainier and tougher Anna. Should he rob a bank and in the process kill a man, he would tell Anna but not Fred, because "Life to [Anna] was not a breathtaking mystery, but rather a clearly drawn diagram; confusing perhaps at a glance, but perfectly simple once you got the hang of the pattern."

The four became involved with the students, and Hank discovered that collegians' as well as field workers' conversation was "about Roosevelt, Hitler, Mussolini, strikes and revolutions. ... Their opinions were such as one finds in liberal newspapers and magazines." Anseley pilloried the failings of Russian communes, which the students had celebrated, arguing, "When we engage in a selfless undertaking, we not only rid ourselves of private greed but also of private responsibility. By keeping clear of the guilt of selfishness, we deprive our conscience of its voice and we commit atrocities and enormities without shuddering and without fear of remorse. ... A sense of duty and of devotion to an ideal often produces a brand of selflessness more ruthless and harmful than extreme selfishness." Hoffer would enshrine that sentiment in *The True Believer*.

Hoffer's inexperience as a fictional storyteller came through as he related the contrived back-story of the novel: Fred had been involved in Baltimore with a young man who, because of devotion to honor, felt the need to marry a dying woman. Abandoned, Fred had fled to Chicago, worked in a pickle factory, and met Anna on a picket line. Finely matched, they came to California to hone their skills toward eventually setting up shop as power brokers between workers, unions, business, and government. Anseley's past, also mysterious, remained hidden until he became an aide to Professor Stilton on the chlorosis of lime trees, and his actions revealed him as a patrician with a master's degree from Cornell. Several other Hoffer stories also contained a well-bred man who fled from his natural surroundings and found solace as a migrant.

In this novel, after a time at the college, to escape the women's machinations that would keep them there as academics, Anseley and Hank eventually escaped to the road. They met old comrades, to whom Hoffer gave capsule versions of stories in his list of ten, which they told around campfires. The women chased after them and there was a reunion of the four at which the big secret was finally revealed: Anseley was the beau who had broken Fred's heart in Baltimore; they had been trying to get back together, but Fred's very deep tie to

Anna was in the way. Anseley and Hank promised to return to the college and the girls in the fall to take up new lives, but until then they wanted to be on the road. As they jumped from one boxcar to another, Anseley was killed and Hank was maimed. Coming to in a hospital, he found Fred caring for him, as he recuperated, with greater affection than he expected.

Fred hinted that Hank could join the university and that the two of them could become more deeply involved. Hank mused, "it occurred to me that any woman, beautiful or not, who told me that she loved me—was lying. And if, as she kissed me, she closed her eyes in ecstasy—she was pretending; and her passionate trembling and panting was play-acting. I felt that words had no meaning; that they were hatched at the root of the tongue."

Anna protested that the three of them could craft a satisfactory arrangement in which Hank and Fred could marry and have a blissful sexual relationship, but he dismissed this possibility by observing that between Anna and Fred there was no space for a man. Furthermore, "I am at heart a tramp. ... I can't harness myself to a life of effort and achievement. ... What I need is hunger, toil, and fear, and a marriage to Fred would [not produce] the kind of suffering that steels a man's soul." The ladies, agreeing that his destiny lay elsewhere, and without "bitterness or resentment," packed him off to his mother.

In "Chance and Mr. Kunze," Hoffer painted characters even more reflective of his already-crystallized philosophic and political views of life, the social contract, capitalism, the need for iconoclasm, and the varieties of survival. This time the narrator was unnamed, an observer in the story but not a participant.

He informed readers that Arthur Kunze was born poor but by the end of the Great War had become rich from holdings in lumber, hardware, and oil, and by the 1930s was tall, stoop-shouldered, with an awkward gait, "a clumsy, troubled creature" whose appearance belied his retired-multimillionaire status. An actual Arthur Kunze was integral to the settling of a copper-mining area near Death Valley in the 1900s; it is unclear whether Hoffer's Mr. Kunze reflects that historical one—or, for that matter, whether Hoffer's views on such matters as post-war inflation in Germany, the utility of money, and distaste for Roosevelt's social reforms had been influenced by the real Kunze or by some other person with the attributes he gave to his fictional Kunze.

In the 1920s, according to Hoffer's narrator, Kunze became alarmed at the hyperinflation in Germany. "In Mr. Kunze's eyes this was the greatest catastrophe the world had seen, greater than the world war and the Bolshevik revolution. There was a sickening ugliness, and something akin to obscenity about this vanishing of money into thin air. It was as if the world had been stripped, and its nakedness exposed to lecherous eyes." Losing faith in money, Kunze wrote a letter to the San Francisco *Gazette* decrying the situation and predictting chaos: The Allies' currencies would follow the Deutschmark into oblivion, and "Religion will be dead, science will languish, and trade will be no more." To protect himself from such an eventuality, Kunze created near Fortuna a ranch and hired hands to grow their own food and cotton, cut their own timber, and sew their own clothes—a model by which independent farmers could survive the coming cataclysm.

Hoffer was always intrigued by the role chance played in human affairs, deeming it the equal to leadership and ideas in the determining of events. Chance operated in Kunze's life when, of all the migrants he had hired to bring in his cotton crop, he chose to ask questions of the scrawny Al Ebby, known for "his fluency, his remarkable memory for the printed word, and his prowess in drinking." Kunze asked Ebby whether there was a future in the migrant life.

"Future? A man must have a very high opinion of himself to worry about his future," Ebby said, and claimed to be a man who, rather, took his fears to his heart, became comfortable with them, and had thus overcome them. Once men knew such concepts like hunger, destitution, and filth as real things from having dealt with them, Ebby told Kunze, "they lose their awe. ... Man is the toughest animal on earth [because] he has an enormous capacity of getting used to things."

Hoffer would repeat Ebby's notions about no feeling for the future, overcoming fears, and man being the toughest thing on earth in his 1941 letters to Margaret Anderson, in the philosophy that underlay *The True Believer*, and in his 1968 remarks when he began his newspaper columns.

As Ebby left the Kunze ranch for the next reaping job, he accused Kunze of not appreciating the marvelous world that the senses brought to us. Kunze, struck by this remark, plunged into research, advertising for information about migrants, looking into their prevailing wages and conditions, undertaking labor on his own farm to whip his body into shape in preparation for spending time as a migrant, the better to understand how individuals could become independent. Shortly, in "an amazing passage from pretense to genuineness," Kunze became an actual migrant worker. "He felt exhilarated, unencumbered, and ridiculously young. His senses were like kids at a fair." He wondered, "How could even the most successful revolution improve on these tilled lands, the beautiful towns, and the network of highways and railroads?" On the bum, Kunze ran into two antagonists. "Mike Antonovich the Slovenian peasant," unlettered but street-smart, was able to sense that Kunze used to be a boss; and Kunze also bumped into Ebby, who professed not to recognize him. The three spent a gala night out together—during which Ebby pushed Kunze into the diatribe about money not being the root of all evil—and Kunze was so impressed with Mike and Ebby that he revealed his identity to them and hired them to manage his ranch.

The three agreed that the Depression would have a salutary effect on Americans who had grown "soft" during the "get rich quick" 1920s. "It had sapped their courage and powers of endurance. Their helplessness in the face of adversity showed a dangerous lowering of resilience and versatility which once characterized the average American." In a speech to a farmers' association, Kunze said similar things, and then expanded them in letters to the Fortuna newspaper. In one, he advised parents to send their children out to seek work in the fields: "A man who knows that he can go out any time and earn three dollars a day picking cotton, thinning beets, or driving a tractor, will take no lip from any boss. His heart will always be light with confidence and independence."

Now Hoffer threw in a plot point: an aspiring Fortuna area politico, Tommy Hughes, read Kunze's reactionary letters-to-the-editor and decided to make political hay out of them when the right opportunity arose.

Chance made a second appearance, in the form of Kunze happening upon one-year-old child Davy, who captured his heart on a Fortuna street, as did Davy's mother, Lizzy—"deformed" by a childhood accident, she informed him. She had been considered ugly but a man had married her for her money; they moved west when he lost his job, and he then vanished, but at least she had Davy. At Kunze's invitation, mother and child moved to the ranch.

The errant spouse, Roger, soon arrived. Handsome, personable, and currently working for an oil company, Roger took on Kunze, calling him the local worst enemy of the New Deal, and labeling his notions of self-help as "tommyrot." Roger railed that in 1934, "when the government wants to give us back some of our stolen money, the Wall Street pick-pockets raise a hue and cry against the dole and its pauperizing influence." He threatened that a day of reckoning would come. He also confessed to being bitter that Kunze was stealing Lizzy away, because he had always loved her. He had rid himself of their money so they could start a new life: "I felt a surge, a pleasure, when I visualized myself working hard all day long, earning a living for Lizzy and myself."

"A man with grief in his heart is genuine and precious," Kunze responded, and offered Roger a big job. Roger refused; he must "mend" on his own, make enough money for his family to be comfortable, but until then he would permit Lizzy and Davy to stay with Kunze.

Hoffer's plot then galloped to a conclusion. Roger went to Hollywood, almost overnight became a movie star, and let politico Tommy Hughes convince him to sue to retrieve Lizzy and Davy. Kunze fled from Hughes' publicity barrage, along with Lizzy and Davy, and could not be found. In the 1936 campaign, Hughes lambasted Kunze as a reactionary reflecting the "selfishness and ruthlessness of the Republican Party," and won election.

In 1939, Lizzy returned to Fortuna with Kunze's body; he had died in upstate New York, where they had hidden out. The will contained surprises: while the bulk of Kunze's $10 million went to Lizzy, he bequeathed $100,000 each to Ebby, Mike, and Roger, $500,000 to Fortuna for fostering creative work among the middle-aged and older, and $40,000 to enable the town to establish a camp for hoboes.

Hoffer's developing skills as a fictional storyteller might have eventually led him to write novels similar to those of Ayn Rand, featuring dialogues about lofty topics and demonstrating moral and political principles.

Needing to decide whether to pursue or abandon fiction, in the fall of 1939, as World War II began in Europe, Hoffer sought Margaret Anderson's judgment. Drafts of his letters contained hints of courtship in which Hoffer painted himself as a highly moral rebel: "I don't know what you cultured people talk about when you get together. But out here while we work in the fields ride the freight and congregate transit camps, we have now and during the past years our chief topic, If those bastards get away with it," which he then revised as, "The people I meet while traveling on freight trains working in the fields or in WPA projects have the implications of a Hitler victory as their chief topic." He reported feeling "stale," exhausted after finishing with apricots and peaches for this year, but nonetheless heading toward alfalfa harvesting. "My honest opinion is that I'm not worth bothering with and that I'm wasting your time and sympathy. You have perhaps realized already that there is not much in me that can be cajoled or coaxed to the surface and that whatever I write comes more as a dribble than a flood." In each letter, he vouchsafed an additional nugget about his life. In this one he claimed to be a "finished product," with "stomach ulcers, asthma, nervous breakdowns, and violent disorders." Rereading, he crossed out "nervous breakdowns."

In a previous letter she had urged him to let go "the habit of detached distance" and put more of his feelings into his writing. But he was inclined to do the opposite, as Montaigne recommended. "The habit of detached distance … may not be good for a writer, as you imply in your letter, but it suits my nature and I feel almost degraded whenever it is momentarily swept aside by bursts of passion. I must feel a stranger in this world. … Familiarity turns my mind into a graveyard. And it is therefore that I must avoid a secure existence." The novel about Hank, Hoffer confided, should tell Anderson "whether I can write." It was absolutely "not autobiography," but "tells more about me than I can in a dozen long letters." He added that he still had no fixed address and might move again.

When Anderson rejected "Four Years," Hoffer breathed a sigh of relief: having given fiction his best shot—and missed—he could now write essays, a prospect that excited him because the war in Europe and Asia was providing grist for his mill. Events in late 1939 ratified Hoffer's contrary view of Communism and Nazism as similar, and not, as others saw them, as natural enemies: in August, Hitler and Stalin made a pact that allowed them in September to invade Poland and carve it up between them. In December, the USSR invaded Finland. Hoffer's view was further certified by an article in *The Atlantic* in early 1940: Peter Viereck wrote that the invasion of Finland "laid bare the incompetence" of the fellow travelers who had once supported the Hitler-Stalin "non-aggression" pact, and who had insisted (in a broadside in *The Nation*, signed by 400 intellectuals), that "Soviet and fascist policies are diametrically opposed. The Soviet Union continues as always to be a bulwark against war and aggression, and works unceasingly for a peaceful international order."

These world-rending events and their validations of his ideas led Hoffer to make a significant change in his life. He announced in his letter to Anderson of May 14, 1941 that "My travelling days are over," and his plan to spend his remaining years—he guessed he would have ten—"within a narrow compass."

The progress of the war in Europe and Asia thus far gave him reason to believe that his focus was and should be mass movements. Anderson provided a specific audience for him—a woman from the world of high-toned literature who could unlock that world's door for him, should he write something of value. San Francisco should be able to provide him with a steady-enough job and reliable income to enable him to have the time and leisure to write. For two decades he had shunned stability, security, and specific purpose; now, recognizing these as necessary to the writing that would create his future, he took steps to acquire them.

Chapter Three:
On the Docks

The Japanese attack on Pearl Harbor on December 7, 1941 galvanized Hoffer, according to his recollections. Having fulminated about Hitler for years and dreamed of personally killing him, Hoffer volunteered for the U.S. military; then, rejected on medical grounds because of a hernia and chronic gastric problems, he searched for the hardest, most demanding job he could do to further American war efforts. A state employment center sent him to the docks; a surge in shipping was expected because of the need to move military supplies across the Pacific, and more longshoremen were to be hired.

A job as a dockworker fit the bill of being a very demanding job connected to the war effort, but it remains unclear when Hoffer started on the waterfront. He joined the union in 1943, or more than a year after Pearl Harbor, but in between those dates he may have taken temporary jobs, or have been employed as an apprentice before officially joining the union. He had to join the International Longshoreman's and Warehousemen's Union, because the ILWU controlled all hiring along the hundred miles of San Francisco bay waterfront.

"I felt at home in the union from the first day," Hoffer would write, explaining that the ethnic mix of dockworkers was similar to that of the migrants, and so was the nature of dock work—not steady, consisting of various kinds of toil done for many different employers.

Throughout the country, in 1943, membership in unions was high, 15 million workers, one-third of the workforce, mostly concentrated in the economy's manufacturing and transportation sectors.

The ILWU was an industrial union, rather than a trade union such as the cabinet-makers to which Hoffer's father had belonged, and it was part of the Congress of Industrial Organizations, not of the American Federation of Labor.

Harry Bridges, leader of the ILWU, was a firebrand and a Communist, although he never admitted being a Communist Party member. Born in Australia in 1901, he had begun waterfront work on the U.S. West Coast in 1922, and in 1934 had been the key person in a strike that brought about a major power shift that eliminated the stevedoring companies' "shape up," from which the day's workers were chosen, and transferred to the union and its hiring hall the right to dispatch workers to jobs each day. Bridges then formed a new union, the ILWU. Between September 1939 and June 1941, Bridges' sympathies for the Soviet Union led him to publicly oppose U.S. entry into World War II and to prevent his dockworkers from taking actions that might be adverse to the interests of Stalin's partner, Nazi Germany. But after Hitler invaded the USSR in June 1941, and the USSR changed sides and became one of the Allies, Bridges became a strong advocate of American intervention, and after Pearl Harbor he opened the previously closed ILWU rolls to many new members.

Hoffer disliked Communists and second-rate intellectuals—those who were unable to be truly creative and instead threw their energies into seeking and using power; in Hoffer's view, Bridges fit both bills. Hoffer and the union leader quickly developed a mutual dislike. Bridges never permitted the union's newsletter to celebrate Hoffer, and Hoffer in interviews took potshots at Bridges. But Hoffer did not allow his antipathy to Bridges to overrule his admiration for the union and for the lifestyle that its contracts made possible: "You can work when you want to. You have no boss. You can have time for the good things in life—for books, for music, for hobbies. One of the things I have against Harry Bridges is that he cannot see this [independence] as a worthwhile goal, that he tries to lead the men in other directions." Hoffer refused to stand for union office but never missed a union meeting. Occasionally he sketched out in a notebook a speech he planned to give at a meeting. One concerned the question of whether the U.S. should ship extant military materiel to Great Britain and Russia:

> We need <u>time</u> desperately before we are ready to meet the dictators. Once our factories produce airplanes, tanks, ships ... and we have enough trained men to handle the fighting machines we need fear no Hitler or combination of Hitlers. ...We can buy precious time from England Greece Turkey China and even Russia. As long as these countries fight or threaten the Axis powers—we have time to retool, build new factories train more men and build a two-ocean navy. Even if we were to send to Britain and her allies 90% of all our airplanes, tanks, guns, and cargo ships ... it would not interfere at all with ... the stepping up of our defense production to its top capacity.

Arriving each weekday at 6:00 A.M. at the Alaska Fishermen's Union building on lower Clay Street, the ILWU hiring hall, Hoffer awaited dispatch to one of dozens of piers. Not all members who showed up at the hall found work every day, but most did. The tasks in the holds and on the docks were physically demanding; some days, while performing them Hoffer was unable to straighten up for hours at a time. He endured many injuries, beginning in 1943 with the loss of a thumb, which put him in the hospital for nine months while doctors grafted onto the stub a piece of his rib and skin from his thigh. Later he joked that it took as long to make a thumb as to bring a baby to term; but the circumstances were more dire. In that accident, two other men lost their lives, and Hoffer was lucky to survive; moreover, the resulting grafted thumb was unsightly, sprouting hair. In later life he would conceal it when being photographed—a small vanity in a man who was mostly without vanity.

According to David Wellman's book, *The Union Makes Us Strong*, ILWU longshoremen, unlike union members in many other CIO shops, could "work with a great deal of freedom," able to reject a particular day's job "without losing [one's] place on the waterfront," and to "choose the amount of work" and the location of the work. Longshoreman Herb Mills remembered dockwork in that era as "only rarely distinguished by an unrelieved monotony" of the sort encountered in industrial plants, and as not too onerous: "The common posture was, 'I don't give a damn what the cargo is.'" "If you're a longshoreman," a third dockworker opined, "that has a stamp on your personality. You're a little tough-minded, opinionated, sentimental and pretty easy with money. And probably a little arrogant."

Although Hoffer objected to being perceived as sentimental, he exhibited all these attributes with the exception of being "easy with money," as he carefully limited his expenses so that he need not work more than four days a week in order to have enough money and time off to write. He resided in a $25-a-month furnished room in McAllister Street with a pull-down bed, stained yellow wallpaper, a second-hand phonograph on which to play his Beethoven records, and no mirror, as he claimed not to need one, even for shaving. His major regular purchase, outside of food, was tobacco, cigarettes, cigars, and pipe-tobacco. To write he put a board across two chairs. The cast of mind that kept him alone in a gang of workers—composing in his head sentences about lofty subjects while unloading a vessel—also served to rationalize his avoidance of acquiring a wife and children. The only family to which he belonged was the union, and he became an admirer of the ILWU's street smarts and fairness. The union members' genius, he judged, replicated that of the Skid Row denizens who had built a road in the San Bernardino mountains—able to do a competent job on any task with a minimum of supervision.

The ILWU also changed Hoffer's ideas about the nature of capitalism. In the 1930s, one of his basic tenets had been the sense that individuals must earn their own living and provide for their own future without relying on a group of peers, or on government intervention, safety nets, or regulations. But at heart more of an enthusiast for free market capitalism than a doctrinaire anti-unionist, Hoffer, once he started working under the aegis of the ILWU, acknowledged benefitting from the union's prior successes in having forced concessions from management. He also liked the union's fairness in dealing with slackers, miscreants, and other internal problems. So in the 1940s he revised his argument, that capitalism was a natural activity of human beings; he widened his pantheon of normal human traits to include the equally natural activity of workers bargaining collectively for wages and benefits. This led to one of his central insights, that workers and management were eternally opposed, and that while they would always clash, they needed to work together to create ways to get the tasks done and to make a sustainable enterprise.

During his time off Hoffer read voraciously, in the public library, in books borrowed from it, and in a few that he bought, copying passages from them into daybooks. He would let references in one reading lead led him to the next. That was how he happened upon a 1943 translation of Jacob Burckhardt's *Force and Freedom: Reflections on History*, from which he learned a great deal about mass movements.

Precisely what Hoffer obtained from his reading and how it informed his writing has been a matter of contention. Paul Wesley Batty, in his 1970 doctoral thesis, after comparing passages in Montaigne, Renan, Burckhardt, and De Tocqueville with what Hoffer had written, concluded that those authors only "provided [Hoffer] supporting materials for the theories developed in his own thinking." James T. Baker, in a 1982 biography—as with Batty's thesis, written without access to the Hoffer archives—contended that Hoffer composed *The True Believer* "backwards," hatching his ideas and only then finding authorities to quote because he knew publishers would not accept his ideas without such props. Hoffer himself, in a letter to Anderson, asserted, "the search for quotations was a search for justification. Many of my ideas seemed to me at first sight preposterous, so I had to find some quotation which would seem to support me."

But Hoffer's notebooks reveal a more complicated inter-relationship between his ideas and his reading. From the early 1930s on, he copied out extensive quotes, only a small fraction of which ever found their way into his published works. The quantity and variety of the quotes suggest that while Hoffer's ideas were mostly original, what he read expanded his compass and comprehension, spurring him to thoughts he might not otherwise have reached. As Hoffer told Koerner, "You steal ideas, you steal sentences. If you don't know how to steal you don't know how to create."

Those stealings would fuel his mental processes as he worked out various "problems," his word for the knotty questions to which he sought rational answers. As he would later explain to interviewer James Day,

> If you just hug [the problem], just hang onto it, long enough, some solution will offer itself. ... I believe in familiarity. I believe in living with your problem—sitting with it, eating with it, carrying it around with you. All the time. Some solution will offer itself. ... All kinds of right accidents will happen to you. You'll find out that the whole world—even the newspapers—are talking about your problem, even children will be talking about your problem. The whole world will come to your door and bring mortar and brick for you to build.

Yet Hoffer wrote in a notebook that the creative mind was "a garden infested with ravenous bugs. The moment a seed of thought shows its tender head, it [is] pounced upon and devoured. The precious creative energy within us is distilled from the slime of passions and blind desires. We have to cheat the stubborn and cunning appetites if we want to convert that energy into creative work."

His notebooks reveal the toil of distilling from the grapes of personal experience the wine of universal truths. After recording one day that he had gone about his dockwork dutifully but unenthu-siastically, he generalized, "To shoulder a set of duties and fulfill them gives one the illusion of having mastered one's life and environment." Later in that notebook, Hoffer rephrased that: "Duties are the strings which attach us to a pattern of existence."

Hoffer thought of himself as an empiricist, someone who believes that experience is the main source of knowledge; but he seldom sought to test out his empirically-derived hypotheses by conducting further research among his fellow men. Rather, he was content to hatch his ideas and to leave it to his eventual readers to test out their truths.

In another set of Hoffer notebook entries, he first recorded that one day after work, rather than following his usual procedure of returning home and writing out his thoughts, he had a beer with colleagues; next day in the notebook he castigated himself for having wasted time—but he also plumbed the hiding-out experience and found in it evidence of the perils of cowardice: "It's refuge from our own selves we seek when we run to join the crowd and make noise."

During the last phase of World War II, 1944-45, Hoffer realized that the focus of his as-yet-untitled book had narrowed, and that in his hugging of problems he had found a simple but useful organizing focus for a book: the "true believer" at the heart of all mass movements. This would enable him to discuss the similarities among mass movements, the conditions for recruitment of its followers, and the factors that unified recruits and kept them in harness.

Instantly, the character of his notebooks changed as he began writing out the book as a book, rather than, as he had been doing, as individual, often seemingly unrelated paragraphs. His pace of composition picked up even more as the first phase of the Cold War began— for Hoffer, another American war against a totalitarian government whose followers were true believers. Before the end of 1946 he had fleshed out 125 sections, each subdivided, for a total of about 500 subsections. Given the subsections' density and complexity of thought, his rate of composition, about one subsection per day, was phenomenal, made possible by drawing on drafts that he had been composing since the mid-1930s.

On December 13, 1946, he summed up on a single notebook page a decade's worth of thinking. Asking rhetorically what a mass movement does for its followers, he answered:

It takes them out of themselves.
It gives them a future.
It fills their lives with activities.
It frees them of responsibility for their own lives; frees them of the killing strain of competition.
It frees them of loneliness.
It gives them a cause for pride.
It fills them with hope.
It gives them a sense of righteousness,
It gives them courage and banishes fear from their hearts.
It gives them a sense of superiority over those not in the movement.
It gives them a sense of growth and development; a feeling of success.
It gives them the feeling that they are useful, wanted, important.
It gives them the illusion of might and fills their souls with grandeur.

Hoffer finished writing *The True Believer* while he and his fellow dockworkers were out on strike. During World War II, the ILWU and many other unions had adhered to a no-strike pledge, but after the war pushed hard for better pay and working conditions—one-third of all unionized workers walked off their jobs during 1946. In June, President Harry S. Truman settled one huge strike by ordering the Army to take over operation of the railroads if their unions did not sign new contracts; the railroad unions signed and the strike was averted. But when Truman threatened to have the Navy similarly take over the ships and docks if the longshore and seafarer unions struck, the ILWU and other maritime unions prevented that takeover by having unions abroad pledge not to handle any cargo loaded by the Navy. Even so, the longshoremen still felt the need to strike.

The decision to walk out was still pending when Hoffer jotted down in a notebook what he wanted to say about the issues at a union meeting. Conceding that most longshoremen worked mainly to make money, he argued that, nonetheless, some wished to work on the docks until their dying day. Therefore, he reasoned, factors more important than pay had to be addressed in the negotiations. "I don't love work," he asserted. "But it's something I can't get rid of. It's like a chronic disease that will prey on me till I die. So I say let's make the best of it. Let us make it as pleasant and as easy as we can. Of course we will fight for higher wages. But before anything else let us concentrate on making the job less unpleasant, less wearisome, and less killing than it is."

Hoffer, in other words, wanted the settlement to concentrate on the present; he was also exploring, just then, in his draft of the book, how true believers related to the present: "All mass movements deprecate the present, mask its reality, and employ every device to divert the gaze of their followers from it. They depict the present as a mean and shameful prelude to a glorious and noble future." Ever his toughest editor, he immediately shortened and improved the thought: "They depict the present as a mean prelude to a noble future."

As for his own future, the evidence in the notebooks is that he had finally decided to plan his own, as he had never done as a migrant, perhaps because now he had something to live for. In the same notebook, he sketched out a budget for the next year that had him spending more money on buying books than on rent.

Ten years later, Hoffer would note in the margin of the August 1947 to January 1948 notebook that while he could not remember his precise emotional condition at its time of writing, "I must have been at my fluent best."

The fluency can be seen in his steps toward what would become three sub-sections of The True Believer regarding "doctrine." In shaping these and many other sections, Hoffer adopted the plan of scientific researchers, who assert that the investigator's largest task is to properly frame a question, because once that is done the answer often comes readily. After years of thinking about mass movements, Hoffer posed one such question, in pen: "What happens to a doctrine when it is adopted by a mass movement?" Below that he wrote "a, b, c," and left space for filling in those blanks. He already had the "a" and "b" answers: "It is dramatized" and "It is dogmatized." But "c" eluded him for a while, perhaps no more than a few hours, until he affixed "c," in pencil: "It is vulgarized."

Hoffer's method included debriefing himself as Montaigne had, but while Montaigne frequently looked first for clues in the writings of Latin and Greek authors, Hoffer was unwilling to consult the classics first or to rely too much on anyone else's thinking at any point in his process, even that of authors he admired. In a diary entry— occasionally the notebooks became diaries—he explained why he did not consult others' work first: "It's a delight to approach a problem without preconceived ideas. One is animated by sheer curiosity and a benevolence toward the facts. We know that the situation has its inner logic and we want to detect its outline and pattern. ... We are eager to be surprised and willing to be shamed by our proven ignorance."

Wondering whether all mass movements had a holy book, he quickly listed a few: the Bible, the Koran, the writings of Marx and Lenin, and Hitler's *Mein Kampf*. Trying to figure what these tomes had in common, he wrote in a rushed hand his startling conclusion: "All mass movements have a Devil." Not satisfied with that expression of the insight, he mulled it over until he wrote, "There are mass movements without a God, but none without a Devil." Reworked as "Mass movements can rise and spread without belief in a God, but never without belief in a devil," this became one of his most quoted lines.

That same day he wrote another diary paragraph on a related subject and then crossed it out with the comment, "rotten writing." The following day he warned, "Don't let your penchant for the paradox and extravagant run away with you." And on a later page of the notebook, he judged an aphorism "not so good."

He occasionally veered from his main subject with coruscating musings. One contended, "To the prostitute, the differences are not between persons, that is to say between essentially similar units, but between penis and vagina—things totally different. And in one's attitude towards something of a different order there can be no personal element." But he never let that insight see print. Dinner companions would note Hoffer's vulgarity, as would interviewers—but only when the cameras and tape-recorders were off, since he was careful enough not to let his vulgarities mar his public image.

Sometimes he would write down in his notebook what it was he could not find, and by doing so further his quest for an insight: "I assume that though the contents of a doctrine can be as fantastic and absurd as one can well imagine and still be effective, it yet has to have some practical component or kernel which is the spring of its effectiveness. Just what this is I don't know. Perhaps it is a formulation of the impossible. Better: the formulation of a promise which cannot be verified or refuted by experience." A few hours later, he realized that his contention that a doctrine must have some practical component was "hardly so," for a doctrine "is a catalyst only. Its substance does not partake of the nature of the movement. It is impossible to judge the nature and strength of a movement from its doctrine."

Needing to verify this insight, he could not do so by querying himself or his mates on the dock; and so he did some research in books that might cover the subject of what happened to a doctrine when it was new. The most obvious target was religion, and the Protestant revolution. He found a gloss on John Calvin and his teachings, read it, and from it deduced, "Doctrine then is a token of certainty—a password to heaven. Does a password have to be intelligible? One's life depends on repeating the password precisely as it is given. You can't change one syllable without robbing it of its potent charm." Now he understood: "Absolute certainty = unintelligible or vague or unprovable (therefore irrefutable)."

He pushed on, asking, "Are the frustrated more ready to accept a doctrine than people who are not frustrated?" and "What are the peculiarities of a particular doctrine?" To properly answer the second question, he noted, he should look into Catholicism and into national and social revolutions. After reading Henri Bergson's 1935 book, *The Two Sources of Morality and Religion*, he concluded, "The key is in the precise words of a doctrine, not in their meaning." He also looked for wisdom about doctrine and social revolutions in the works of British Marxist Harold Laski and in philosopher Alfred North Whitehead's 1936 *Leadership in a Free Society*. Eventually he would answer his first question, whether the frustrated were more ready to accept a doctrine, by positing, "There is apparently some connection between dissatisfaction with oneself and a proneness to credulity. ... There is no hope for the frustrated in the actual and the possible. ... They ask to be deceived."

Reading about Calvin did not completely answer his queries, so he moved on to Martin Luther. Later, Hoffer would assert that the "table talk" of important people was more revealing than their formal utterances because when they were being casual they were more direct in their phrasing and vocabulary; from a biography of Luther he copied out a particularly revelatory snippet of Luther's table talk: "So tenaciously should we cling to the word revealed by the Gospel that were I to see all the Angels in Heaven coming down to me to tell me something different, not only would I not be tempted to doubt a single syllable [of the Gospel], but I would shut my eyes and stop my ears, for they [the angels] would not deserve to be either seen or heard." Now he was able to conclude that a mass movement's doctrine was the key to belief, the controlling ideology. Continuing to search for information about its function within a mass movement, he found in a 1946 book, *Why They Behave Like Russians*, by Jack Fischer, an apt quote from an official history of the Communist Party: "The power of the Marxist-Leninist theory lies in the fact that it enables the Party to find the right orientation in any situation."

Such doctrinaire followings of the Party line, in Hoffer's view, had sent American Communists in precisely the wrong direction. A new era in union activity had begun with the passage of the Taft-Hartley Act in June 1947; Taft-Hartley required that to be eligible for union office, candidates, including current office holders, had to sign affidavits that they were not Communists. Now the CIO leadership, to Hoffer's satisfaction, was in the process of pushing out eleven of its unions dominated by Communists, including the Harry Bridges-led ILWU, and curtailing those unions' license to negotiate contracts. Hoffer was all for cutting back the ability of leftist ideologues to use unions for their purposes, and in a 1948 notebook observed that Communist-led unions had not been achieving much, of late, and had taken a thrashing from such anti-Communists as Walter Reuther, leader of the United Auto Workers. Hoffer assessed the Communists' negotiating techniques as "obviously wrong ... and it would have been very interesting to discuss it [in the meeting]. But as I felt my way I found that their attitude is: 'Let the heathen rave.' They don't realize that they are more handicapped than Lenin was and that they ... will remain almost blind if they go on aping Stalin's tactics." He chortled over the spectacle of Harry Bridges at last being forced to play a different role in negotiations with the new management representative: "They acted like haranguers and not class antagonists. Bridges seemed to like his new role: no declamations, no fireworks, just shrewd horsetrading. ... We won a very good contract and I can't see how class consciousness could have gained us more."

In Hoffer's engagement with union issues, as in his correspondence and in the book he was writing, he scrupulously avoided assaying events, individuals, and trends in political terms. He was not apolitical—his political views were settled, and right of center—but he made a concerted effort to understand the world through the eyes of an analyst of human nature rather than through the interposed lens of political calculus.

Hoffer and Anderson had an informal arrangement: she assisted him by making editorial suggestions and by acting as his agent; should the book sell, Hoffer would split the money with her in an as-yet unspecified way. In June 1948, at her request, he sent her the introduction and a detailed chapter outline. Hearing nothing from her before the end of the year, he hardly knew what to think. She surfaced again in February of 1949; in the interim, Louis Adamic had committed suicide and Anderson had had to take over the editorship of *Common Ground*. It had required all of her time, but when she returned to her duties as agent, she was able to tell him that Harper liked the outline and was conditionally willing to publish, should the completed manuscript be satisfactory.

Drafts of sections flew back and forth between Hoffer and editor Elizabeth Lawrence throughout 1949, until on November 10 he sent off a finished manuscript to Anderson along with $100 for typing. She typed it and sent it to Lawrence, who was happy with it. But Harper publishing decisions were made by an editorial committee, and Lawrence had to have that committee's agreement on what might well be a controversial book; potential objectors included Jack Fischer and Evan Thomas. Thomas, then 29, a son of Norman Thomas, perennial Socialist Party candidate for president, had been with the publisher for just a few years. Fischer, then in his forties, was the author of several books, a fixture at *Harper's* magazine, and on track to become the book division's editor-in-chief.

Evan Thomas, near the halfway point in reading of the manuscript, expressed to Lawrence his admiration for the unknown author's "gift of expression and apparent insight," and his feeling that he would vote to publish. But upon reaching the manuscript's end—he wrote in a memo—he felt "quite the opposite. This is basically an extremely cynical work. And cynicism coupled with a felicity of expression, plus a plausibility of hypothesis. ... I wish to deny the author's plausible cynicism with everything in me." He recommended against publication. Jack Fischer judged it differently; although his memo pointed out a dozen sections requiring revision, it closed by saying, "This seems to me an important piece of original thinking and I very much hope we can work out a contract to publish it." That opinion carried the day.

Receiving a telegram from Harper & Brothers that they would publish the book, Hoffer experienced what he later contended was his life's "only moment of unalloyed happiness. ... I felt like a darling of fate, an immortal raised above the common run of humanity. There were no doubts about my worthiness and no fear about the future."

The moment passed quickly, he later also said, in part because he had no one to share it with. He may have communicated that to Margaret Anderson, because shortly she came to San Francisco. She would much later recall that they walked through Golden Gate State Park, his favorite ramble, and Hoffer repeatedly reached into his pockets and pulled out note cards from which he would declaim quotations and his own aphorisms, seeking her reaction.

They may have had an affair; Hoffer confided to Tomkins in 1966 that Anderson had sent him some "crude letters," indicative of a prior intimate relationship. He recalled his impressions of her in San Francisco in 1949-50: "very American ... an elderly maid" with a surprising "desire to dominate."

Affair or not, they had business to conduct—what to ask for in the publishing contract. Most publishers offered authors an advance against royalties. But in a notebook draft letter to Anderson, Hoffer instructed her that, like children, they should have "no defenses" and must trust the publisher to "not take candy from a baby."

> No one has ever lost any money on me since I have been on my own—and surely it is not fit that so unpleasant a thing should happen for the first time ... with this book. Once Harper has its money back it is up to the publisher to decide what our rightful portion should be. I didn't write the book for money. I wrote it to justify your faith in me and also for the salvation of my soul—which is probably one and the same thing.

His avowal that he would not accept a penny from Harper until they made back all they might spend to publish the book was an unusual stance for a writer, but then, Hoffer did not think of himself as a writer, and he very much wanted his actions in regard to publishing the book to be congruent with his vision of the right and proper thing to do. How he envisioned himself, just then, was revealed in another entry in this notebook, in which he adopted a variant of Alfred North Whitehead's "hierarchy of values." Whitehead had famously argued that each individual inculcates or invents a "hierarchy of values" and uses its rankings to decide between life choices, usually opting for the action that aims toward the higher value. Hoffer wrote, "A man has to work out a hierarchy of self-valuation. He has to find out what he is first, second, third and so forth. In my case: I am first a human being, second an American, third a workingman, fourth a longshoreman, fifth a thinker, sixth a writer."

Hoffer had more work to do before *The True Believer* could be published; he was sent copies of the Thomas and Fischer memos, which contained queries and suggestions on a dozen or so specific sections.

"I enjoyed your devastating criticism," Hoffer wrote to Thomas in a notebook draft of a response. "Your memo crystallized several vague thoughts in my mind, and this is always a cause for joy. I know of no better way of answering your memo than by these newly crystallized thoughts." He inscribed in the notebook revamped or new sections on freedom, deprecation of the present, and—one asked for by Fischer—on foreign influences on mass movements. Several of the new thoughts hatched in this exchange became central to the finished book: "We have more faith in what we imitate than in what we originate. We cannot derive a sense of certitude from anything that has its roots in ourselves," and "It is probably better for a people that its government should be overthrown the moment it begins to show signs of chronic incompetence—even though such overthrow involves a frightful waste in lives and wealth—than that it should be allowed to rot and crumble and fall of itself." In notes to himself during the revisions, he warned that he must "guard against ... textbook completeness. ... Any aspect of a problem which does not seem to offer a chance for original thinking should be left out."

During the last phases of the revisions, Hoffer and Anderson sent letters and sections back and forth daily. Hoffer complained of having to rush the writing of the end of the book; although satisfied with the result, the process gave him "deep misgivings," since his "habit" was to write a section, then put it away for months, and then to look at it again, find the holes, and fix them. Short-circuiting that process made him nervous, but he thanked her profusely for helping him to complete the revisions in the time allotted.

She also helped him devote more attention to elements of the craft of writing that made an essay more readable—phrases and sentences that tied ideas together, that directed the reader's attention, and that varied the pace, intensity, and tenor. Agreeing to some of that language, he also insisted to the publisher,

> It is not possible to think in understatement. Thought is a process of exaggeration. To think about a problem is not unlike drawing a caricature. You have to exaggerate the salient point and leave out that which is not typical. ... As to the quantity of absolute truth in a thought: it seems to me that the more comprehensive and unobjectionable a thought becomes the more clumsy and unexciting it gets. ... I wrote the book not as a moralist but as a technician. My object was not to pass judgment but to find out how come and how things are done. The true believer is everywhere, we have to cope with him, and it is well that we should know all we can concerning his nature.

During the last stages of the publishing, the printer had difficulty fitting some sections on the pages and asked that a couple of sections be shortened. Anderson shaved them. Hoffer, in closely examining the galleys discovered the changes and, enraged, sent a stinging telegram to Elizabeth Lawrence demanding that she put back in anything that Anderson had taken out. Lawrence did so.

Despite this uproar, before publication Hoffer journeyed east just to see Anderson in her rural New York home near Lake Erie, and there, he later confided to Tomkins, they encountered the same difficulties as they had in their San Francisco meeting; he concluded, "I suppose high-strung intellectuals, high-strung women are not my meat."

Part of the book's appeal, Harper & Brothers knew, was that an unschooled manual laborer could write such a wide-ranging, deeply intellectual book that cited the Bible, Luther, Renan, Dostoevsky, Montaigne, Pascal, Hitler, Trotsky, Yeats, H. G. Wells, Homer, and de Tocqueville. To gauge how the book would be received, Harper showed galleys to opinion leaders. An early version of the jacket copy suggests the answers they obtained:

> Judging from early reactions to this book, *The True Believer* is very likely to make a lot of people angry—<u>not</u> just Communists and Fascists and the kind of people who search for a modern "man on horseback," but some devout Christians and honest people with pet convictions to defend. It is a highly original piece of writing—by turns stimulating, exasperating, exciting—in which a migrant worker and longshoreman looks into the phenomenon of mass movements with the detachment of a Machiavelli.

Harper sent copies of the book to newspapers and magazines, for publicity as well as for reviews. One went to the San Francisco *Examiner*, which assigned reporter Dick Pearce. In "Longshoreman Writes Book About Philosophy," Pearce adopted a man-bites-dog tone—how amazing that a lowly longshoreman could write a book!—but could not be entirely dismissive, because its contents impressed him.

Pearce spoke with other dockworkers to try to fathom Hoffer, but did not get much. Hoffer had acquaintances but no close friends on the docks, partly due to his solitary nature and partly in consequence of his workday pattern. Rather than toil regularly with the same partner or gang and move together from job to job, he allowed the union to assign him a different partner each day. Although Hoffer and his work partners would frequently disagree about "union matters and human behavior," as he put it in a diary, a few had attempted to befriend him. The first to do so was Olaf Olsen, an immigrant with a wife and a passel of children but also a roving eye for the ladies; another was Bob O'Brien, a well-read Catholic; and, in the interim between completion and publication of *The True Believer*, Selden Osborne.

A son of a miner and his wife, born in Arizona in 1911, Selden Osborne had grown up on a ranch near the Mexican border and San Diego. In a brief 1935 autobiography, he related that due to the ranch's isolation, he and his siblings had not attended school until halfway through the primary grades, and at home were taught independence and self-reliance. During his high school years, spent in La Jolla, the pastor of his Protestant church aimed him toward "action on the basis of conviction. ... I was quite personally ambitious and more or less regarded myself as a savior of humanity. I planned to study law, and to go into politics in order to become a great political leader, to lead the way to the establishment of a perfect society." He worked as a laborer and joined his first union before matriculating at Stanford in 1928. As an undergraduate he roomed for a time with Clark Kerr, future president of the University of California system. He gravitated to the YMCA, where there were discussion groups as well as gymnasium facilities. The one at Stanford, he discovered, was full of campus radicals, and he adopted their pacifism and socialism. After college he completed graduate work with the intention of becoming a teacher and continuing his socialist endeavors. There were no teaching jobs available. He organized a conference against war, but because he refused to take a position of absolute pacifism, many friends regarded him as a Communist, a label and a creed that he rejected. Unemployed, he continued to organize for the Socialist

Party in various California locations. By 1935, he confessed in this autobiography, written for a Socialist summer leadership institute, "I have got over the idea that I, an intellectual, can show the workers the way out. ... My experience in Los Angeles has done a great deal to cure me of my desire to be a 'Big Shot', and I would much rather be a follower, working under the complete direction of someone in whom I had real confidence."

Between 1935 and 1951, Selden spent time in jail for his beliefs, worked on the waterfront, joined the ILWU to participate in its radical unionism, and started and failed at various schemes. The woman whom he would marry in 1944, Lili Fabilli, had also been involved in union organizing, of fish cannery workers, before matriculating at Berkeley in 1937, where she worked as a housemaid to earn money, and was one of a group of free-spirited poets, painters, and what another member called "self-declared anarchists," able to parse the differences between Stalinists, Trotskyites and Lovestonites. By 1951 Lili and Selden had two children, Tonia, six, and Stephen, two. Selden was known among the longshoremen for his passionate radicalism, but they had repeatedly refused to vote him into office. He attributed his defeats to Bridges' animosity. He openly admired Eric Hoffer, and invited Hoffer to accompany him to lectures, among them one by Max Shachtman, a former Communist theorist who was becoming an anti-Stalinist but who had not shed his radical beliefs. Selden and Hoffer got along well enough for Selden to invited Hoffer home to meet his wife and family.

Lili at 34 was a tall, big-boned, full-figured woman with sensuous lips and eyes, outgoing, vivacious, good-looking, smart, and motherly. One of four daughters of an Italian Catholic immigrant farming family from the San Joaquin valley, she had organized workers in her sardine factory, had worked in an airplane factory during World War II, and would become a teacher for children with disabilities. To Hoffer— who believed in the role of chance and was delighted when circumstances seemed to conspire to make his predictions come true—Lili combined the attributes of the two women in his autobiographical novel, the beauty and warmth of "Fred" and the intellectual savvy of "Anna." Hoffer was quite a bit older than Lili, a big man with a booming voice, a big laugh and big appetites, newly confident because his book was about to be published and he might well become a celebrated thinker, and—despite all that—very emotionally needy. Lili would later tell Tomkins that in her first conversation with Hoffer, on the telephone as he inquired about dinner arrangements, she recognized in him a *paisano,* the sort of Italian workingman from Italy who boarded with Italian-American farmers like the Fabillis in the expectation of making money to send to his family back home. A *paisano* would become incorporated into the family household, a stranger yet an intimate.

The Osbornes and Hoffer, as they would soon be saying, "adopted" each other, with Hoffer regularly coming to the Osborne home for weekend dinners and outings. Selden Osborne and Eric Hoffer became close friends and would remain close for the rest of their lives. And—perhaps by design, perhaps by chance—Eric Hoffer and Lili Osborne, viscerally attracted to one another, became lovers.

Chapter Four:
The True Believer

Cold War events were in Americans' thoughts and World War II was still a fresh memory in the early spring of 1951, when *The True Believer: Thoughts on the Nature of Mass Movements* was published. On the Korean peninsula, U.S. armed forces battled against Communist armies being supplied by the USSR and Communist China; Mao Zedong had recently forced Chiang Kai Shek's partisans off the mainland and was courting Stalin for a non-aggression pact. There were new revelations about prior Nazi atrocities, and former Nazis were being pursued in Europe and South America in an effort to bring them to justice. Nationalist movements had recently birthed the new countries of India and Israel. Senator Joseph McCarthy was hunting Communists in government and in academia, and the House Un-American Activities Committee was exposing Communists in Hollywood. Julius and Ethel Rosenberg were about to stand trial for passing atomic bomb secrets to the Soviet Union. Communism was of such concern that contestants for the Miss America crown were asked to comment on Karl Marx.

The True Believer enjoyed as near-perfect timing and circumstances as any author could wish for. The book argued for equating America's prior, Nazi enemy with its current, Communist enemy on ethical, moral, and psychological grounds. And it did so just when those on the right looked for a justification of belligerence against Communism, and when America's "non-Communist left," as Arthur Schlesinger, Jr. styled them, desperately sought ways to be against Communism without rejecting the positive social progress achieved through leftist ideas in the U.S during the New Deal and post-war years.

Readers opening *The True Believer* found a preface that began boldly: "All mass movements generate in their adherents a readiness to die and a proclivity for united action; all of them, irrespective of the doctrine they preach and the program they project, breed fanaticism, enthusiasm, fervent hope, hatred, and intolerance." Many readers had sensed similarities between the country's former and current enemies, but not the movements' inner connections. Now this unknown writer was identifying the connections in language that was dense yet that promised a comprehensible treatment of the subjects. But Hoffer soon moved beyond readers' comfort zone as he spoke of "a certain uniformity in all types of dedication, of faith, of pursuit of power, of unity and of self-sacrifice. ... He who, like Pascal, finds precise reasons for the effectiveness of Christian doctrine has also found the reasons for the effectiveness of Communist, Nazi, and nationalist doctrine." Some readers would have found this an unpalatable comparison, so to buttress this provocative thesis Hoffer identified antecedents of today's mass movements in a dozen different cultures and historical ages, and summed up their common element in an aphorism that contravened the prevailing wisdom, "A mass movement attracts and holds a following not because it can satisfy the desire for self-advancement, but because it can satisfy the passion for self-renunciation." Hoffer then refuted another widely held notion, that mass movements succeeded because they trashed the established order; he argued that if the Communists won in Europe or Africa, it would not be "because they know how to stir up discontent or how to infect people with hatred, but because they know how to preach hope."

By the end of *The True Believer*'s first section, readers knew Hoffer's basic points: mass movements were peopled by individuals who had been failures in one way or another until the movements gave them something beyond themselves to believe in and fight for as a "holy cause"; mass movements' leaders manipulated true believers by means of their fears, failings, and hopes; and holy causes were not only those that readers loathed, Communism and Nazism, but included some that some readers embraced—fervent religiosity, socialism, and ethnic nationalism. Many critics and readers would later say that they were amazed to discover that while they had not previously thought of these matters in the ways that Hoffer analyzed them, Hoffer's positions were so persuasively articulated that they found themselves largely in agreement with him.

His analyses also gave to Americans two things that no current political leader or writer provided. In detailing the human weaknesses of the true believers who peopled the mass movements, Hoffer definitively linked America's past and present enemies, and he ratified American readers' belief in the inherent superiority of an American way of life based on democracy, capitalism, tolerance, equal opportunity, and individualism. By doing these things, the book provided even more reason for Americans to back the government's efforts to seek the downfall of the Soviet Union. With a single stroke, Hoffer rationalized and re-energized American anti-Communism.

The book's middle chapters took readers deeper into human nature than they might have expected to go. Few readers would have sensed, in advance of reading the book, that the notion of "true believers" was so integrally related to the role of "undesirables" in human affairs, or that undesirables could be celebrated as the spearhead of change. Hoffer countered potential objections to these ideas by citing examples from the French Revolution, upheavals in nineteenth century Japan, early Catholic Church history, the Reformation, the Puritan Revolution in England, and the philosophic differences between the elitist Confucius and Mo-Tzu, the advocate for the poor.

Sophisticated readers might recognize that Hoffer's analysis owed almost nothing to the two major tools of contemporary analysts, Marxist economics and Freudian psychology. As *Time* magazine would later write, in 1951 economics was the primary way that experts explained all of history and contemporary affairs: "Men were seen as voting or revolting or going to war according to the dictates of 'the pocketbook nerve.' The Constitution of the United

States was viewed solely as a set of compromises between economic interest groups. Hitler was seen as an instrument of the Ruhr Industrialists, [and] the world was divided into have and have-not nations." Just then, as well, psychologically based treatises were explicating mass man through Freud's principles—William Reich's *The Mass Psychology of Fascism* asserted that Germans submitted to Hitler because of their fear of sexual inadequacy.

Hoffer had deliberately avoided reading Marx and Freud. Dismissing Marx as out of touch with real workingmen, he would similarly write of Freud, "I had a vague feeling that familiarity with psychoanalysis would make it easy for me to substitute terms for thoughts and this might offer an escape from the laborious task of thinking things through on my own." But Hoffer did function as a depth psychologist—as in the book's most oft-quoted line, its Section 8, "Faith in a holy cause is to a considerable extent a substitute for the lost faith in ourselves"—and as a macro-economist, as in its sections about the poor. He analyzed the poor from the point of view of someone who had always been poor and chose to remain so: refusing to lump all poor into a single category defined by income level, or to dismiss them as powerless, he instead sorted the poor by their varied routes to poverty and their attitudes toward money. "The new poor" had recently been middle-class and were more angry than "the abjectly poor;" "the free poor" were essentially slaves, while "the creative poor," artists and thinkers, did have some power. He also explained the inducements offered by a mass movement to amalgamate them all into "the united poor."

In unflaggingly direct prose, he wrenched the reader in unexpected directions. Discussing the "free poor," he tackled the myth that freedom was always desirable: "We join a mass movement to escape individual responsibility, or, in the words of the ardent young Nazi, 'to be free from freedom.'" Discussing slavery, he opined, "The segregated Negro in the South is less frustrated than the non-segregated Negro in the North," arguing that African-Americans in the South were less stressed because they gave up striving for integration, reasoning that the goal could not be achieved, but that African-Americans in northern cities continued to push for and believe in integration—and, blocked from achieving it, became more frustrated.

Why had Soviet citizens been able to stand up heroically to the advances of Hitler's armies, but offered no resistance to the depredations of Stalin's secret police? Why had some Jews fiercely fought to establish the state of Israel, while their relatives went in a seemingly docile manner to Hitler's gas chambers? Hoffer posited the same answer for both questions: that the Soviets when facing Nazi armies had been united as a group, but scattered as individuals when facing Stalin's secret police, and that the Jews had been united when fighting the British in Palestine, but assimilated and scattered when facing the Nazi secret police.

By the book's middle chapters, it became clear that Hoffer's target was not only the true believer, but everyman—not *them*, but *us*. "Our frustration is greater when we have much and want more than when we have nothing and want some. We are less satisfied when we lack many things than when we seem to lack one thing." Such truths hurt, and Hoffer knew it, describing them as "perplexing and unpleasant." He also knew that he made many readers uncomfortable with his dismissals of modest materialism, ambition, and the desire to belong to a larger community. Yet he continued to dissect and seemingly to denigrate concepts that comforted many people who did not think of themselves as true believers, such as "glory" and "self-mastery" and "honor." Shakespeare's Falstaff had decried honor as no more than "air" and "a mere scutcheon," phrases fully as dismissive as Hoffer's, but Shakespeare's judgment on honor, perhaps because it was uttered by a fictional character, felt less offensive than Hoffer's.

Much more in *The True Believer* was uncomfortable reading: when Hoffer asserted, at the end of a section about how mass movements substituted new allegiances for previous ties to homes and families, that "the proselytizer who comes and says 'Follow me' is

75

a family-wrecker," it was hard for any Christian not to be offended by this deliberate undermining of Christ's directive. Only later in the book did Hoffer warn readers that he habitually overstated his cases and used "half-truths" to make points. Hoffer's exaggeration quotient was more obvious in such lines as, "Failure in the management of practical affairs seems to be a qualification for success in the management of public affairs," than when, after parsing the difference between individuals' actions and those of "corporate" groups like armies and mass movements, Hoffer asserted, "The torture chamber is a corporate institution."

Conscious that the book said very little that was positive about mass movements, Hoffer tried in its last parts to remedy that lack. "Rare leaders such as Lincoln, Gandhi, even F.D.R., Churchill, and Nehru," he wrote,

> ... do not hesitate to harness men's hungers and fears to weld a following and make it zealous unto death in the service of a holy cause; but unlike a Hitler, a Stalin, or even a Luther and a Calvin, they are not tempted to use the slime of frustrated souls as mortar in the building of a new world. The self-confidence of these rare leaders is derived from and blended with their faith in humanity, for they know that no one can be honorable unless he honors mankind.

Hoffer stressed that a democratic society must be home to both the majority who were content with the present—the "well-adjusted" autonomous individuals who in a crisis would band together and leap to defend their society—and to a leavening of malcontents, the incipient true believers who were needed to point up the society's faults. He also suggested how an individual could avoid becoming a true believer: through cultivating self-confidence, pride in one's skills, a sense of individuality, and "a dispassionate attitude toward the world." He also suggested that groups such as the best unions could take collective actions that bred "stability and permanence," thereby preventing their society from succumbing to the lures of true believership.

In his final section, "Useful Mass Movements," Hoffer celebrated as salutary what had happened during World War II, when the U.S., Great Britain, and its former colonies in Canada, South Africa, and Australia had briefly become a mass movement to release Europe and Asia from vassalage to the Axis powers. Throughout history, he asserted, mass movements had often brought stagnant periods to an end and thus advanced human progress. Seeking to identify what made a nation "virile" and properly aimed at a self-sustaining future, he posited that it must have a goal that was palpable, distant, and not overwhelmingly concrete, rather than an unrealizable "sublime" goal such as universal equality. In conclusion, Hoffer cited J. B. S. Haldane's observation that one of the world's most important inventions was fanaticism—the heart of any mass movement. "And it is strange to think that in receiving this malady of the soul the world also received a miraculous instrument for raising societies and nations from the dead—an instrument of resurrection."

In early 1951, ahead of publication of *The True Believer* or distribution to regular reviewers, Harper & Brothers had sent copies to noted authors for blurbs, among them the liberal historian Arthur Schlesinger Jr., and the conservative historian Peter Viereck. Both were impressed, Schlesinger writing of the book, "This brilliant and original inquiry into the nature of mass movements is a genuine contribution to our social thought," and Viereck—whom Hoffer had quoted in the book—praising its "devastating originality of social psychology," and opining, "Almost like Nietzsche, Hoffer's scintillating insights left me with amazed delight even though I often disagreed."

When regular reviews were published, they echoed Schlesinger and Viereck's initial impressions. Richard Rovere, a former writer for the leftist *New Masses* who had become a leading anti-communist, wrote in a lengthy review in *The New Yorker* that the book dealt "severely and brilliantly" with its theme, political fanaticism, and labeled Hoffer "a born generalizer, with a mind that inclines to the wry epigram and the icy aphorism as naturally as did that of the Duc de La Rochefoucauld." This lengthy review quoted hundreds of words from Hoffer's text. By contrast, in the same issue of *The New Yorker*, Hannah Arendt's *The Origins of Totalitarianism* received a brief and not entirely favorable review. *The New York Times* reviewed *The True Believer* twice, in the daily paper and in the Sunday book review; daily reviewer Orville Prescott lauded the book as "a harsh and potent mental tonic" that "glitters with icy wit," and in the Sunday *Times*, novelist E. B. Garside marveled, "All [Hoffer's] observations are incandescent. The book has no soft places, every page is hard and clear and crystalline. ... The writing itself is a marvel. Line after line is quotable."

Reviews in smaller-market newspapers and magazines were equally laudatory. As important to the publisher, the book enjoyed good word-of-mouth; readers would underline it, repeat its lines aloud to friends, and recommend it—sure signs of the book's wit, perceptiveness, and relevance. As syndicated newspaper columnist Georgie Anne Geyer would later recall about her experience of reading *The True Believer*, "One of the striking things about Hoffer is the personal response he evokes in people who read him. They've been watching the apparent madhouse of the modern world with growing confusion of spirit. Then they read Hoffer, and suddenly there's a framework for it, and a sense about it."

Around this time, Harper & Brothers began to refer to their author as the "longshoreman philosopher," a handle that stuck, even though Hoffer did not think of himself as a philosopher and in his book had studiously avoided instructing people (as he thought philosophers did) on how they should live. His reluctance to instruct did nothing to dispel his aura of mystery. Like some hero in a Greek myth, he seemed to have sprung into being fully armed.

Novelist Garside, seeking to understand him, studied his photograph on the inside back flap of *The True Believer*, and pronounced it a nice American face, one whose benevolence was the only balance to the toughness of the book. The photograph showed a smiling Hoffer with his trademark cap, and wearing a shirt with enormous lapels and no tie. He was clearly not a young man, in this photograph, but not yet an old one, with a smile more enigmatic than benevolent.

The lines beneath that photograph, on the inside back flap, only deepened the mystery by quoting Hoffer about his blindness in childhood and his determination, on heading to Los Angeles, to remain poor and independent. Here was a man seriously different from the authors that readers were used to encountering, and perhaps more formidable because of that differentness.

The New Yorker decided to wade into the enigma of Eric Hoffer. Two weeks after the magazine's rave review, its "Talk of the Town" section did a short piece on Hoffer. They obtained some information from Hoffer's early letters to Anderson, and Elizabeth Lawrence passed along more, including Norman Thomas's impressions from a lunch with Hoffer in San Francisco: Thomas described Hoffer as big, bold, thickset, strong, tie-less, "a bit awkward, but in manner active and eager." Anderson told the story of finally meeting Hoffer, "a great, friendly dog who radiates good will and exacts good will in return."

Not everyone liked *The True Believer*, or Hoffer. The San Francisco papers were less enthusiastic than those in Eastern cities, and in academia the book was for the most part ignored. Neither Hoffer nor his book had the academic cachet of *The Lonely Crowd*, by Harvard sociologists David Riesman, Nathan Glazer, and Reuel Denney, published in 1950, which dissected the "other-directed" people who made up that crowd of Americans, or of scholar Arendt's *The Origins of Totalitarianism*, which traced Nazism and Stalinism to anti-Semitism and imperialism, or of Bauhaus philosopher Theodor Adorno's *The Authoritarian Personality*, published in 1950, which deconstructed the personalities of Germans who so readily submitted to Hitler.

Six months after *The True Believer*'s debut, reporter Richard Donovan summed up the book's impact and the critical reaction in a four-page article in the monthly magazine *The Reporter*, "Migrant with a Message: How a longshoreman named Eric Hoffer began confounding the philosophy professors." Donovan wrote that public interest in the book had taken off because of "the hard shine of its reasoning, plus Hoffer's ability to turn an aphorism," but public interest was equally aroused by knowing that "'one of the most significant studies of our time' was not written by a famous scholar but by an unknown San Francisco longshoreman and part-time migrant worker." Neither Donovan nor any other reviewer mentioned Hoffer's rather complete anti-Communism; his stance was so in tune with the temper of the times that it did not warrant comment.

Academia's ignoring of Hoffer and the book might have been lessened had Bertrand Russell's review of *The True Believer* been published at the time of the book's American debut rather than a year later. In *The Observer*, the 79-year-old philosopher, the recipient of the 1950 Nobel Prize in literature, wrote of Hoffer, "Eschewing erudition, [he] applies an almost uncanny psychological insight to the explanation of the motives which throughout the ages have gene-rated the many different kinds of mass movement known to history." Russell then went into the specifics, agreeing with and repeating Hoffer's contentions:

> When a man joins in a mass movement he is persuaded that the movement is wholly good and that its virtue is reflected upon himself. His load of sin, on the other hand, is ejected onto an opponent's movement. In this way he is able at the same time to love his co-religionists, to hate the infidels, and to feel that sense of personal worth which, as an individual he had lost.
>
> Fear of the outer world and hatred of self are thus essential ingredients in the psychology of those who become converts to mass movements. ... If Mr. Hoffer's analysis is right, as I am

convinced that it is, the only cure for fanaticism lies in self-respect. ... A collection of abject individuals can be turned into a cruelly fanatical society; but only a community of self-respecting individuals can practise freedom and tolerance.

All this and much more will the reader find in Mr. Hoffer's book, which, in spite of its brevity and because of its simplicity, seems to me as sound intellectually as it is timely politically.

Re-reading *The True Believer* sixty years after its initial publication affirms that our culture has fully incorporated Hoffer's explications of Nazism and Communism into our basic understanding of that now long-past era. Today, Hoffer's comments about those regimes and their fanatic followers seem judicious rather than controversial, on a par with his many other observations of earlier historic eras such as that of the French Revolution.

More potent in the twenty-first century than when the book was first published are Hoffer's identification of the weaknesses and vulnerabilities that cause people to become true believers, and his revelations about how true believers relate to their world, their communities, and their leaders. His insights into the character of fanatics provide a window into the most perplexing "true believers" of the twenty-first century, the suicide bombers and al Qaeda members bent on destruction in the service of their holy cause, but also into the fervent beliefs that energize the partisans of many contemporary causes, from that of the Tea Party to ardent environmentalists and fanatical soccer fans. Through Hoffer we can understand how, as the economies of the world increasingly interlock, and as communication technologies enhance the ability of leaders and would-be leaders to influence our thoughts, more and more people are pressured to act against their own interests—as well as learn about what each individual can do to prevent succumbing to such pressures. On re-reading it today, *The True Believer* takes an honored place as an essential guide to a timeless subject: how to recognize and to resist the enemies of freedom, individuality, and personal responsibility.

In 1951, *The True Believer* was selling well enough for Harper & Brothers to plan further printings and to express interest in whatever Hoffer might write. Hoffer was eager to tout to Elizabeth Lawrence, as a next opus, a book of aphorisms that he had already compiled: "The thoughts deal with society, government, God, war, nations, economies, public figures and so on. They are not stuffy pieces but flashes of insight which may or may not be valid."

Hoffer expected to make, from American hardcover and foreign sales of *The True Believer*, about $4,000 to $5,000 in the book's first year, an amount greater than his annual $3,000 waterfront wage. He also had invitations to speak, and possible articles to write that might well have made it possible for him to henceforth make enough to live on as a writer and lecturer. But he decided not to quit his day job. Beyond his real need of a safe source of continuing income, it was important to Hoffer to continue as a working member of the working class, perhaps sensing that this connection, in addition to aiding his legitimacy, also made him more unlike other writers from impoverished or difficult backgrounds who at the first opportunity left behind those surrounds and manual labor jobs.

Sketching out a letter to Margaret Anderson, he pushed back against being rushed to produce a new book: "I loathe excitement, hurry, and the common restlessness of ambition. ... You can't help seeing life as a race. You have placed your bet on me and I am supposed to run and make good. I think you'll spare yourself many disappointments if you'll realize that I am not running."

Anderson, alarmed at the prospect of losing her influence over him, convinced *Harper's* to look again at the rejected "Tramps and Pioneers." The magazine now agreed to run the article in shortened form as "The Role of the Undesirables" in its December 1952 issue, commissioning a half-dozen line drawings as a way of pointing up its importance.

As a result of *The True Believer's* good sales and critical reception, Hoffer's life changed in some ways that were immediately perceptible and in some that only later became apparent. Though he would continue to deny that he was an intellectual, he now had the evidence that he could write an intellectually stimulating book and could hold his own with people who made their living dealing with ideas. As one consequence, he allowed his relationships to some of those whom he had known in his migrant and early longshoring days to fade. For years he had made an annual visit to Bob Dale, a barely literate pal in Santa Cruz; now several years elapsed between visits, causing Dale to send plaintive notes of invitation; Bob O'Brien wrote to him a lengthy critique of an early draft of "Tramps," rejecting the central tenet equating California pioneers with tramps, and citing the evidence in Chapter Ten of Hubert Howe Bancroft's *California Inter Pocula*—and Hoffer let his friendship with O'Brien attenuate.

According to Lili, around this time Hoffer also had a definitive falling out with Margaret Anderson. The trigger may have been Hoffer's rage over Anderson's last-minute attempts to rewrite sections of *The True Believer*, and/or to her releasing Hoffer's early letters to reporters. But underlying these reasons was something even more basic to Hoffer: he was a man who did not like to be beholden to anyone for anything, and a continuing connection to Anderson would make him feel obligated to her, perhaps even dependent on her—after all, he had dedicated *The True Believer* to Anderson, "without whose goading finger which reached me across a continent this book would not have been written." In later years, Hoffer would muse that he might have produced many more books had he married Anderson. But in the period just after his book was published, whatever romantic spark existed between Hoffer and Anderson fizzled out, supplanted by Hoffer's burgeoning involvement with Lili. Thereafter Hoffer dealt with Harper & Brothers directly.

Shortly after *The True Believer* was published in 1951, Brigadier General G. T. Lanham, the U.S. Army's chief of public information, gave out many copies to friends, among them one to his superior, General Dwight D. Eisenhower. The commanding general, shortly to become a candidate for the presidency, read the book through more than once and, as was his habit with books that engaged him, made extensive notes in the margins. For instance, he underlined a Hoffer line, "For men to plunge headlong into an undertaking of vast change, they must be intensely discontented," and wrote, "Which explains the demagogue! Huey Long. Hitler. Hundreds of others since the time of Alcibiades about 2250 years ago." On some issues in the book, the general disagreed: to Hoffer's contention that, "All forms of dedication, devotion, loyalty and self-surrender are in essence a desperate clinging to something which might give worth and meaning to our futile, spoiled lives," Eisenhower wrote, "This, I think is demonstrably false. For example, devotion to country can be simply a clear realization that group tasks become so important that all of us must devote himself unreservedly to their accomplishment." Some years later, in a letter written to a constituent, Eisenhower explained that Hoffer's understanding of Fascism and Communism was important because he "points out that dictatorial systems make one contribution to their people which leads them to tend to support such systems—freedom from the necessity of informing themselves and making up their own minds concerning these tremendous complex and difficult questions." In 1951-52, Eisenhower discussed the book with Dr. Gabriel Hauge, his aide for economic affairs, and used it as a basis for some campaign speeches. He also brought it up in conversation with Pulitzer-Prize winning war correspondent Marguerite Higgins, and gave her his annotated copy. Shortly after the landslide that elected Eisenhower as president, in late November 1952, Higgins told friends in the reportorial community about Ike's admiration for *The True Believer*, and word seeped out. By early 1953, Secretary of Defense Charles Wilson, former CEO of General Motors, and other Eisenhower administration officials were keeping stacks of the book in their offices to give out to visitors. Eisenhower was immensely popular, and his indirect endorsement of *The True Believer* accelerated its sales.

Proof of Eisenhower's enthusiasm, in the form of a typed excerpt from a letter from Hauge to another author, and an article quoting Higgins, were part of a scrapbook of reviews and articles about Hoffer that Margaret Anderson sent to him in an attempt to patch things up between them.

Chapter Five:
Between Big Books

Longshoremen were becoming objects of public curiosity. A 1949 series of articles about corruption on New York's waterfront won a Pulitzer Prize and was the basis for Budd Schulberg's script for Elia Kazan's film *On The Waterfront*, as well as for Arthur Miller's play *A View from the Bridge*. Tennessee Williams' play *A Streetcar Named Desire*, while not about longshoremen, also featured an intelligent though unlettered working-class protagonist. All contributed to public eagerness as to what "longshoreman philosopher" Eric Hoffer might say in his next book.

American culture was notorious for conspiring against an author's "second act" by overly celebrating with praise and money an initial play, novel, or non-fiction book, but then insisting that the second become as celebrated. Most second outings produced under this kind of pressure were judged as not the writer's best. In the early 1950s, novelist Norman Mailer was having a tough time following up *The Naked and the Dead*, and playwright Robert Anderson, *Tea and Sympathy*. In Europe and South America, serious literary success was not deemed to be the same as commercial success, and so writers were presumed to make their living from something other than writing while building a reputation through a series of small triumphs—a process that ameliorated European and South American authors' second act difficulties. But in America the hurdle existed, cemented into place by an axiomatic belief in capitalism that commingled literary value and moneymaking activity.

For Eric Hoffer, the problem of needing a second success was perhaps more acute than for other writers because his first book had transformed him from anonymous dockworker to "longshoreman philosopher." Should he prove unable to follow up his triumph well enough, he could slip back into an undistinguished existence, which he might well find painful. His problem was exacerbated because he didn't have a new subject to concentrate on, and felt that on the subject of mass movements he had already expressed all he wanted to say. He did not know what else he could write about that would have equivalent resonance. He had not yet understood that for him the subject of mass man was an "inland sea," as he would later characterize it, and that it would remain the source and the context of everything he wrote. So he searched for a new great theme and in the summer of 1951 thought that he had identified it, "enthusiasm." He confided it to Bob O'Brien, stressing the aspect of his basal distrust for passion, which he called an "intensification" of enthusiasm.

Soon, however, he decided that there was not enough in enthusiasm for a full book. He tried to tell Anderson that he was in no hurry to find the next big theme, almost taunting her by his report of "groping" for it. "My eyes have regained their sight but my mind is still blind," he explained. "When I have to deal with a new subject I am like a blind person who has to guess by feel the nature of some wholly strange object."

But by November 1951 he was able to list in a notebook the chapter titles and subjects of a proposed book on social change: "The Reformer. The Idealist. Cynicism (meaning the Intellectual), The Psychological Component, The religious impulse, Great expectations, Change and Consequences (soul, plasticity, explosiveness), Instances of drastic change. ... The Idea of a Chosen People, The Awakening of Stagnant Societies, Self-Esteem, Cynicism and Faith, and Some Thoughts on the Nature of Enthusiasm."

Those chapter subjects would become the substance of *The Ordeal of Change*, published in 1963, which Hoffer eventually judged to be his best book. Yet this second big book took him more than a decade to complete. What delayed him so long?

For one thing, his measured pace of composition. Writing *The True Believer* had taken many years, and even though he had already amassed quite a bit of material that might go into the new book, he was unwilling and, he thought, possibly unable to hurry his composition process. "How terribly hard and almost impossible it is to tell the truth," he would write; "We deal with truth as the cook deals with meat and vegetables."

A second reason was his insularity, which translated into reluctance to obtain guidance from an agent, editor, or intellectual peer who might have helped him define his focus. Hoffer liked to quip that having someone else do his thinking for him was akin to having someone else eat his food for him; but this notion also prevented him from accepting advice. Then too, he was intent on finding that subject within himself: self-awareness was all, he would write; without it, there was "neither sensitivity [nor] intellectual integrity, nor a genuine feeling for one's fellow men."

A third reason for delay involved his eagerness to accept assignments from magazines. He had never before composed on a deadline or on a commissioned subject, but after *Harper's* published "The Role of the Undesirables," other magazine editors solicited him. He was ecstatic at a request from *The New York Times Magazine*—it was ratification of his intellectual worth—and liked the subject, "Why Captive Peoples Revolt," but when he finished the article he was not sure that it represented his best thinking. He was happier with *The Reporter*'s non-specific request: editor Max Ascoli, a fan, wanted any article he cared to do, and so Hoffer wrote about "The Awakening of Asia," home of the "stagnant" societies that he was investigating; even so, it took him eighteen months. Meeting the *Pacific Spectator*'s deadline for "The Intellectual and the Masses," he would later say, was the hardest thing he had ever done.

A fourth reason for delay was his fondness for aphorisms. He was attracted to the idea of a book of them, in part because he wanted to be known as an aphorist like Montaigne and De La Rochefoucauld, and in part because the form relieved him of the need to provide fuller explanations of his thoughts. Most aphorisms are generalizations, which he liked to make, and the form favors the overstatements and deliberately provocative comparisons of his argumentative style. "An aphorism states a half-truth and hints at a larger truth," he later explained. "To an aphorist, all facts are perishable. His aim is to entertain and stimulate. Instruction means the stuffing of people with perishable facts. And since in human affairs the truthful is usually paradoxical, aphorismic writing is likely to prove helpful." Then too, as a man who composed on his feet, while doing manual labor, Hoffer was more comfortable with the short paragraph than with the extended disquisition.

Trenchant aphorisms tend by their brevity and completeness to shut off further discussion, as in these by De La Rochefoucauld, "Before we set our hearts too much upon anything, let us examine how happy those are who already possess it," and "Hypocrisy is the homage which vice pays to virtue," and in these by Montaigne, "A man who fears suffering is already suffering from what he fears," and "Everyone rushes everywhere, and into the future, because no one wants to face one's own inner self." Some Hoffer aphorisms fit readily into the same category, as in his already-famous line, "Faith in a holy cause is to a considerable extent a substitute for the lost faith in ourselves," and newer ones such as "There is always a chance that he who sets himself up as his brother's keeper will end up by being his jailkeeper." But many of Hoffer's most significant observations require more than a single line, and spur readers to think further rather than foreclosing the argument: "There has been a gradual shrinking of the range of predictability during the past 2000 years. In the heyday of Christianity predictability reached the utmost limit: it predicted the life beyond. In the idea of progress, which took the place of millennial prognostication, predictability is much narrower." "The moment we are seized with a passion to be wholly different from what we are, we are in a religious mood. Remorse, a vivid awareness of our weakness or worthlessness, a craving for pride, fame and glory—all ... involve a rejection of the real self and a reaching out for a new identity."

The real difficulty for a publisher, in a book of Hoffer aphorisms, was the potential readership's preference for narrative. While Renaissance-era readers of Montaigne and De La Rochefoucauld were connoisseurs of aphorisms, modern readers were neither used to aphorisms nor primed to appreciate them, looking instead for story-telling and sequentiality, which were in short supply in *The Passionate State of Mind*. Moreover, as Harper & Row would soon acknowledge in its flap copy, Hoffer aphorisms were not "comfortable reading."

A fifth and last reason for the delay involved Hoffer's increasingly tangled relationship with the Osbornes—daughter Tonia, aged nine in 1953, and son Stephen, aged six, in addition to Selden and Lili. Hoffer used his writing income to assist the chronically underfunded family. An undated letter to him from Selden returned $200 borrowed to tide the family over during an enforced thirty-day vacation period in which Selden had no income. He thanked Hoffer for regularly extending such assistance: "You have helped us in so many big ways, and are so generous in so many little ways also! It is not that I forget to say 'thank you' but that sometimes it seems out of place to thank you for so many things you do." Although Hoffer was confiding to his note-books around this time that he must do "as little harm as possible," keep desires in check and "guard against self-dramatization, a feeling of importance, and the sprouting of expectations," he was acutely aware, as he would put it many years later, that he had "invaded" his friend's "nest" and "taken" his wife.

In that same later time frame Selden would admit that before Hoffer arrived, his and Lili's relationship had cooled, and imply that Hoffer's intrusion, while not precisely welcome, did provide a way out of a marriage that had soured. Yet the Osborne divorce did not occur until 1968 and Selden remained in residence with Lili and the children until 1966. Lili wrote to Tomkins that while she and Selden still shared "attachment, affection, and mutual concern," for a long time they had not had a real marriage.

The triangle was a complex matter, not least because of Selden's admiration for Hoffer and because of the work that Selden put into remaining friends with him. After an altercation, Selden wrote to Hoffer: "You certainly have no more reason to apologize to me than I to you. We clash, and the clash hurts me because of my situation." The note reminded Hoffer of his having spoken many times of "the importance of doing the important thing," but cautioned that "in many circumstances [that] means hurting other people." "The leverage of life's immediate demands," Selden added, in the short run prevented him from doing that important thing, but he believed that such leverage would attenuate over time. In closing, he wrote, "You make me very angry but I really love you."

In 1955, Lili announced that she was pregnant. Hoffer, delighted with the pregnancy, predicted that the child would be a boy, asked that he be named Eric, and promised to treat him as his beloved grandchild and to assist in every way in underwriting his life. Selden and Lili agreed to name the boy Eric Osborne.

"Passions usually have their roots in that which is blemished, crippled, incomplete, and insecure within us," Hoffer asserted in the first of the 280 short sections *The Passionate State of Mind and other Aphorisms*, thereby setting out the 1955 book's purview, style, and tone. The book differed broadly from *The True Believer* in not being about mass movements per se, and in saying nothing directly about Nazism or Communism and very little that was historically specific. It's strongest observations held a bright mirror to illusions, as in 263, "Suffering cleanses only when it is free of resentment. Wholehearted contempt for our tormentors safeguards our soul from the mutilations of bitterness and hatred." Many of them also provided a sense of how he viewed his role in the world as in 17, "There is perhaps no better way of measuring the natural endowment of a soul than by its ability to transmute dissatisfaction into a creative impulse."

Having thought earlier of a book about enthusiasm, and abandoned that as too narrow a compass, in this book he positioned enthusiasm as one passion among many, all of them suspect. Popular culture celebrated passions as positive, romantic emotions, but Hoffer did not, defining the "passionate state" as the state of being unduly and unwisely carried away from reason. He offered suggestions for transcending it: the skilled worker could cultivate a feeling of ease in going about the job, the artist could become caught up in the creative process, and the man of action could undertake activities that benefitted society.

He was particularly insightful about leaders who used followers' passions for dastardly ends, as in the quotable tag line of 95, "All leaders strive to turn their followers into children." His section 42 stood Lord Acton's famous dictum on its head by asserting that weakness corrupted just as absolutely as power; his 30 suggested that the "most difficult" path to acquiring a sense of worth was self-realization. He contrasted "self-esteem," based on personal achievement, and "pride," based on identification with things outside the self and containing elements of "fear and intolerance."

Most readers had no inkling that many of the book's sections reflected Hoffer's personal fears, because all they read were impersonal, witty aphorisms. But for those few who knew his biography and private life, those underlying fears were palpable. In 21, he stated, "Lovemaking is radical while marriage is conservative." In 27, he warned, "confidence and self-esteem" were "extremely perishable, and must be generated anew each day," because "an achievement today is but a challenge for tomorrow." In 70, he confessed, "We lie loudest when we lie to ourselves." In 130, he chafed at "the playwrights and stage managers of our lives [who] cast us in a role, and we play it whether we will or not," and worried, in 189, "We are never really sure of the genuineness of our convictions, feelings, tastes, and desires."

As such lines also demonstrate, the aphoristic form is best suited not to appreciating life's bounty but to deflating man's illusions.

That inherently cynical attribute of aphorisms hurt the book's reception. Moreover, since Hoffer provided no chapter headings or other connective materials, readers searching for patterns found unintended ones; many readers over-linked the current book's concerns to those in Hoffer's previous book, and judged *The Passionate State of Mind* as only extending or merely repeating the basic insights of *The True Believer*.

Professional critics' reviews were mixed. Although *Time* lauded Hoffer as a "Dockside Montaigne" with a bent for "near 17th century-style brooding on 20th century problems," Richard Rovere of *The New Yorker*—a champion of *The True Believer*—was less enthusiastic. He praised the "pretty powerful effect" of the new book's "cool, mocking iconoclasm" and "massive suspicion of the righteous," but expressed disappointment at what he deemed its paraphrasing of De La Rochefoucauld's maxims and of Hoffer's own earlier work. But even other reviewers who preferred the first Hoffer book interpreted the second as affirming Hoffer's talent and insightfulness.

Read today, *The Passionate State of Mind* has many insights into the individual that still reverberate, particularly those concerned with the nature of fear and its consequences, the psychological fault-line in the self that Hoffer labeled the source of all creativity, and the relationship between an individual's creativity and his or her ability to withstand the negative pressures of passions. His comments on these matters are more helpful to individuals today, in a world that features a greater number and variety of temptations to indulge in "passion" than there were in the less information-saturated world of 1955.

At his publisher's request, Hoffer had met with various important people who came through San Francisco, such as Norman Thomas and Joyce Cary. But he had not been impressed by Norman Thomas, who counseled him to study Buddhism and the religions of the East.

Cary, best known for his novel *The Horse's Mouth*, shared an editor with Hoffer, Elizabeth Lawrence, who perhaps believed, on the basis of Cary's classic non-fiction study *Power in Men*, about freedom and liberty, that he and Hoffer had common interests and would become friends. Hoffer and Cary shared a meal but no correspondence ensued. However, after *The Passionate State of Mind* appeared, when Hoffer was asked to entertain, separately, Saul Alinsky, Hannah Arendt, and Eugene Burdick, he did so, and developed good relationships with all three.

Alinsky, the author of *Reveille for Radicals* and a biography of mineworkers' leader John L. Lewis, was a social theorist who put his ideas to work as a community organizer in Chicago. Though he was considerably to the left of Hoffer politically, they found plenty of areas of agreement. Afterwards, Alinsky wrote to him, "Those kinds of evenings and conversation companions and the feeling which prevails through that kind of a night is one of the most precious things in life." They corresponded, and in later years when Alinsky passed through San Francisco, they would meet and talk. Hannah Arendt, after a walk with Hoffer through Golden Gate Park, was as complimentary:

> Like a king who shows his realm you showed me San Francisco; you are king bounty not only to your godson. I think I never understood the Walt Whitman side of this country so clearly before I met you and you told me how you used to wander and live with the elements, where every man is your brother and nobody is your friend. I love the book you sent me [*The Passionate State of Mind*] because it has the same quality. You won't know that; it is the side of ourselves which must remain dark to us and can appear—shine really—only to others. It is the same sovereignty, the majesty of solitude which shines through every sentence.

The aspect of Hoffer that Arendt identified as Whitmanesque, featuring his charisma and ability to seduce, was coming to the fore.

It was on display, notably, in a 1957 appearance at Berkeley. Hoffer had occasionally lectured at this citadel of intellectuals since shortly after the publication of *The True Believer*, invited to do so by political scientist Norman Jacobson.

Shortly after Jacobson defended his doctoral dissertation in 1951, he had been given a copy of Hoffer's book. Reading it quickly, he had been incensed at Hoffer's dismissal of professional political scientists; then, possibly at the urging of his friend Eugene Burdick, with whom Jacobson would collaborate on some screenplays, he read the book again, recognized its brilliance, got in touch with Hoffer, and began a friendship. The political science department at Berkeley was then a notable bastion of "the non-Communist left," those who were to the left of the political center on economic and social matters but who were adamantly not Communists. Jacobson and Hoffer disagreed on most issues, but Jacobson admired Hoffer's depth of learning and power of reasoning, and thought students ought to be exposed to him. After this particular Berkeley appearance in 1957, he wrote to Hoffer, "It was more than merely a virtuoso performance. It was to most of us a masterpiece. The students were deeply touched and stimulated and I still hear comments from them."

Hoffer and Jacobson shared a fondness for the Old Testament and the history of Judaism; partly through Jacobson's encourage-ment, Hoffer became a public supporter of Israel, and learned enough Hebrew to recite Psalm 104 in that tongue to a Jacobson class. Hoffer would later write, in a letter recommending tenure for Jacobson, "Several fruitful trains of thought which occupied me for ... years have had their inception in conversations and correspondence with Norman." Hoffer also brought Hannah Arendt to a Jacobson seminar, where she was quite taken with the level of discourse, the students' "responsiveness to original trains of thought," and their warm respect for their professor.

Eugene "Bud" Burdick, a psychologist with close ties to the Berkeley poli sci department, was co-author of the best-seller *The Ugly American* and sole author of other novels noted for their social analysis. He interviewed Hoffer for the first serious examination of Hoffer's work, a twenty-page article in *The Reporter*, published in February 1957, and they remained friends for the rest of Burdick's life. Max Ascoli, founder and editor of *The Reporter*, was the impetus behind the Burdick article, and he also commissioned articles from Hoffer. In Italy, Ascoli had been a leading anti-fascist before his forced emigration in 1932; in the U.S., he had written *The Power of Freedom* and founded *The Reporter*, a liberal magazine with an international perspective that, like Ascoli and Burdick themselves, was steadily moving rightward by the end of the 1950s.

Burdick asserted that both of Hoffer's books (*The True Believer* and *The Passionate State of Mind*) contained material that to readers was "unnerving" because they did not want to think

> ... that the glint in the eye of a liberal reformer might harden into the glaring certitude of a Lenin or a Hitler. We are disturbed to think that selflessness is often a mask that justifies ruthlessness ... and we shy from the idea that our impulse to mold and save and change—which we consider to be our noblest passions—may really spring from a dry rot of rage against others. And yet we have the slight gnawing sensation that something about this is true.

Burdick also pointed out, as no one previously had, Hoffer's considerable appeal to the right. Some of Hoffer's more quotable lines, Burdick wrote, would nicely

> ... flesh out a speech by an outgoing president of the National Association of Manufacturers or, indeed, anyone who wished to lambaste contemporary socialism. The conservative would also be nourished by Hoffer's view that "Great evils befall the world when the powerful begin to copy the weak." And he would applaud the notion that "from the drive and action of the strong the whole society benefits, and the arrogance of certitude is a small price to pay for the benefits."

Burdick observed that all sorts of ideologues selectively quoted Hoffer to berate their opponents. That was a reference to what had happened in the spring of 1956, when Eisenhower was running for re-election, and a *Newsweek* article on what the president read featured *The True Believer*, with close-up photos of Eisenhower's copy and his written comments. *Look* had followed with a photo spread, "Ike's Favorite Philosopher," that shows Hoffer actively participating in burnishing his legend, contemplating deep thoughts in his sparsely furnished room, stalking regally with his grand walking stick through Golden Gate Park, and, on the docks, trundling cargo with a fellow worker and then posed on a pallet in solitary contemplation of a small book. But Eisenhower's interest made him uneasy; he would later quip that it had ratified his decision to make the book's language easy enough for a child to understand.

Despite such wisecracks, Hoffer was now closer to Eisenhower in political outlook, having rejected the vestiges of liberalism that he had accepted in the 1940s as a concomitant of his union affiliation. In 1955 Eisenhower had welcomed the re-uniting of the AFL and the CIO with a short speech that identified three labor principles on which he and the new organization agreed: one, "the ultimate values of mankind ... include liberty, human dignity, opportunity and equal rights and justice," interpreted as the right of labor to organize; two, the economic interests of employers and workers were for "mutual prosperity;" and three, "labor relations will be managed best when worked out in honest negotiation between employers and unions, without government's unwarranted interference." Although some AFL-CIO officers disagreed with Eisenhower's summary of principles, Hoffer's view of unions was precisely that of the president. Then too, like Eisenhower Hoffer was disdainful of intellectuals; like Eisenhower he was fervent in his anti-Communism; and like Eisenhower—and like Mr. Kunze, in the story Hoffer wrote twenty years earlier—Hoffer was increasingly convinced of the centrality of the profit motive in human progress. A society lacking "the acquisitive motive," Hoffer wrote, was "likely to develop into a combination of army and school."

For such heresies, Hoffer was increasingly derided by the left, a drumbeat that would continue throughout his career. It was not simply his apparent drift to the right that upset the left; it was his distance from the stance that they expected of members of "progressive" unions and of working class writers. But that expectation itself was suspect. After the Taft-Hartley Act and the expulsion of Communist-led unions from the CIO, the ILWU among them, there was an increasing schism between the leaders of unions, who tended to be quite progressive, and the regular members, who were much less so. Hoffer's sentiments were more in line with rank and file than with the leadership.

That split was highlighted when Hoffer participated in a union-sponsored panel discussion at a small college. Audience members were asked to write their impressions of the panel. Harry Bridges was in that audience, and while he acknowledged that Hoffer could "say in a few sentences what takes most professors ten lectures," he carped that Hoffer "has unfortunately put himself in a position of seeming to be an apologist for the status quo." Evaluations of Hoffer from others in the audience, unionists and college students, were more positive, and none echoed Bridges' categorization of Hoffer as an apologist.

Hoffer did not much like being on a panel, any panel; he preferred being alone on a podium, and in the late 1950s he was provided with one ideal setting for such a lecture, a theater at Stanford's Center for the Advanced Study in the Behavioral Sciences that held several hundred people yet because of its large windows felt open to the air and the rolling hills. This milieu, and the eagerness of the audience to listen to him, and the company of Lili Osborne, induced Hoffer to set aside prepared remarks and speak extemporaneously about how he came to write *The True Believer*, giving details of his childhood, migrant work, and the like. When he told the story of the El Centro camp, he paused and asked if anyone there was from El Centro, and when a hand went up, Hoffer asked if there was anyone from Modesto, and from other towns where he had worked.

They answered, and Hoffer realized that the audience was hanging on every word, and felt that were he to ask them to follow him in action, they would.

In that moment, Hoffer realized that Hitler's seductiveness as an orator had been the source of his power. Lili later emphasized that aspect of Hoffer by referring to what happened in that auditorium as "making love in public." The persuasive power that Hoffer felt frightened him, so much so that he resolved never again to lecture in public.

Hoffer's interest in contemporary events continued to rise. He became intrigued by the tides of nationalism in Africa and East Asia, the collapse of the Fourth Republic in France, and the USSR's launch of Sputnik in October 1957. He was bothered by the United States' inability, in the late 1950s, to emerge from the throes of a long recession and make headway in foreign affairs. Eisenhower and Secretary of State John Foster Dulles seemed unwilling to address these problems, and Hoffer thought they ought to be doing something—in contrast to his earlier judgment that the U.S. was best off under unexceptional leaders who did not experiment to fix current crises. In the spring of 1957, discomfited because events had proved his judgments wrong, unnerved by his success at lecturing, and still searching for his next subject, Hoffer decided to keep a diary. "I had to sort things out, talk to somebody," he later explained. It would run to seven notebook volumes, and although not initially meant for publication, when he rediscovered it, Harper & Row would publish it in 1969 as *Working and Thinking on the Waterfront*.

He began on May 20, 1958, and in his second entry confided that what usually floated around his head, when he was not contemplating large concepts, were thoughts about "Little Eric," two-and-a-half, the apple of his eye. He had to fight the urge to spend more time with the boy and Lili than the weekly visits they had agreed upon, holding in check the impulse to see the child as he exited a nursery school class. Hoffer tried to transmute this emotion into a generality: "My attachment to the boy is being reinforced by a sense of loneliness. Men feel lonely when they do not do the one thing they ought to do. It is only when we fully exercise our capacities—when we grow—that we have roots in the world and feel at home in it."

Reading *Letters from Jerusalem* by May Clawson, published recently, he marveled at her sunniness and sensitivity—terrific attributes of Americans, he judged, and observed, "Under similar circumstances, I would have been neither delightful nor fine. Here she is among total strangers and she does not carp or criticize, nor betray the least trace of bad temper."

On May 23 he resorted to a favored investigative tool, inverting an accepted historical explanation to test its validity. Progress, he wrote, was "not a continuous struggle of the common people since the beginning of time but the [product of] unceasing reaching out of the educated for power and prestige which began almost with the invention of writing." He conflated his anger at Communism with his anger at intellectuals—in the USSR they were now the tools of represssion, and outside of it, no more than parrots of the Party line. He recounted a union meeting whose first half was devoted to hashing over the case of Morton Sobell, an engineer convicted of espionage for the USSR along with Julius and Ethel Rosenberg, and who was trying to rally support for release from prison. "The intellectual dishonesty of the Commies and fellow-travelers [in the union] was of the crudest" during this discussion, Hoffer noted, but was pleased to report that in the second half of the meeting, devoted to how to deal with "chiselers" at the union hall, "The solutions offered were original and wonderfully simple. The simplicity con-veyed an impression of subtlety."

He worried in other entries about becoming unduly deprecating of intellectuals. "It is strange that this attitude should become pronounced in me at a time when the creative flow is at its thinnest." What he judged proper for intellectuals was ideology-free analysis and, in fiction, constructing interesting characters, plots, and descriptions. In his view, most would-be intellectuals, failing at these tasks, settled for being pseudo-intellectuals and substituted a yearning for political and supervisory power for lack of creative power.

He was a very tough observer. Paired on the docks with a man from Montenegro, Hoffer dismissed him to the diary as "communistic in his sympathies, bitter about this country, and chock-full of grievances." Hoffer was currently reading a book that encompassed the Montenegrin's home area, Charles Diehl's *Byzantium: Greatness and Decline*, and arrogantly asked the longshoreman a historical question about his home country. Only upon receiving the correct answer, Hoffer wrote, did he discuss with him how and why nationalistic churches differed from the Catholic church, and how this might transfer to communism's ability to spur the nationalities under it to independence. But whatever dialogue the men had was not recorded in the diary—the entry simply repeated what Hoffer had told the Montenegrin, not the man's responses.

Hoffer was as caustic about the celebrated writers he read, such as Neitzsche: "Surely, the man has not written a single sentence that was not animated by a passionate craving to make up for something he had missed in life. [His work is] a conglomerate of flashing insights embedded in a matrix of preposterous bunk." He judged Thomas Carlyle's famous book on *Chartism* as far too wordy, although containing some beautiful passages. Tackling Leon Trotsky's *Diary in Exile*, he found in it added evidence of the negative effects of intellectuals; Trotsky, he wrote, was "convinced that people cannot be decent unless they have a great idea which raises them 'above personal misery, above weakness, above all kinds of perfidy and baseness.' To a Trotsky, the mass of people who do the world's work without fuss and feathers are morally debased."

"I am increasingly aware of how much I have to watch myself," Hoffer confessed in another entry, but he did not police himself in terms of reining in his biases, principal among them a long-simmering mistrust of those he persisted in calling "Negroes." Just then the ILWU was struggling to incorporate a large number of African-

Americans, and many of Hoffer's fellow white long-term members were resisting the influx. In June, Hoffer mused that African-Americans, more so than whites, seemed to present exaggerated, "stereotypical" characters, such as "the unctuous hypocrite, the barefaced cheat, the windbag, the lecher, the miser," and he decided this must be attributable to their need for "play-acting" to get by in a white society. In another entry, he wrote of beginning to read *An American in India*, by Saunders Redding, an African-American state department employee, and initially judging it as "a perplexing and depressing book. A sick man writing about sick people. When facing the most preposterous questions and defamatory insinuations he remains speechless." Next day, having read further, he altered his assessment: "Saunders Redding's book is worth reading for its de-tailed recording of the talk of the Indian intellectuals both young and old. He reproduces minutely their arguments, rudeness, sarcasm and self-righteousness. Since he seldom essayed a rebuttal his recording comes out sharp and forceful." The following day, having completed the book, he called it "a fascinating puzzle. Imagination could never synthesize for us the state of mind of a Negro in a white environ-ment," and he wondered "whether a Negro intellectual can feel himself truly and wholly an American."

To Hoffer's credit was his willingness to alter an initial negative judgment on the basis of further evidence. But his bias did not abate. While elsewhere Hoffer wrote that when people were biased they looked for evidence that ratified their bias, he now did just that, complaining to the diary on July 22 that African-Americans, although late arrivals to his union, held a disproportionate number of its higher posts. "They have achieved much without having to fight for it. Yet the Negro longshoreman sounds bitter and frustrated." He tried to deny bias by recording that he knew several African-American dock-workers to be "gentle, quiet, conscientious, and highly competent. I would give much to [know] their life histories—how they manage to go through life without being tainted and blemished." Hoffer seemed unaware that this characterization, too, was the product of bias.

How could a man who had written so insightfully about America having been built by undesirables, by immigrants from the lowest rungs of society, refuse to award any percentage of truth to the similar assertion made by African-Americans, that black slaves had been the South's engine of wealth? And, when confronted with the former colony of Gold Coast becoming the independent nation of Ghana, disparage the possibility that this triumph could do for blacks everywhere what the founding of Israel had done for the Jews? "The crucial question," Hoffer wrote in this entry on Ghana, "is whether the Negro will ever give up the alibi of discrimination. You do not give up the unperishable advantage of an alibi for the short-lived exhilaration of achievement." Although Hoffer believed his judgments to be based on analysis of facts and supported by evidence, he regularly selected to report on aspects of an event—as in the founding of Ghana—that upheld his previous views and rejected any need to take into account contravening evidence such as the hampering legacies of slavery and colonialism that underlay what he dismissed as an "alibi."

Hoffer's bias toward African-Americans was exacerbated, during the year recorded in this diary, because he was plagued in his rented rooms by noisy blacks who moved in above and below him, disturbing his sleep. In reaction, after sixteen years in this flat Hoffer felt forced to decamp to another furnished apartment, on Clay Street in Chinatown, at the top of a steep hill. It was much quieter, for which he was grateful.

More trenchant and truthful entries of the diary recounted his readings. He lambasted several articles in *The New Yorker* that purported to be expert analyses but had been contradicted by recent newspaper headlines and were thereby exposed as ideological speculations. "No matter how often the predictions of experts and soothsayers are proven wrong," he noted, "we go on reading them [because] we simply need the momentary illusion that we know what's ahead."

Studying the early histories of Christianity and Islam, he concluded, "Islam is almost without inner contradictions—between church and state, profession and performance, the spirit and the flesh." People assumed, he continued that such contradictions would bring about the breakdown of a society, but because Islam fulfilled all of its adherents' needs, it had a "tranquilizing effect" whose "end result was stagnation." Contemplating this, he reached a central idea: "Vigor and creative flow have their source in internal strains and tensions. It is the pull of opposite poles that stretches souls. And only stretched souls make music."

The diary contained the seeds of many later articles, book sections, and Hoffer basic tenets, such as that "every drastic change recapitulates to some extent the change from boyhood to manhood," that no country is very good for its young, that he has a "savage heart" and must fight against it, and that the desire for freedom and the desire for power over other men are polar opposites.

He inscribed the diary at night, often with thoughts originally noted during the day in a daybook. In a daybook entry from this period, after mulling over the possible ways that a faith could be spread, he reached a thought so important that he indicated it by a blast of exclamation points: "!!!!! Thus a faith or a way of life may be most readily transmitted to alien populations in a movement which comes into being as a dissent and a challenge. And it is thus that heresies may often play a vital role in the diffusion of a religious or social system." Passages like these revealed Hoffer's mind working at its best, unearthing the underlying causes of events and the previously hidden connections between what had elsewhere been portrayed as disparate entities.

Although by this method Hoffer acquired the certainty that he was correct in his analyses of the world, he continued to worry, through the diary, about the propriety of his actions toward Eric and Lili. When the three had nice outings, he noted his pleasure—an odd but satisfying one for a man who had had no touch with family for forty years. He was also of two minds about being overworked on the docks, looking forward to a ten-day vacation in October but during it becoming annoyed as he spent it recovering his strength rather than writing.

He chronicled "an unpleasant falling out with Selden," after Selden opined that people were prone to detect in others their own faults, and wondered if his characterization of the union officials as "lazy and dishonest" meant that he also had such failings. Hoffer writes that he hid his real thoughts: "I did not tell him that his sin of laziness was in not making the efforts to utilize the training and knowledge he had been given at Stanford, and that his dishonesty manifests itself in crass self-righteousness." But he antagonized Selden anyway by turning the conversation to pretentiousness; then at midnight in his room Hoffer admitted that had been "tactless and stupid." Nonetheless, he thought Selden constitutionally unable to respond to criticism, so in Selden's "present state of mind, seeing things as they really are might be fatal. He perhaps has to be self-righteous in order to survive." Hoffer concluded that Selden was the idealist described by Nietzsche, "A creature who has reasons for remaining in the dark about himself, and who is also clever enough to remain in the dark concerning these reasons." Hoffer wrote quite a bit in the diary about his dislike of intellectuals—with Selden and Harry Bridges as unidentified examples of the sort that he could not stand.

Two weeks after the "falling out" there was a family dinner at the Osbornes that Hoffer began to recount to the diary by a summation, "How hard it is to know what is really happening to us." During the dinner, the boy became overly boisterous, and when Hoffer tried to quiet him down, yelled, "You not belong to the house anyhow!" In reaction Selden had "a peculiar smile" on his face. "This is the most complex household imaginable, with everyone pulling in a different direction. The moods swing wildly from one extreme to the other, and so do the attitudes toward me." Hoffer loved all the Osbornes, he wrote, but wondered what his favorite anthropologist, Laurens van der Post, would say about the family. At moments with them, he wrote, "I am convinced that I am being drained and bled. ... With Selden's somber sulking, Tonia's epilepsy, Lili's spells of utter thoughtlessness anything may happen. Steve's hunger for security may be typical of boys his age, but it has a quality of foreboding. Even Little Eric with all of his innocence and robustness fills me with misgivings."

The next morning, he worked at breakfast "on a section dealing with the antagonism between action and creativeness," possibly spurred by the previous evening's tensions. "The thwarted impulse toward action ... works itself out in creativeness," he judged, and asserted that thwarted people "tend to become either revolutionaries or writers, artists, etc. ... Where there are no talents, tension vents itself in a variety of action."

In a diary entry soon thereafter, Hoffer warned himself against lumping all intellectuals into one category, and to avoid over-generalizing. But this entry was followed by a reminder that a "hefty chapter" would have to deal with intellectuals' bad-mouthing of the United States.

At five one morning, he noted his dread of having to meet a group of journalists from Southeast Asia later that day at the behest of the American Press Institute of Columbia University, but after the event wrote, "It was a hell of a meeting with a pack of biting, hissing, pseudo-intellectuals. I pushed their noses in the dirt!" He did so, he wrote, to redress "the sort of baiting [Saunders Redding] had to endure without hitting back. ... Bill Stuckey [of the API said] they had needled and baited everyone from Dulles down. It is good that an American workingman let them have it."

Hoffer knew he was sometimes unduly angry and over-critical—for instance, of Tonia, then completing high school, and of the other Osborne children—and sought ways to overcome anger. "Fair play is primarily the practice of not blaming them for anything that is going wrong with us. We tend to rub our guilty conscience against others the way we wipe our dirty fingers on a rag. This is as evil a misuse of others as the practice of exploitation." Perhaps as expiation for himself blaming others, he toiled to better his relationships to "the boy," whose antics and intelligence he was beginning to understand. Hoffer was unused to parenting—for that matter, unused to living with another person, even part-time—and was often ham-handed in his treatment of Lili, Eric, Stephen, and Tonia. But spending time with Lili and Eric gave Hoffer joy; and, although he had not been used to such an emotion, over the months chronicled in the diary he came to the realization that he needed such emotions in order to write well.

By the end of 1958, perhaps through writing out his problems and straining to describe and understand his emotions, his thinking had become more cogent. His December 30 entry succinctly summed up many new ideas: "Once man was tamed by the manipulative magic of Priest and King he stopped tinkering with and probing the world around him and became a beggar—begging Gods for good crops and good fortune. With the birth of the new Occident, man resumed to question nature and pry answers from her. He became a miracle maker, and ceased to believe in miracles." Happy with this, he confided to the diary, "It is strange that utterly dejected in the morning I now sit at my table wholly at peace with the world. When my head works at all, all is well."

A new union hiring hall opened in mid-January 1959, and Hoffer was mildly disconcerted by the change in routine. Moreover, "The renewed riots in the Belgian Congo make me wonder whether there can be a peaceful transition from Colonialism to independence. Indeed can any abrupt transition, any drastic change, be peaceful?" Reading about Nikita Khrushchev's "shenanigans" over Berlin—he had issued an ultimatum to the Western powers to get out within six months—Hoffer labeled them "juvenile," and decided that while mature people preferred change that brought steady growth and that proceeded imperceptibly, juveniles judged "continuity and gradualism as synonymous with stagnation," and lusted after drastic change "as a mark of dynamism, vigor, and freedom."

By March 16, 1959, he realized that all the articles he had written—those on the role of the undesirables, on captive peoples, on the awakening of Asia, and on the intellectual and the masses, even "God and the Machine Age" for *The Reporter*, "A Workingman Looks at the Boss" for *Harper's*, and "Thoughts on the Brotherhood of Man," for *The New York Times*, fit a pattern:

> My subject is obviously change; why it is so difficult and explosive in the communist countries and in the new nations. The intellectual is trying to master and direct this process. If I manage to write a few more articles—on the readiness to work, the connection between technical modernization and social primitivization, and others I will have a book. ... A comprehensive theory of change should be applicable not only to the change from backwardness to modernization but also to the passage from boyhood to manhood, from poverty to affluence, from subjection to equality, and so on, even to the menopause.

Having identified his big subject, Hoffer felt no more need for a formal diary, and shortly brought it to a close, almost in mid-sentence. The final entry concerned the new influx of men to the docks, an arrival of young people that made him feel good.

Hoffer seemed unaware, when he put away the seven notebooks of his 1958-59 diary, that in them he had created one of the most candid and intellectually startling of twentieth century diaries, more powerful as literature than many of his other works.

Chapter Six:
Change and *The Ordeal of Change*

Momentum toward explosive social change had been building in the United States since World War II. Between 1959 and 1963, Hoffer's period of new composition for *The Ordeal of Change*, the "baby boom" generation entered college, eager to break out of the docile followers' mold of their parents' cohort; the birth control pill was making possible an escape from prior sexual mores; African-Americans were demanding racial equality; and technological advances were revolutionizing work and leisure.

In his early sixties, and although finally enjoying his dockwork and accepting himself as a full-time workingman rather than as a migrant, Hoffer wondered to his diary,

> Have I missed much by spending my life with barely literate people? Could I have written *The True Believer* when surrounded by articulate people, well read and skilled in argument? ... Intellectual isolation was in my case a decisive advantage. The question is whether now contact with well-informed people might not prove stimulating. Many things one gets along without when young become desirable when old.

He became closer to intellectuals and artists such as Norman Jacobson of Berkeley and finepoint etcher Alex Stern, but nonetheless continued to work on the docks and took pains not to differentiate himself from fellow ILWU members. Lili recalled waiting for him some afternoons as he finished work and noting how closely he resembled the other longshoremen—middle-aged, large-framed, a bit bulky, and comfortable-looking in his work clothes and reinforced boots. Hoffer continued to try out his opinions on coworkers and to listen to them closely during union meetings.

Automation in the form of "containerization" was radically changing the way all American longshoremen worked. "Moving along the waterfront like a tornado through a town, the container transforms everything it touches," David Wellman wrote in *The Union Makes Us Strong*. The containerization era began with a single ship in June 1958 and was codified in the 1960-61 M&M (mechanization and modernization) contract. Part of the M&M was a union agreement to the restructuring of the workforce and its benefits packages, giving to older workers added medical benefits and incentives for them to retire and withholding them from younger workers; Hoffer was upset by this latter aspect, telling a union meeting, "This generation has no right to give away, or sell for money, conditions that were given to us by a previous generation." Nonetheless, under the M&M cargo size and the weight of loaded cargoes quintupled, while the number of longshoremen and the hours they worked decreased almost as precipitously.

The M&M contract was part of an economic turning point for San Francisco that brought similar changes in manufacturing; thereafter, the city declined rapidly as a base for blue-collar work. Most containerized shipping left the San Francisco piers for Oakland, and San Francisco began its transformation to a white-collar, corporate headquarters, and service-industry city with an emphasis on tourism. In 1955, the re-amalgamating of the AFL and CIO, which had taken place that year, had been seen as a point of upward take-off for unionization, by 1963 that event was beginning to be understood in retrospect as the commencement of precisely the opposite—of a steady decline in unionization of the American workforce, exacerbated by the deterioration of manufacturing.

Cut completely through an orange at several angles and you produce slices of differing thickness, diameter, and content—some with more flesh and others with more rind—but all are circles, echoes of the orange's spherical form. The sixteen chapters of *The Ordeal of Change* each similarly addressed a different aspect of the basic subject, systemic social change, from various angles and to varying depths. As Hoffer had told his diary in 1959, change had been his subject since *The True Believer*, and "every article I have written fits into a pattern. ... If I manage to write a few more ... I will have a book." But articles as a form of writing necessitate the author presenting a subject in a few pages; a non-fiction book usually requires the author to develop a thesis and a narrative over the course of multiple chapters, and to provide the resulting book with a distinct beginning, middle, and end. *The Ordeal of Change* felt and read more like a collection of articles/essays about the subject than a book-length inquiry.

Blurbs from sociologist Richard Bendix, who had written about Karl Marx and Max Weber, and from Harry Overstreet, co-author of *What We Must Know About Communism*, suggested that the book was an anti-Communist screed. It was far more. Hoffer argued that large-scale social change was more explosive, more radical, and more transformative than any revolution or evolution, and therefore that it warranted closer examination than anyone had previously paid to change. Actually, he had been paying attention to change throughout his career; more so than mass movements, social change was Hoffer's "inland sea."

His main insight was to understand social change as being inextricably tied to the fault lines within individuals; that linkage was why people feared change, why "every radical adjustment is a crisis in self-esteem," and why groups embracing drastic change were made up of "misfits" who "substituted faith for self-confidence, pride for self-esteem, and fusion with others for individual balance," producing "a proclivity for fanatical attitudes, united action, and ... an atmosphere of revolution."

Critical Cold War clashes had recently taken place over the building of the Berlin Wall, the emplacement of Soviet missiles in Cuba, and for influence on the future of new nations in Asia and

Africa. In 1960 alone, seventeen former colonies in Africa became independent, and at issue in their emancipations was whether they would embrace democracy and capitalism, or choose a communistic system. Chapter Two, "The Awakening of Asia," reflected Hoffer's great interest in this subject. What, he rhetorically asked, did the "ill-fed, ill-clad, and ill-housed masses in China, India, Indonesia … deeply desire?" Not better food, clothing, or shelter, he argued, but collective "pride"—lacking because colonization had destroyed the patriarchal, clan, and tribal cultures that had previously fostered an existence in which an individual "never felt alone, never felt lost, and never saw himself as a speck floating in an eternity of nothingness." This analysis owed much to Van der Post.

Unsettled Africans and Asians, Hoffer argued, became easy prey for pseudo-intellectual rabble-rousers from the same background who had nonetheless developed "a horror of manual labor" and a hatred of a social system that denied them positions of command. Such men quite readily succumbed to Communist propaganda that promised them "membership in a ruling elite." While Lord Acton had famously posited, "Absolute power corrupts absolutely;" Hoffer argued that "power corrupts the few, while weakness corrupts the many," and then used this idea to critique foreign-aid programs that were not working well because they tried to "win the weak by sharing our wealth with them," rather than by teaching the weak to help themselves in ways that would augment pride.

Chapters Three and Four contained the essence of Hoffer's argument: that a fundamental chasm existed between "Deeds and Words," that this split exacerbated change, and that it was affected by "imitation." Later in life, Hoffer would judge this analysis as one of his most important.

It was one of his most central, most visceral, and most personal set of insights, the one that birthed others such as his dissection of intellectuals. As such, it may have had deep psychological roots, perhaps in Hoffer's relationship to his father. Knut Hoffer possessed many books, and—according to Eric—adopted atheism as an intellectual pose; but Knut did little to demonstrate his intellectual leanings, which may well have raised in his only child the suspicion that he was merely a blowhard, and birthed Eric's lifelong suspicion of and antipathy to professional intellectuals.

Sham intellectuals were always of interest to Hoffer, and he was keen to identify them and to draw conclusions from their actions and lack of actions. He did so, notably in this book, in regard to Third World intellectuals' imitation of and adoption of American trappings while at the same time voicing acute anti-Americanism. He characterized this type of imitation as not the sincerest form of flattery but rather as demonstrating the imitators' fear that "the American way" of democracy and capitalism threatened their existence.

Such turnabouts occurred, Hoffer suggested, because of the change in the relationship of intellectuals to their society. Throughout most of recorded history, from the time of ancient Sumer and Egypt until the Middle Ages, Hoffer wrote, intellectuals had either been members of the ruling elite or closely allied to those elites; since the Renaissance, intellectuals, although out of power, had roiled the Western world by their "passionate search for an acknowledged status and a role of social usefulness," which had led them to "pioneer ... every upheaval from the Reformation to the latest nationalist or socialist movement."

Hoffer's analysis, which deprecated intellectuals, was profoundly anti-establishmentarian. Just then Richard Hofstadter, in *Anti-Intellectualism in American Life* was writing that derision of intellectuals, a characteristic of the early Eisenhower years, had reached its height during the heyday of Joe McCarthy and had since been reversed by the celebration of scientific striving engendered by the launch of Sputnik in 1957. Hofstadter contended that anti-intellectuals displayed "a resentment and suspicion of the life of the mind and of those who are considered to represent it; and a disposition constantly to minimize the value of that life." There were critics who wanted to apply that description to Hoffer, and he had often been charged with being anti-intellectual. Rejecting the charge, Hoffer emphasized that he disliked only certain aspects of what intellectuals did and the roles they chose to play in society. What offended Hoffer about intellectuals had little to do with "resentment and suspicion of the life of the mind"; rather, it was that intellectuals behaved like aristocrats and monarchists, embracing exclusiveness, and—above all—that they were unduly dismissive of the importance, the integrity, and the genius of the masses. This last, to Hoffer, was the unforgiveable sin.

Hoffer similarly rejected the idea that he *represented* the working class; rather, he said, he was *of* the working class, and saw part of his job as articulating working-class antagonism to all academics, bureaucrats, and managers who sought to lord it over manual laborers. He exempted from his bile the legitimate entrepreneurs of Western industrial society, whom he cherished. He admired democracies that were full of men of action—deed-doing workers and businessmen; the problem was that such societies provided few niches for intellectuals, whereas Communist countries had plenty of niches for them as government functionaries. Communist societies' many word-brandishing intellectuals were overjoyed that they and their ideas were taken seriously, even if that meant that some of the intellectuals were imprisoned for those ideas.

Hoffer's most unexpected insight was to identify imitation as a species of heresy. Imitation of American lifestyles, as practiced by people in Third World countries, did not automatically make the imitators "identify ... wholeheartedly with the model," which was why he labeled it a heresy. Throughout history, many countries and religions had been deeply changed by the very heresies that they had forcefully rejected, as these became "vehicles for the transmission of [their] ideas, attitudes and ways of life." Judaism, by not accepting the heresy of Christianity and by refusing to become assimilated in a Christianized world, reinforced Jews' integrity as a group and their survival and influence; India, in its rejection of Buddhism, exported that religion to the rest of Asia, where it flourished, nurturing Indian culture and ideas.

The main example of a modern heresy, Hoffer wrote, was Communism. Historian Arnold Toynbee had famously contended that Communism was a heresy of Christianity because it was deliberately godless; but Hoffer labeled Communism a heresy of capitalism: Russia and China were one-employer states that had exactly the same aims as a monopoly did, "to turn the captive population into skilled mechanics and so shape their souls that they would toil from sunup to sundown, thankful to be alive and blessing their exploiters."

For Hoffer to situate in Communism all that he disliked was somewhat of a trap. By 1963, his monolithic view of Communism was dated; it ignored the Sino-Soviet split and the significant effects of the death of Stalin and the impact of Khrushchev's reforms—evidence that could have countered his positions. The emphasis on Communism also muddied his focus; for instance, in the opening of Chapter Five, "The Readiness To Work." Hoffer began by comparing the difference between Communist and capitalism societies on that subject, quipping that the chief problem for Communists was "how to make people work" while for capitalists, it was "how to find enough jobs for people who want to work."

Very quickly, in this chapter, he left behind this pat formulation and its artificial dichotomy between Communism and capitalism in regard to work, and took up his main themes: Which individuals were the most ready for work? Whence came the idea of working hard as an element of a successful life? In classical times, Hoffer noted, work was looked down upon as toil done by slaves. That posture changed in medieval Europe as monks were forced to work as a concomitant of their thinking and praying, an idea furthered as Luther and Calvin "infused a new seriousness into man's daily design." Hoffer admired those who were eager to work, labeling their zest as the essence of enterprise and of an individual's separation from the group. But not everyone sought an "autonomous existence," which was "beset with fears" and required "confidence and self-esteem." Rather, "It is only the few who can acquire a sense of worth by developing and employing their capacities and talents. The majority prove their worth by keeping busy. A busy life is the nearest thing to a purposeful life."

Had the masses, "energized and activated by freedom," ever created anything "worthwhile"? Never, prior to the birth of the United States, the first and only mass-directed society. While all other civilizations had been "shaped by exclusive minorities," the U.S. had been shaped by the masses. He attacked "the deprecators of America" for wrongly deriding America's defects as those of a business civilization. Not so, he wrote: they were those of a mass civilization: "worship of success, the cult of the practical, the identification of quality with quantity, the addiction to sheer action, the fascination with the trivial."

Having acutely identified America's faults, Hoffer immediately let the reader savor his equally-well-observed list of America's virtues: "A superb dynamism, an unprecedented diffusion of skills, a genius for organization and teamwork, a flexibility that makes possible an easy adjustment to the most drastic change, an ability to get things done with a minimum of tutelage and supervision, an unbounded capacity for fraternization." Wondering why it was that although "the people I work and live with are lumpy with talent," such talent had not been widely utilized in the arts, he concluded that American society was not yet one that encouraged and trained everyone to be an artisan. Renaissance Florence's system created workingmen artisans, some of them major artists, who never lost "intimate contact with everyday life." There was potential for America to repeat this success, since "the increase in leisure due to the spread of automation makes the participation of the masses in cultural creativeness ... more feasible."

In Chapter Six Hoffer juxtaposed "The Intellectual and the Masses." By intellectuals he meant second-rate men of words who required "the sanction of ideals ... in order to act forcefully," and who then used these ideals to lead other men into the bondage of true believership, allying with autocracies, becoming "the most formidable taskmaster[s] in history," and using the masses in their experiments. He quoted Karl Jaspers, Ralph Waldo Emerson, and even Renan, all of whom saw the masses as needing to be controlled, an attitude resembling "that of a colonial functionary toward the natives." True creatives did not try to exert authority over ordinary people; but intellectuals incapable of great creativity—pseudo-intellectuals—tried to "imprint [their] mediocrity and meagerness on every phase of cultural activity" in their effort to "rule the roost."

Hoffer's need to stress the practical aspects of civilization over the activities of intellectuals fused with his solidifying conservative understanding of how capitalism operated, in Chapter Seven. While Hofstadter, a member of the upper-class, university-based intelligentsia, investigated *Anti-Intellectualism in American Life,* Hoffer examined precisely the opposite, "the anti-practical bias of the intellectual," a bias all too apparent to manual laborers but seldom discussed in print. The practicality of the workingman was integral to Hoffer's way of looking at capitalism; whereas most academy-based intellectuals analyzed capitalism by examining the capitalist or by identifying who controlled the means of production, Hoffer looked at it from the point of view of the worker. Progress, he asserted, depended on a practical sense because that was the key to a society's willingness to experiment and innovate. He saw that operating, for instance, in the invention of writing, which was originally fashioned to carry on commerce; he saw it in action in the rise of the Moslem civilization in the Middle Ages, and in the trading-based Netherlands empire of the sixteenth century. The most important triumph of the practical sense, he wrote, was the rise to power of the United States, a country created by "emigrants from the Old World, and the ceaseless movement of population inside the continent," all very practical people. He contrasted America's rise with the "scribe-dominated" societies throughout history, those who in his view had derived "a rare satisfaction from tearing tangible things out of the hands of practical people" as they sought to "separate the trader from his wealth."

Although Hoffer may have thought he was only giving an historical analysis, in formulating this essay he leaped into the political arena. In accusing anti-practical-sense societies of separating the trader from his wealth, he positioned laissez-faire economic policies—policies that let the trader do as he pleased—as essential to the success of democratic societies. This equating of laissez-faire economics with democratic governance was not a fact; it was a thesis championed by the more conservative economic and social analysts of Hoffer's time. If in 1951 Eugene Burdick had to point out that Hoffer's philosophy had much in it that could have come from a speech by the president of the National Association of Manufacturers, a dozen years later, what Hoffer wrote meshed even more closely with the free-market, anti-government-intervention economic philosophy articulated by such men as Milton Friedman, in his *A Monetary History of the United States, 1867-1960*, also published in 1963.

Chapter Eight, "Jehovah and the Machine Age," was another historical foray. Prompting and guiding the men who were at the birth of modern science, Hoffer wrote was "a particular concept of God," a Jehovah conceived as the grand engineer of the universe, who combined intellect and practical sense, and whose principles Renaissance scientists discovered and imitated.

In Chapter Nine, Hoffer returned to the concerns of Chapter Seven, discussing "Workingman and Management." One of his best essays, it was closely reasoned, personally referenced, and deeply felt. The general philosophical climate of Hoffer's day was heavily influenced by Marxist analyses; in this chapter he presented a diametrically opposite point of view, a view from the actual workingman rather than from the theoretical workingman about whom Marx had written. Marx believed that all workmen aspired to become managers; Hoffer categorically disagreed. He wrote that he and the men he worked with had long since understood that they were "eternal workingmen" and would be "bossed and managed by someone, no matter who owns the means of production." Hoffer also termed inevitable and necessary that workers and management should clash, and that neither group should win all of the time.

"A fiercely independent labor force," Hoffer concluded, was "not incompatible with efficient production."

Nor was such a labor force opposed to automation. Taking on the modern counterparts of the Luddites, Hoffer welcomed automation on the dock and in the factories, as it could relieve workers of what De Tocqueville had labeled "the disease of work," the sort of toil, Hoffer explained, that had "tortured humanity since the first days of its existence." In a lively leap of reasoning, Hoffer asserted that automation was "the culmination of vying with God" that he had spoken of in Chapter Eight, a battle that had begun in earnest during the Renaissance but that he saw as now figuratively shifting back in time to the gates of Eden. The "blasphemous multitude with their host of machines" was threatening to bring to an end the toil that had begun with the expulsion of Adam and Eve from Paradise—the toil of having to do arduous manual labor to earn one's daily bread. But should the "disease of work" cease to exist, he summed up, labor and management would still remain at odds, knowing that were they ever to lie down together like "wolf and lamb," the resulting society would be "stagnant."

Chapters Ten, Eleven, Twelve, and Thirteen dealt with other instances, aspects, and conditions of change: "Popular Upheavals in Communist Countries;" the brotherhood of man; the need for individual freedom; and the relationships among scribes, writers, and rebels. In a sense, these chapters fleshed out Hoffer ideas introduced in earlier books.

"Popular Upheavals in Communist Countries" was prescient about what would eventually cause the downfall of Communism—the slow introduction of small liberties, the resurgence of religious observance, and the desire for material goods—but it only briefly touched on such subjects.

The central tenet of his chapter on brotherhood, "The capacity for getting along with our neighbor depends to a large extent on the capacity for getting along with ourselves," was an extension of *The True Believer's* already-famous sentence, "Faith in a holy cause is to a considerable extent a substitute for the lost faith in ourselves." The "unattainability of self-respect" pushed people toward the sort of pride that lauded one's own group at the expense of others, undermined the brotherhood of man, and led to wars and change.

In his chapter on "individual freedom," Hoffer quoted Pascal's (and Montaigne's) dictum that virtue was made not from a love of virtue but from "the counterpoise of two opposite vices," and went on to expand on another belief he shared with Montaigne and Pascal, that the clash of opposites provided fertile ground for change and progress—as he had explored in earlier chapters about the clashes of word vs. deed, workingmen vs. management, and practical sense vs. intellectual sense.

In the book's final few chapters, Hoffer explored "the playful mood" and "the unnaturalness of human nature," subjects that would increasingly intrigue him. He asserted that all of human invention came from people playfully trying to make their lives better—a prime source of change. "'Great' thinking consists in the working out of insights and ideas which come to us in playful moments," he wrote, with autobiographical relish; "It is doubtful whether a mind that is pinned down and cannot drift elsewhere is capable of formulating new questions." By contrast, mass movements were "fits of deadly seriousness" brought on by "sterile pedants possessed of a murderous hatred for festive creativeness."

All power, he wrote, sought to curb freedom. Therefore, "every device employed to bolster individual freedom must have as its chief purpose the impairment of the absoluteness of power." This central contention of Chapter Fifteen brought together all of the book's themes—the split between words and deeds, the influence of the ancient Hebrews, heresies, the need of man to conquer and exceed animal nature, the approaching leisure society, and former colonies "vaulting" from "the paralysis of centuries ... onto the stage of history."

But Fifteen was not the last chapter. That position was occupied by Hoffer's earliest non-fiction work, the truncated "Tramps and Pioneers" essay that *Harper's* had printed in 1952 as "The Role of the Undesirables." Although fascinating, and definitely about undesirables as the engines of change, when read as a culminating chapter of a book it seemed markedly out of place—more of an introduction than a summing up.

The Ordeal of Change garnered mostly good reviews from the professional critics, though not the sort of raves that had greeted *The True Believer*. Loren Baritz in *The Nation* acknowledged its "flavor of genuine intellectual excitement," and Maurice Dolbier in the *New York Herald Tribune* found in "almost every chapter closely reasoned arguments that can convince you that assumptions you have always carelessly held are not true, and that open new and promising lines of thought." But some critics panned it as only an extension of *The True Believer*, or were bothered by its repetitiveness, which, they charged, stemmed from the book's being a collection of magazine pieces rather than integrated chapters; Robert R. Kirsch in the *Los Angeles Times* characterized the book as evidence that "the whole is sometimes less than the sum of its parts." John Radosta in *The New York Times* called it a "love letter to common men, including outcasts, failures, drunks, and jailbirds," a description that fit Hoffer's final chapter but not the rest of the book. *Newsweek* called the book "stimulating despite its burden of dismay," and quoted from it liberally, because, the magazine said, "The quality of Hoffer's thinking, his independence and freshness, can be conveyed only by quotation." *Time* included it in a "best reading" trio.

The most cogent analysis came from Garry Wills, in the pages of the *National Review*. After congratulating Hoffer on surviving the embrace of Eisenhower, Wills dismissed the idea that Hoffer was only a writer of icy aphorisms, and discussed him as a thorough romantic whose strength was that his were the ideas of a man who worked on the docks, a man who embodied his ideas rather than one who simply talked and wrote about ideas.

The book's ultimate accolade came from the National Institute of Arts and Letters, which the following year honored Hoffer as an "aphorist, moralist, observer of the human condition."

The Ordeal of Change might have fared better with the critics, and possibly with the public, had it been labeled a collection of articles with a common focus. Hoffer should have been asked to rework the articles to consolidate material, for instance, on the birth of writing, in one chapter rather than leaving it scattered in three chapters, and he could have provided interstitial material—he had already worked through the linkages among the chapters, telling his diary on April 1, 1959, "The problem of change is ... intermixed in my mind with the problem of man and nature. The human plasticity required by drastic change involves some dehumanization. Juvenilization, infantilization, barbarization are phases in a 'return to nature.' A diminution of human uniqueness. In a sense, to become plastic, man must become matter—malleable clay." A tougher editor would have urged Hoffer to update his articles to prevent chapters written in the Fifties from being dismissed; his observation about not attempting to win over "weak" countries by giving them our wealth was more appropriate for Truman's Point Four program than for the Peace Corps, which was doing what Hoffer had suggested, teaching the weak to help themselves.

If *The True Believer* appeared at precisely the right moment to maximize its impact, *The Ordeal of Change* appeared at precisely the wrong moment, the cusp of a new era that instantly made its contents seem outdated. The ascension of John F. Kennedy to the presidency began a period in which intellectuals were in favor; since the populace tends to like what the president likes, Hoffer's anger at intellectuals felt out of phase. The deeper trouble was that a far more unsettling ordeal of change than what Hoffer outlined had already begun, although it would continue largely unnoticed until the assassination of President Kennedy, six months after the book was published. That shock initiated a ten-year period of assaults on the body politic and on America's social structures that would violently thrust aside the ideas that had sustained American society through the Depression, World War II, and the immediate post-war era. In 1963 Hoffer was still perceived by the public—and continued to be positioned by the publisher—as the soul of anti-Communism, at just that moment when the onrushing "decade of shocks" forced the rapid receding of the anti-Communist tenor of the 1950s. Similarly, he was perceived as a workingman just when automation of the sort that put his kind of workingmen permanently out of work was embraced as the route to the future; as an anti-intellectual when intellectuals were in favor; and, finally, as a romanticized loner when the future increasingly appeared to belong to people cohering into groups.

Nearly fifty years after its publication, when the pace of change has accelerated to warp speed, our general appreciation of how rapidly and how thoroughly our lives change every day makes some parts of *The Ordeal of Change* enlighten and resonate perhaps more so than they did for readers in 1963. Particularly relevant are Hoffer's insights about human frailties and their relationship to change and to power, his description of the bases for innovation, his identification of imitation as heresy, his elucidating of the connection between progress and man's need to continually conquer nature, and his celebrating of the sense of play as fundamental to invention and to the proper use of leisure time.

Hoffer's chapters about the prevalence and influence of intellectuals in governance were also ahead of their time. In 1963, Hoffer thought that only authoritarian regimes were troubled by an overabundance of intellectuals; today, all governments, especially those of the democracies, increasingly rely on the expertise of specialists in all fields of endeavor and, as Hoffer predicted, ordinary people are even more at their mercy—for example, when governments choose fixes for their economy, or when they decide what scientific innovations and weaponry to pursue, or what strategies to use to fight crime.

When the reception of the book that Hoffer thought of as his best did not reflect his assessment, he altered two long-held patterns, his reticence to allow others to know his background and his reluctance to be interviewed. He agreed to a series of six interviews with James Day of KQED, San Francisco's educational television station, and under Day's gentle prodding spoke freely about his background as well as his ideas. Breaking a third pattern, in those interviews he commented on contemporary as well as on historical trends. After the first set of six half-hours, the nascent public broadcasting system—not yet a broadcast network, only an affiliation of independent stations that bicycled films and tapes from station to station—asked for more, until a series of twelve was readied, to be seen nationally in 1964-65.

Hoffer had told friends that longshoring was increasingly exhausting even as he confided to a diary, "I have finally become a genuine worker. Though all of my life a manual laborer, I have until the last two years thought of myself primarily as a human being, and many a time I would lay off weeks and months until I spent the last dime saved. Now when I lay off three or four days I start loading ships in my sleep and get up in the morning as tired as after a hard day's work." To obtain time for Hoffer to write, KQED urged him to apply for a Guggenheim Foundation fellowship and offered to smooth the way, but Hoffer would not go along, perhaps not wanting to complete the long application, prevail on friends for recommendations, and politick for votes on the committee. Aiming to provide more income to Hoffer, Norman Jacobson consulted Clark Kerr, the university's president (and long- time Hoffer acquaintance, through Selden Osborne) who recommended that Jacobson seek for Hoffer an appointment at Berkeley in Jacobson's department. Chairman

Robert Scalapino agreed that Hoffer should become part of the department, which also included Aaron Wildavsky, whom Hoffer came to like. Kerr then signed off on the arrangement. In late November 1963, Berkeley offered to hire Eric Hoffer—who had never been to grade school, let alone to college—as the equivalent of a full professor. Jacobson assured Hoffer that the appointment would be whatever he wished, "full-time, half-time, third-time, whatever," and not at all a burden to Jacobson, as Hoffer had worried. As to precisely how Hoffer would earn his $12,000, "I know you will trust your profoundest instincts, and that you will speak accordingly. We'll all listen, and you will not disappoint any of us, least of all me. I only want what you want for yourself."

Hoffer was not sure if he wanted a Berkeley post. As he would shortly tell a reporter, he worried what would happen should the intellectual establishment get its claws on him; they might "destroy him by feting him, dissipating his energies, trying to make him believe he is something he is not." But what Jacobson and other supporters hoped to gain from Hoffer being at Berkeley was just the opposite, a benefit to the students of having them encounter a fresh, non-academic voice that could shake them up. That was certainly what happened to the students at Lewis and Clark College in Portland, Oregon, when Hoffer, for the first time since his 1958 vow to stop lecturing, appeared at a large public forum at the college. A student summed up his impact:

> Last week Lewis and Clark had the good fortune to be invaded by an exciting and dangerous person who by his presence seemed to challenge our ritual, our regular habits of speech and thought and some of our common assumptions about ourselves. All of us [would-be academics] felt this in the presence of Mr. Eric Hoffer, this professed non-academic and non-intellectual ("I'm just shooting off my mouth"), a rare and invigorating personality. ... A sort of natural phenomenon who allowed no one to be indifferent to him—whose personality compelled reactions from all.

Hoffer wrote to Jacobson's mother, Jeanne, on the leaf of a December, 1963 Christmas card, "The offer from the university, due largely to Norman's influence, frightened the daylights out of me. To let go the waterfront would leave me suspended in the air. I must somehow keep my identity as a workingman. I shall probably accept a fraction of an appointment so that I can go on working. I shall not be a professor." He agreed to come to Berkeley every Wednesday afternoon and use Jacobson's office as a base. His duties would be to talk with anyone who showed up; and, a few times each semester, to lecture to the hundred or so students and faculty of the political science department.

He decided to cut back on the number of days that he worked on the docks, to no more than three a week, until he reached the union's mandatory retirement age in 1967. He grumbled to whoever would listen that the arrangement with Berkeley would be the first time in his life that he would be paid for doing nothing. Then, with the Berkeley appointment set, with KQED's series of half-hour interviews scheduled for national viewing in 1964-65, and with article assignments on contemporary topics from *The New York Times Magazine* and *Harper's* in hand, Hoffer turned his attention more to the present day and to current social problems than he had ever done.

Chapter Seven:
Becoming Controversial

The years between early 1964, when Eric Hoffer began to teach at Berkeley, and late 1967, when his interview with Eric Sevareid was broadcast and he met with President Johnson at the White House, held for him as many difficult moments as exhilarating ones. An increasing level of controversy over what he wrote and said tempered the acclaim for him produced by his media appearances.

For the nation, these were years of upheaval during which college students, minorities, and women actively challenged prior conceptions of their proper places in American society and old assumptions about the country's military, economic, and moral place in the world. College campuses became focal points for these clashes. Hoffer arrived at Berkeley, the most populous campus in the country, just as student protests about American involvement in the war in Vietnam and about the university's military-funded research were becoming more strident. They had not reached the level of being disruptive, their moderation attributable to the U.S. still having fewer than 25,000 troops in Vietnam, and to draft quotas that had not yet been raised to provide twenty times that number. Nonetheless, actor Ronald Reagan, preparing to run for governor, could already label Berkeley "a hotbed of liberalism," since ten percent of the students had taken part in civil rights activities and the campus had sent the most graduates of any school into the Peace Corps. Yet even at Berkeley in 1964, most students, as with their counterparts at other colleges across the country, approved of continued American involvement in the war in Vietnam.

Hoffer, an enthusiastic supporter of the United States' military mission as necessary to preventing a Communist takeover, began to have disagreements on Vietnam and on other current issues with some who dropped by his Berkeley office on Wednesday afternoons. "Most of the students I have been talking to do not think much of America," he informed Jeanne Jacobson that spring:

> They have all sorts of clippings which tell how silly, thoughtless, and even depraved Americans can be. The assumption is that most Americans are what [those] clippings say they are. I lose my temper now and then. I always knew that America is not a country for the old. Now I am discovering it is not a country for the young. Yet to me America always looked good, though I saw it from below. But you cannot tell twenty-year-olds that they haven't seen anything and know nothing first-hand.

However, in his next letter to her he was able to report, "I am discovering in retrospect that I actually admire the kids at the university. ... Many of those who raved against this country came later to tell me how much they loved me. Grandfather image." Two who agreed with Hoffer's positions and became close to him were Stacey Cole and Denis Doyle, whom he lauded to Jeanne Jacobson as brilliant. Doyle recalls that he had been in a seminar with Norman Jacobson, who had recommended that he drop in on Hoffer. The young man was entranced and Hoffer was impressed; the two struck up a friendship that endured through the rest of Hoffer's life. "Hoffer was the first important published author I'd met, and his acceptance of me helped me believe I could take my place among authors and thinkers," Doyle remembers.

"The award [from the National Institute of Arts and Letters] somehow makes me feel like a fraud," Hoffer confided to Jeanne in the spring of 1964; unwilling to travel to New York to accept the award, he reserved tickets to the event for her. That spring he chose to acknowledge the significance of his career in a different way, donating twenty-three of his 1940s notebooks to the San Francisco

Public Library's new division devoted to manuscript collections. The library also invited Hoffer to take part in a panel about writing and labor with Kenneth Rexroth, a poet and former IWW organizer, and Robert Kirsch, literary editor of the Los Angeles *Times*. On the panel, Kirsch was more complimentary to Hoffer than in his dismissive review of *The Ordeal of Change*.

Around this time, while riding a bus Hoffer read about student riots in Istanbul, Tokyo, Saigon, and Mexico City and, "snorting with disgust," muttered to himself, "History made by juvenile delinquents." He deemed his insight worthy of further examination; it became allied in his mind with those derived from "observing two willful godchildren in action," and birthed two realizations: that the juvenile was "the archetypal man in transition" and that the current age was "a time of juveniles."

For the next few years Hoffer pursued these notions. They meshed with his longer established tenet, that what separated men from boys was that boys had never worked for a living. Men who performed steady work, he further held, resisted change and provided the backbone for society. This led him to an odd crusade. "Something strange happened to me," he later wrote. "I found myself running around ... telling people of an impending crisis, a turning point as fateful as any since the origin of society, and warning them that woe betides a society that reaches such a turning point and does not turn." Formerly against appearing in public, he now sought every venue—campuses, Kiwanis clubs, and conventions—to trumpet his worries. The crisis that he foresaw was automation, and it not only augured ill for dockworkers but for all of his sort of American workingmen, who within decades would be "unneeded and unwanted." Although he recognized that history was cyclical, and that at various points certain classes of people fell by the wayside—currently "businessmen" were "superfluous" in the Soviet Union—he was nonetheless staggered, and believed others should be, by the thought of the masses in America becoming superfluous. The statistics that alarmed him showed several million jobs being lost to automation each year, and an equivalent number of young people entering the labor force without specific jobs to go to—and all of this occurring as the cost of creating a job continued to rise. The experts promised that a growing economy would absorb the unemployed and new workers, but to Hoffer that was "a pipe dream. ... We shall wake up one day to find twenty million or so unemployed in our midst." He was not worried that this crisis would produce widespread poverty, since America's resources were large and no one need starve. Rather, what scared him was that skilled, competent, and resourceful workingmen—his kind of people, the ones he thought of as real Americans—would be unable to find jobs. This situation could become "explosive," so he hoped that the "potent irritation" of those twenty million unemployed would lead to innovations that could ameliorate this terrible problem by providing work for the skilled. Hoffer was not alone in such thinking; industrialist John Diebold had recently said that American society had "yet to perceive the true nature of the momentous change automation is effecting in our lives ... far greater ... than has yet been realized." A bank manager reported that 75 employees plus new machines now did twice the work that used to be done by 400 employees. Nikita Khrushchev had boasted, "Automation is good. It is the means we will use to lick you capitalists."

Hoffer's analysis and alarm were not misguided. Only his timing was off. Daniel Bell would not announce until 1973 the "post-industrial society," with its transition from "a goods-producing to a service economy," the rapid decline of the blue-collar proletariat, and the "preeminence of the professional and technical class," all elements that Hoffer had predicted. During the quarter-century following Hoffer's sounding of the tocsin, the transition to a service economy and the addition of jobs using computers and other communication technologies provided enough new employment to offset losses from automation. But Hoffer was not wrong about the crisis attendant on skilled workers losing their jobs—that crisis had simply been postponed. It arrived in late 2008, and since then, job loss has been substantial, throwing more than ten million people out of work and making all the more difficult the creating of new jobs for them; many economists believe that the absorption of all who want to work may not be fully accomplished until the "baby boomer" generation retires.

In the fall of 1964, Hoffer's problems with rebellious students at Berkeley grew, in tandem with their growing discontent, fueled by rising draft quotas. By then his department had moved into the eighth floor of a new building. The college's dean, yielding to pressure from a conservative publisher, issued a memo forbidding political demonstrations on a 26-foot strip of sidewalk near the main entrance; in reaction, student Mario Savio, returning from a summer with an integration group in Mississippi, founded the Free Speech Movement, and the campus began to implode with protests. Hoffer listened to students curse the professors and "let it be known that any punk that came to my class and called me a motherfucker I was going to personally throw down those eight flights of steps, and then I was going to jump after him to be sure he found the bottom. So everybody was very polite." The demonstrations and disruptions escalated. Chancellor Clark Kerr tried to effect compromises but by Thanksgiving things had gotten so out of hand that Governor Pat Brown sent police to the campus, resulting in arrests. In reaction, 16,000 students shut down the university. Hoffer was appalled by the students' flaunting of authority and their apparent desire to do anything but study.

In the spring of 1965 the U.S. began bombing North Vietnam, spurring many college professors to become overtly anti-war and to begin teach-ins at several universities. This political advocacy by some professors upset many others, including Hoffer's boss at Berkeley, Robert Scalapino, who was the main "hawk" speaker at one of the first teach-ins, at George Washington University in Washington, D.C., opposing the main "dove," a Cornell political scientist. Scalapino, a noted Sinologist, warned that a retreat in Vietnam would embolden Chinese Communist aggression throughout Southeast Asia.

By the summer of 1965, Hoffer was continually sparring verbally over the war with students and with a few dockworkers. Most longshoremen were still in favor of the war, and perhaps that emboldened a rumored Hoffer action that journalist Ernest Zaugg reported in an article that summer, a fistfight between Hoffer and one particularly anti-war dockworker.

Polls in mid-1965 showed the majority of college students, as well as union members, still in favor of the U.S. actions in the war in Vietnam; some 48 percent of the general-public sample polled by Gallup thought that the U.S. was handling the war properly, and only 28 percent thought it was not. These numbers then shifted rapidly as, on campuses, anti-war sentiment increased steadily when the number of young men drafted each month climbed—184,000 American military would be in Vietnam by the end of 1965, and twice that number by the end of 1966. By mid-1966, about 60 percent of adults polled felt that sending troops to Vietnam was a mistake; some 71 percent of young people felt that way, although only 48 percent of those over fifty did so.

Complicating Hoffer's views of the excesses and the glories of the young were his relationships with the Osborne children. He got along well with Stephen but continued to clash with Tonia and to worry about Eric. When Tonia graduated, Hoffer paid for her graduation dress. She sent him a note of thanks from New York City, to which she moved, telling him that she was doing well in her job. But in 1966 she died there from an epileptic seizure. The loss was devastating for her parents and siblings, and her younger brother came to believe that Hoffer's needling had been an element in Tonia's moving away and into a vulnerable situation.

Hoffer's developing friendships with Cole and Doyle, and the positive responses he received from students at his lectures at small colleges in out-of-the-way places, also provided reasons for him not to stereotype all collegians as arrogant kids handed the world on a platter yet insistent on rejecting it. Hoffer put the onus on their professors' anti-Americanism. Max Ascoli was making similar charges in The Reporter, taking the professors to task for opposition to American involvement in Vietnam:

Do they know what they are doing to their country, these professionals of reflection and expression called intellectuals? Do they think that by having set themselves apart from the major venture in which America is engaged they have become a separate and sovereign state? No matter whether connected or not with campuses, there are enough of [them] to inflict the punishment of loneliness on those of their peers who refuse to go along.

Those, like Ascoli and Hoffer, who did not "go along" with the growing anti-war sentiment were increasingly out of step. For Ascoli the consequences were dire: within months of his articulating his most advanced views of the professoriat's anti-war tilt, his magazine began losing advertising dollars and paid subscriptions so severely that within a year it had to stop publication.

Even more difficult for Hoffer to understand and accept than the youth uprising was what he labeled "the Negro Revolution" in his November 1964 article in *The New York Times Magazine*, "The Negro Is Prejudiced Against Himself." Although in this article he tried not to appear biased, Hoffer knew he was a man of prejudices and made no apologies for that; later he would label his prejudices the "testicles" of his mind, and construe them as a source of his strength rather than as a reason for readers to reject his thoughts. Montaigne exhibited a similar braggadocio about his blatant prejudices—against women, against Protestants and Muslims, against certain ancient Greek thinkers whom he judged as less sagacious than the Romans. But since Montaigne wrote for an audience that did not disagree with those prejudices, his biases did him little harm during his lifetime or subsequently; Montaigne's misogyny, for instance, did not deter Virginia Woolf's admiration for his essays. Conversely, Hoffer suffered public disdain because of what he wrote and said about those he insisted on continuing to call "Negroes," because his utterances and writings felt highly biased at the precise moment in time when

American society was striving to get beyond color bias and to seek ways to meet the country's obligations toward providing all of its inhabitants with equality of opportunity.

Hoffer's bias seeped through diary entries such as this one in the spring of 1964:

> I cannot understand how a large number of American Negroes could ever swallow the Muslim hogwash ladled out by an Elijah Mohammad. ... James Baldwin and Malcolm X have been running all over Europe and Africa telling people that the Negro has done all our work for us. Actually if all the twenty million Negroes in American stopped doing a thing ... I doubt whether the rhythm of everyday life in America would be critically affected.

Hoffer's prejudice toward the descendants of slaves, people who were still daily contending with debilitating discrimination, seemed all the more illogical when juxtaposed to his long-term, well-expressed sensitivity to the downtrodden in history. But he believed that each individual must earn the right to be taken seriously by society, a tenet seated in his experience of always having had to scramble for a living. As Hoffer put it in the 1964 article, he and those men he had toiled with on the docks and in the fields had "started to work for a living in our teens," had "been poor all of our lives," and

> ... our white skin brought us no privileges and no favors. For more than twenty years I worked in the fields of California with Negroes, and now and then for Negro contractors. On the San Francisco waterfront ... there are as many black longshoremen as white. My kind of people does not feel that the world owes us anything, or that we owe anybody—white, black, or yellow—a damn thing. We believe that the Negro should have ... the right to vote, the right to join any union open to us, the right to live, work, study and play anywhere he pleases. But he can have no special claims on us, and no valid grievances against us.

More personally, Hoffer's animus toward African-Americans seems to have stemmed from his clashes with individual blacks over a period of many years, exacerbated by his recent problems with the blacks who became bad neighbors to him in McAllister Street, and with the black longshoremen who were awarded full memberships in the ILWU before, in his view, they had earned that privilege. In diary entries from the 1930s to the 1960s, he reported instances in which his negative assessment of African-Americans seemed to be upheld by events and individuals' behavior. But these were really instances in which his supposedly objective observations were filtered through his already-extant willingness to believe the worst of people with dark skins. Used to drawing generalities based on his own experience, Hoffer refused to acknowledge that there might be experiences so different from his that they would contradict his generalizations or not fit comfortably within them—this was particularly true for the lives of African-Americans.

Nearer the end of Hoffer's life, in an unpublished manuscript of comments on quotations culled from books, he gave his fullest explanation of the more legitimate source of his prejudice. He compared the "emancipation" of the "Negroes" to that of the Jews in Europe in the first half of the nineteenth century:

> After centuries of discrimination the Jews were granted equality grudgingly—as a gift rather than as a right. Both gentiles and Jews took it for granted that the Jews still had to prove themselves worthy of equality. This assumption generated a creative ferment that pushed the Jews to the front rank in almost every field of human endeavor. The Negro, on the other hand, is now entering the mainstream of American life as a creditor. He not only claims equality as a right but demands compensation for what he had been deprived [of] in the past.

Similarly, his 1964 article asserted, "Only when the Negro community as a whole performs something that will win for it the admiration of the world will the Negro individual be completely himself." Such sentiments formed the basis of Hoffer's agreement with Chicago community organizer Saul Alinsky. But the article did not mention Alinsky; rather, Hoffer stated, as though it was a fact, that group accomplishment was the *only* legitimate basis for collective pride, a notion that Alinsky and others in close touch with the black community would have rejected.

Even so, Hoffer's article offered plenty of insight and sensitivity, for instance in his observation, "That which corrodes the soul of the Negro is his monstrous inner agreement with the prevailing prejudice against him." Such telling points were obscured by paragraphs advocating that African-Americans should stay in their Southern rural enclaves and transform them into grand cities to earn respect for their group. "If it be true that the only effective way to help the Negro is to help him help himself, then the Negro's aversion to, or perhaps incapacity for, a self-starting, do-it-yourself way of life makes it questionable whether he can ever attain freedom and self-respect." Hoffer was adamant that poor leaders were leading African-Americans astray, and that "even if discrimination were wiped out overnight," blacks would still be under "enormous handicaps" and have only "meager opportunities for self-advancement," because it was a "fact that in America, and perhaps in any white environment, the Negro remains a Negro first, no matter what he achieves." He saw their predicament as "a crisis of identity" that could not be ameliorated by Elijah Muhammad's separatism or Martin Luther King Jr.'s exhortations to take pride in their black brothers' accomplishments in Africa. Hoffer would later explain to Denis Doyle that he thought Martin Luther King Jr.'s program of passive non-violence was "a cop out," inappropriate for achieving the sort of pride that Hoffer believed to be essential for blacks or any other group.

"The Negro Is Prejudiced Against Himself" generated many indignant letters-to-the-editor and began to fix Hoffer in the public mind as a deprecator of African-Americans, as an opponent of civil rights, and—in conjunction with his opposition to the student protesters—as a reactionary.

Rather, Hoffer, along with most other Americans over the age of thirty-five to forty, Americans who had endured the Depression and World War II, shared the core beliefs of what sociologist Lauren Langman would label "western industrial man," which she listed as 1) a belief in rational explanations; 2) self-reliance, independence and individualism; 3) hard work as a moral calling; 4) domination over nature; and 5) future orientation. On each of these points, Langman contended, the "countercultural child" of the 1960s held opposite views.

Hoffer's strength lay in his articulation of western industrial values, and his appeal was increasingly to the sharers of those values—manual laborers, first- and second-generation immigrants, and middle-class adults older than the kids who intoned "Don't trust anyone over thirty." At the center of Hoffer's thought, and, he believed, that of those who shared his values and concerns, was the notion of work as necessary and ennobling, and of nature as something that had to be dominated and controlled. This was the core of the western industrial values, those descended from the Old Testament and the Protestant ethic, those that had made modern civilization possible, those that continued to enable progress.

As the Sixties wore on, the fault lines between people who embraced western industrial values and people who did not, between more recent immigrants and those whose grandparents had been born in the U.S., between age and youth, and between left and right continued to widen. Hoffer and those who believed in the values as he construed them, viewing the upheavals of the decade as unwarranted rebellions, became increasingly conservative.

While Hoffer was volubly and publicly articulating his rejections of the countercultural child and of that child's professors, he was also positing a future in which a substantial fraction of the adult population would remain in school. Hoffer admired the world of learning as only a man who had never been to school could. Accordingly, he positioned academia as an ideal to which all of society should aspire. He argued that in the automated-factory future, since there would not be enough work to keep people busy, the best thing would be to set aside a state—he proposed northern California and a adjoining part of Oregon—and relieve it and its inhabitants of the necessity to produce or manufacture anything, so that they could devote themselves to university-type education. "If we are to awaken and cultivate the talents dormant in a whole population, we must change our conception of what is efficient, useful, practical, wasteful, and so on. Up to now in this country we are warned not to waste our time, but we are brought up to waste our time." The main goal of his university-state was to educate people so they could live up to their artistic and intellectual potential, but it also aimed to neutralize the power of intellectuals by training many more people to be intellectuals, thus diluting their impact. Hoffer was angered by those who yearned for artistic glory but who could demonstrate only minimal talent:

> There is nothing in contemporary America that can cure or alleviate their chronic frustration. They want power, lordship, and opportunities for imposing action. Even if we should banish poverty from the land, lift up the Negro to true equality, withdraw from Vietnam, and give half of the national income as foreign aid, they will still see America as an air-conditioned nightmare unfit for them to live in. ... What [the intellectual] cannot stomach is the mass of the American people—a mindless monstrosity devoid of spiritual, moral, and intellectual capacities. ... [He] rejects the idea that our ability to do things with little tutelage and leadership is a mark of social vigor.

Hoffer's clashes with the counterculturists in 1964-67 taught him two things: that by commenting on contemporary matters he was stepping into the political arena; and that thereafter his statements would be judged as political statements were, not solely on the basis of their insight or lack of it, but much more on the basis of whether his hearer or reader agreed or disagreed with the statements' political bent. Hoffer had previously shied away from the political arena but now embraced it to the point of becoming more overtly theatrical. He posed on the steps of Berkeley's Sproul Hall—site of many student protests—to declaim loudly and with bold physical gestures against Mario Savio, and against the anti-war battalions, and against those who allowed six million Jews to die in World War II—all, with a reporter there to record his bravado.

At the same time, a whisper of self-doubt began to creep into his thoughts. In the 1930s and 1940s similar doubts had troubled him, but since the acceptance of his first book he had kept them at bay. They informed his mid-1965 response to a query from *Saturday Review* editor Norman Cousins, that he was not willing to sum up his life's lessons for a series that would include thoughts from Dr. Albert Schweitzer and other "major contemporary thinkers," some of whom Hoffer admired. Cousins wrote back, "I've always been bemused by what might be called the malocclusion between a man's own idea of his worth and the world's idea of it. If you don't consider yourself a major contemporary thinker, that's all well and good; but you'll have a hard time convincing the rest of us. ... Your modest declination of my invitation has, incidentally, left me with greater respect and admiration for you than ever." Hoffer, flattered but still only willing to write what he wanted to, sent Cousins "The Return of Nature," which ran as part of the "What I Have Learned" series in a February 1966 issue.

Spurred by self-doubt, by the urge to perform, and by the need to explicate his tough positions on contemporary issues, Hoffer released more details about himself. Nearing the end of one KQED session with James Day, Hoffer asserted, "Creativeness ... needs cesspools, it also needs grievances, it needs nightmares, it needs memories, unpleasant memories." In response to this heartfelt statement, Day warned Hoffer that in their next conversation, "I'm going to ask some personal questions of you, and have you tell us something about the experience, something about your own memories."

"I shall be glad," Hoffer responded, "I shall be glad."

He had originally agreed to the public broadcasting interviews in the expectation that they would aid the sales of his next book, *The Temper of Our Time.* That book included Hoffer's fantasy about a university-state and his recently-published articles about "the Negro revolution," the youth uprising, the opposition of man and nature, and about automation—a half-dozen articles, some unchanged from their earlier publication, others lightly annotated to explain their origin or to add data from events that occurred in the interim between their first publication and late 1966.

The Temper of Our Time established Hoffer as a true contrarian. His prior perch as an anti-establishmentarian had been over-run by the countercultural forces, and he no longer wished to be defined by his anti-Communism. Hoffer's new essays positioned him as the voice of the skilled working class that he believed still made up the majority of American citizens—at a moment when the country's airwaves and printed pages were increasingly dominated by a different set of Americans, those espousing anti-establishment positions that he objected to as wrong-headed and because they featured put-downs of the working class.

As later studies of the body politic at that time have revealed, it was also a moment when a large proportion of those groups of white ethnics whom President Nixon would later label "the silent majority" were coming around to the belief that Hoffer had so forcefully expressed in his 1964 article, "The Negro Is Prejudiced Against Himself." According to a later article by professors Thomas J. Sugrue and John D. Skrentny, "The ethnic revival took the form that it did in response to black militancy and the government policies that were developing in its wake. Although whites, including ethnics, supported (at least by the measure of public opinion surveys) laws that forbade racial discrimination, they equated remedial and race-conscious public policies as 'special treatment' for blacks."

But in 1966, the silent majority was as yet unidentified.

Three groups of ethnics, however, had already become enthusiasts for Hoffer, at a moment, after the publication of *The*

Temper of Our Time, when Hoffer was either being ignored by liberal book reviewers or chastised by them. As he would tell friends, the Jews delighted in having such a non-Jewish public defender of the state of Israel and of the Jewish heritage that underlay the Christian world; the psychiatrists liked his contention that human beings had to subdue nature both within and outside of us; and—the most important group to Hoffer—the monsignors at the University of San Francisco admired his contention that God and the devil battled not in heaven but in each individual's soul, and his defining of God's influence as anything that humanizes people. The Jesuits thought of him as a theologian, he told friends, wining and dining him so they could listen to him talk; their attention helped Hoffer with Lili's devout family, who had previously looked askance at him as a non-believer but now addressed him playfully as Eric Cardinal Hoffer.

The Temper of Our Time was only sparsely reviewed, but the James Day series of interviews on public broadcasting channels did aid its sales, and also gave Harper & Row impetus to publish a new edition of *The True Believer*, which had sold 400,000 copies and was heading toward a half-million.

The continuing popularity of *The True Believer* and the public broadcasting exposure spurred *The New Yorker* staff writer Calvin Tomkins to suggest a profile for the magazine. Tomkins had been a general editor for *Newsweek* before joining *The New Yorker* in 1960, and while his expertise lay mostly in the visual arts, he was keenly sensitive to a wide range of people engaged in artistic endeavors. He set out the rationale for the article in a note to his editors on March 28, 1966: "This solitary, self-taught man retains a hatred of the academic world, yet in his strange lifetime he has come near to the academic dream of encompassing all knowledge in an age of specialization. His books—really one long essay built on aphorisms—seem likely to take their place among the few truly original structures in Twentieth Century thought."

To be profiled by *The New Yorker* was to be enshrined in the pantheon of artists whose works were notable as well as broadly popular. For a week in April, Hoffer met with Tomkins daily, showed him his apartment and workplace, and took him to Sunday dinner at Lili's, with Selden, Eric and a friend of the boy's. By then Tonia had moved to New York and Stephen was out of the country, in the Peace Corps. Tomkins spoke to Lili, somewhat less to Selden, and also interviewed longshoremen, union officials, Norman Jacobson, and others. During that week Hoffer was at his performing best; his KQED interviews and regular Berkeley sessions had given him confidence in conversationally articulating his ideas and in revealing slivers of his background.

Months ahead of publication of *The New Yorker* article, Tomkins sent Hoffer the manuscript so that he could correct any errors; Hoffer refused on principle to read it or to suggest emendations, informing Tomkins in a note, "The profile will be as much, if not more, about you than about me. ... You could not have found anything worthwhile in me unless you already had it in you." The article appeared in the January 7, 1967 issue. "Profiles: The Creative Situation," consisting mainly of long quotes from Hoffer, condensed from tape recordings that Tomkins had made, was positioned just after a short story by Jorge Luis Borges, and its text columns were flanked by advertisements for Mercedes-Benz, Colonial Williamsburg, and sundresses for women on winter cruises. Tomkins well conveyed the sense of a man of large enthusiasms, intellectual range, and an abiding passion for deep thought, at home on the docks and comfortable as the voice of his fellow workingmen.

Editor William Shawn now wrote to Hoffer; asserting that his magazine did not "usually publish aphorisms (or essays)," he nonetheless asked Hoffer to submit some aphorisms. Hoffer did; Shawn tried to make arrangements to publish them, but eventually thought better of the idea and did not.

Selden and Lili Osborne wrote separate notes of thanks to Tomkins. Selden thought the article nicely captured his friend, as did

Lili, who wrote that she was "grateful for your forbearance, compassion, and generosity in dealing with the tenuous nature of our household."

The Tomkins' profile soon attracted Eric Sevareid, for the interview that would be filmed by CBS in May and broadcast in September, and *Life* magazine, for a photo-filled profile printed in March, as well as other visitors to Hoffer.

The full Sunday-dinner-at-Lili's treatment was increasingly offered to select Hoffer guests. Her home on Clayton Street, which predated the 1906 earthquake, was festooned with succulent plants inside and out, and decorated with her paintings—Tomkins, an appreciator of art, thought them quite good—as well as with craft objects from Mexico, the Caribbean, and around the world. For the "feasts," Lili would spend an entire day preparing German, Italian, and American dishes and a plethora of desserts; the wine and after-dinner drinks lubricated conversations that would go on for hours. Lili, now a teacher for learning-disabled children, was a full participant in the discussions. Such treatment positively swayed guests, not just by the cornucopia of the food but by the intensity of the opinions ventured and by the sense of Hoffer displaying himself as he would for a valued friend. Gloria Doyle, wife of Denis, recalled the atmosphere of those Sundays, for which Lili cooked and Hoffer provided the "best" liquors and cigarettes for the eight to twelve people around a table, with Hoffer at one end and Selden at the other. Lili's house, she recalled in a memoir,

> ... was a chaotic jumble, filled with children, pets, plants, pottery and folk art. Lili presided over this lived-in domesticity with ease [and] relished the role as hostess to Eric. ... To Lili's table Eric brought friends and intellectuals—writers, artists, professors, graduate students and an occasional longshoreman. ... Eric did most of the talking. He had an enormous personality, brilliant, charismatic, and passionate. With his singular view of the human condition, he drew us in.

Tomkins' thank-you to Lili, after his first Sunday dinner, said that experiencing Hoffer in such surroundings provided a depth of understanding "that could never have come otherwise, so much so that at the moment I'm in a sort of despair about ever being able to get any of it down on paper. I'll try hard, and I'll be writing with you and your husband and your son in mind!" Selden's attendance at the Tomkins dinner in the spring of 1966 may have been among his last, as he left the house completely within a few months, around the time of Tonia's death.

Another 1967 visitor who experienced the full Sunday dinner treatment was Georgie Anne Geyer, a 32-year-old Chicago newspaper reporter about to head off to an important assignment in Moscow. Saul Alinsky had made the introduction to Hoffer for her. In an article in the Chicago *Daily News* she described Lili, then 50, as "totally beautiful. Her dark hair falls naturally into careless curls, her eyes are silky and her mouth slow and sensuous." Lili and the "warm and passionate" Hoffer were "all big, vital people. ... Nothing about him is quiet or unrestrained. His voice booms, his laugh is proclamation."

Years later Geyer recalled that night in 1967 as one of her most memorable evenings; Hoffer was "larger than life," a formidable drinker and eater as well as a thinker, befitting his identity as a workingman. "I was delighted to be able to back up his theories about the working class and the intellectual class and their special proclivities" by examples from her previous posting in South America, where, she reported to him, the intellectuals were anti-American but the masses were pro-American. Hoffer claimed to distrust intellectuals because they were "too theatrical" and they hatched theories and then adduced facts to support those theories, whereas he began his analyses with facts and then fashioned theories to explain them. Geyer and Hoffer were of a like mind, she thought, and promised to stop in San Francisco on her way back from Moscow.

Hoffer continued to receive invitations to speak at schools and colleges, but accepted only a few, usually to institutions that were relatively small or of minor academic status. He lectured at the John

Burroughs preparatory school in St. Louis, and his thank-you to the dean conveys why he preferred such venues:

> The visit to Saint Louis ... was an immersion in the America I cherish: the mysterious continent where people are wonderfully kind, wonderfully intelligent, and wonderfully competent. The children I saw are the finest human beings I ever met. Up to now I judged America by the people I worked and lived with. I found them good. But now when I think and speak of America I shall think of the people I have met in Saint Louis.

He was also receiving letters from strangers, some forwarded by KQED or Berkeley or his publishers; he only chose to answer those that piqued his interest, most of them from celebrities or fellow writers. A Protestant minister in Dallas, E. C. Rowand, became a close friend after introducing himself as also having eye problems that might soon leave him blind. Hoffer, Lili, and the Rowands, both ministers, traded ideas and visits for years, with the Rowands reading aloud in their church some of Hoffer's letters and articles as stimuli for discussions. In the years to come, Hoffer would particularly value the correspondents who had reached out to him before Sevareid made him famous.

"A man could speak and write all his life and not accomplish what Hoffer accomplished in that one hour," Sevareid told the San Francisco *Chronicle* soon after the CBS broadcast. "What Hoffer does is to cut through the scab of doubt about this country, its purpose and its future, to touch the nerve of faith about ourselves and our nation. It is something like Churchill talking to the English people in dark times."

That aspect of Hoffer's interview interested the White House, as did his vocal support for the president and his expectation that Johnson would go down in history as the most important president of the twentieth century. Though Hoffer had been saying and writing similar things for years, when he uttered these sentiments on CBS, the White House invited him to meet with the president.

Since the publication of the *Life* article, "Docker of Philosophy," in March 1967, administration insiders had been urging Hoffer's books on President Johnson; Secretary of Agriculture Orville Freeman had sent the president a note on March 31, quoting lines from *The True Believer* about hope, unduly raised expectations, and the like, and touting Hoffer's lines as a good explanation of why Johnson, who had done so much for the people, was declining in popularity, and what could be done about it. Jack Valenti, a former confidante of Johnson's who had become president of the Motion Picture Association of America, sent a note suggesting that the Johnsons invite Hoffer for a small dinner at the White House. Valenti and Bill Moyers, the former press secretary, had been deeply involved in the increasingly difficult task of finding intellectuals to support Johnson. Annotations on the Valenti note show that a White House aide agreed that Hoffer should be invited to a function, but vetoed the Valenti notion that Hoffer should have a one-on-one talk with the president. An invitation to a dinner in June with Prime Minister Harold Wilson of Great Britain was sent to Hoffer, but he declined to attend, perhaps because he had been informed that he would not have any chance to speak with the president in private, or perhaps because Hoffer was very much opposed to the path that Great Britain had taken in recent years.

In September, in advance of the CBS broadcast, Sevareid wrote to Press Secretary George Christian that he hoped the president would see it, "because I have a hunch it would be a tonic to his spirits. What Hoffer says, with power and eloquence, about the President and about the intellectual critics of the President and this country ought to fortify the President and will shake up a lot of other people who understand neither Mr. Johnson nor America."

Other documents in the White House files suggest that Johnson did at some point watch the broadcast. Many White House staffers did as well, one noting afterwards that Hoffer was "so great, I am amazed the Republicans haven't asked for equal time." Moyers, who had become publisher of Newsday, sent a note urging Johnson to talk with Hoffer. Sevareid advised that Hoffer was to be in Washington on October 3, and a White House invitation was issued. Before Hoffer arrived, the tape was shown several more times at the White House.

The October 3, 1967 mid-afternoon chat between the president and the "longshoreman philosopher," in the Rose Garden on a balmy autumn day, was supposed to last for five minutes and to be primarily a photo opportunity, enabling Johnson to link himself publicly with the workingman's representative—who arrived wearing his customary outfit of workmen's clothing, which delighted the photographers. But Hoffer and Johnson spoke for almost an hour. The best report on what Hoffer told the president is his thank-you for the opportunity. "I felt elated every minute I spent in the White House that a Johnson, one of us, is President. We made this country, and we ought to run it and defend it. Your detractors and tormentors will end up in the dustbin of history." It was a point of view that Johnson seldom heard from an outsider: an appreciation of his intrinsic worth coupled with a plea to him to trust his gut—because the speaker and the other "Johnsons" of the world would have the president's back. In the Rose Garden conversation, Hoffer applauded Johnson's firmness in pursuing the war in Vietnam, and stressed what was good about America—our optimism, our get-the-job-done attitude, our refusal to rest on our laurels, our willingness to fight.

What may have particularly appealed to Johnson was Hoffer's castigating of the president's enemies among the intellectuals. Johnson often felt denigrated by holdovers from the Kennedy Administration who considered themselves intellectually superior. According to Eric Goldman, an advisor hired specifically to find intellectuals to advise Johnson, the Texan was not anti-intellectual but liked to "blast" the intellectuals even as he looked to them for support, "and kept trying to find ones who did not annoy him too much." Hoffer fit the bill: an intellectual who came on as anything but, a man who appreciated Johnson and who was good company over root beer in the Rose Garden. Hoffer recalled for Calvin Tomkins that he had told President Johnson

> ... that Hans Morgenthau would never forgive us [ordinary people] for building the country without asking his advice, and that Hans Morgenthau thinks Americans are not cultured enough to have a foreign policy. Of course in Europe where the Hans Morgenthaus are a dime a dozen they know much better how to manage things than we—they knew how to stop the first world war, the second world war, how to stop Hitler and all those things.

On leaving the Rose Garden, Hoffer told reporters it had been "the finest day of my life." Privately, he assured Johnson by letter, "You will remain my President to the end of my years," and signed his note, "with love and gratitude."

Johnson told Lydia Katzenbach, wife of his former attorney general, "meeting with Eric Hoffer was a memorable experience." He later wrote to a physician friend of Hoffer's, Dr. Donald E. Bernstein, in answer to a letter praising the meeting, "I envy you your Sunday dinners with one of the wisest and best of Americans."

The morning after the meeting, photos of the two men sipping soft drinks in the Rose Garden were all over the nation's newspapers. In a speech that week, Johnson quoted what Hoffer had said to Sevareid, and a week later, White House staffers asked about the session told reporters that Hoffer had put the president "in a relaxed frame of mind for a week." Johnson also spoke to former president Harry Truman about Hoffer and the comfort he had taken from their conversation, and later told Hoffer about this, adding that Truman, too, was a Hoffer fan.

Chapter Eight:
"A Savage Heart"

Now a retired longshoreman, Eric Hoffer would stroll to a café on California and Polk Street for breakfast, then to the waterfront edge of Market Street—a young friend frequently found him there, discussing with a longshoreman or a passing tourist Schopenhauer or America's China trade—and walk six miles each day, visiting construction sites and becoming what he referred to as the city's self-appointed new buildings inspector. Most afternoons he spent at Lili's, in the Haight-Ashbury section, epicenter of the youth revolt, a magnet for "hippies" that provided Hoffer with evidence of the dissimilarity between the visitors' lifestyles and those of working people.

The twin triumphs of the Sevareid interview and the Johnson tête-à-tête assured Hoffer that now, more than ever, he could say and write anything, without adverse consequences. His new popularity proved quite bankable. CBS began negotiations toward an exclusive contract that would have Sevareid interview him once a year for the next three and prevent his appearing on any competing network. Cass Canfield, chairman of Harper & Row's executive committee as well as a senior editor, participated in the negotiations with CBS, and when at dinner in San Francisco Hoffer confided that he and Lili were unhappy with his royalties, Canfield unilaterally raised the paperback royalty from 4 to 6 percent. Since such royalties were normally split fifty-fifty between the hardcover's publisher and the author, Canfield explained in a letter, this was "equivalent to a 12 percent royalty if an outside publisher has these books. And this is a high paperback royalty—well above normal." Canfield also conveyed that Harper &

Row would publish whatever Hoffer sent, and suggested that future books come out at two-year intervals.

A third boost to Hoffer's income came from a weekly syndicated newspaper column. Since mid-1967, Hoffer had done Sunday squibs for the San Francisco *Examiner*, no more than a sentence or two. Among Hoffer's suitors for a longer weekly column he chose the small Ledger Syndicate because he liked the proprietor, John W. Higgins, a one-legged man of energy and enthusiasm. Higgins' winning pitch, made during a six-hour feast at Lili's, was that the country needed a weekly Hoffer column to keep it on an even keel. As with many of Lili's feast guests, Higgins left convinced of his unique relationship with the longshoreman philosopher, and was soon referring in correspondence to Hoffer and Lili as his dearest friends. Hoffer's 50 percent of the gross from the columns could bring him $500 a week. He was selling 1,000 paperbacks a week, at cover prices between 75¢ and $1.25, as well as some hardbacks at a higher price; at the new 6 percent paperback royalty, although he would still make just pennies per copy, he might net as much as another $500 a month. Foreign rights and other fees raised his annual total royalties to near $20,000. His new popularity would boost his 1968 income to $180,000—on which, because he refused to take any tax deductions, he would pay $70,000 in federal taxes.

Calvin Tomkins had remained in touch after *The New Yorker* profile, and when Hoffer's former publisher at Harper & Row, John Macrae III, became president of E. P. Dutton, he commissioned Tomkins to expand the profile into a book. Hoffer was willing, but wanted part of the book to be a section of his aphorisms, likely the ones he had earlier discussed with William Shawn. A Sevareid intro-duction to the book told the tale of the electrifying CBS broadcast. In a letter to Tomkins prior to publication, Lili said that Hoffer wanted him to decide what percentage of its income ought to go to Eric and to the photographers. She also informed him that since Selden had left in mid-1966, hers had not been a "united family," so Tomkins should not imply that the Osbornes were, since they were planning to divorce. *Eric Hoffer: An American Odyssey* took the form of an extended visit to Hoffer by Tomkins, and did not discuss the issue of the Osborne family.

Despite having more income, Hoffer remained at the Clay Street walk-up with no telephone, television, or automobile. Earlier, his non-use of those devices had signaled his relative poverty; now their absence reflected his deliberate iconoclasm and served as a shield to protect him from celebrity-seekers.

"I have a savage heart because I have never been gentled by school marms in grammar school. I think man is the toughest thing on earth." Those Hoffer sentences, offered in publicity materials by the Ledger Syndicate, neatly summed up Hoffer's public persona at that moment and predicted the tenor of his writing in the coming years: containing more overt statements of personal opinion than he had ever ventured, combined with his stock-in-trade, insights into human nature. The titles of some early 1968 columns indicate their roots: "Fulfillment of the Undesirables," "Automation—The New Garden of Eden?" "A Worker Looks at Management," and "Israel Stands Alone."

Hoffer discovered that he could condense his prior full-length articles into 500 word pieces; the insight that came from this process led to his underwriting the Lili Fabilli and Eric Hoffer Essay Prize at Berkeley. For these annual awards to essays, he decreed submissions of no more than 500 words. "Wordiness is a sickness of American writing," he explained to the university, adding that any good idea could be expressed in 200 words but that "if you have nothing to say ... all the words in the dictionaries will not suffice." There was a small dig at his Berkeley colleagues in this explanation; as Denis Doyle later recalled, Aaron Wildavsky had asked Hoffer if he could do a guest column, and Hoffer had agreed, but Wildavsky found it impossible to confine his thoughts on any particular subject to the few hundred words that the column's length permitted.

Increasingly, as 1968 wore on, Hoffer focused the "Reflections" columns on contemporary matters: "Youth Is a Time of Ferment," "The Disease of Rioting," and "The Negro's Vicious Circle."

Construing the present as a time of near-chaos, a consequence of the rapid changes in America since the end of World War II, he saw each hot-button issue as an instance of the larger clash between the elites and the working class, and his duty as upholding the concerns of those first- second-, and third-generation immigrants from Europe who feared the loss of the society they had worked for, fought for, and believed in. A typical column, published June 9, 1968, "The Campus Is For Men, Not Kids," began with Hoffer's report of his joking response when asked why there were so many dogs at Berkeley: "Where there are dogs, there are kids." This "flippant" response led Hoffer to his more serious point, that the dogs were evidence that at present the young people on the nation's campuses were not there to study. Campuses ought to be only for adults who did want to study rather than for kids seeking to rebel. Current college students had not been able to progress beyond adolescence, he charged, because our civilization had no "puberty rites" to smooth the transition between boyhood and manhood. He proposed that before high school graduates became eligible for college, they should perform a couple of years of mandatory manual labor, which would force them to become adults worthy of entry into college. Then, "With a student body made up of grown men and women, universities could become what they are supposed to be: places to learn at leisure, unhurried by examination and supervision."

Many Hoffer columns contained ideas that readers were unlikely to encounter in other newsprint. June 2, 1968: "A nation is not really wealthy when its energies are directed more toward the acquisition of yet more wealth." August 11, 1968: "The Western individual, be he a workingman, a capitalist, an intellectual, a politician, or an artist, is still preoccupied with the salvation of his soul. ... Belief passes, but to have believed never passes."

While writing these columns, Hoffer was also re-examining conclusions he had reached many years earlier, and using the results of his reconsideration in the longer articles he was simultaneously composing. In "Man's Most Useful Occupation," for IBM's publication

Think, Hoffer took on the origins of art in the Neolithic period, showing how the grand cave paintings at Altamira had upset prior notions—his own, included—about how "primitive" early man had been. Neolithic peoples had had enough leisure time to create artistic masterpieces. In "The Birth of Cities," he argued from recent archaeological discoveries that domestication of plants had occurred alongside the birth of cities, providing time and occasion for the inventions of writing and mathematics.

In "The Madhouse of Change," eventually published in *Playboy*, Hoffer explicitly acknowledged his revision efforts. He confessed that even while working on *The True Believer*, "there was something tugging at my mind, making me wonder" whether his observations about the Hitler-Stalin decades were relevant to how nations and people were then changing in Africa and Asia. "The explanation which appealed to me most and which I hung onto the longest" was that "change itself is the cause of the madhouse," yet "all the time I was playing with these explanations I failed to see something that was staring me in the face." The "apocalyptic madhouse" of the Hitler-Stalin decades, he now realized, had been due to attempts by Germany and Russia to "modernize themselves at breakneck speed," in other words, to be reborn; the true engine of change was the longing for rebirth. Mass migrations were iterations of it—"misfits" transferred from Old Europe to New America, he pointed out, to find the resources to aid them in being reborn. A frustrated rebirth was a terrible thing; he saw that happening currently in the "Negro revolution:" because the white majority had been unable to stop judging African-Americans as anything other than black people, despite all efforts, blacks had been unable to achieve a true rebirth. He also now concluded that change for all people had become so rapid and so total that "the present has almost ceased to exist," the future was "so immediate that no one waits for it," and "yesterday seems beyond recall." These alterations set the stage for the take-over of the present by the adolescent mentality, with its inclination to throw out the baby with the bathwater—to reject the positives of their parents' society along with its hampering of self-expression.

As did "The Madhouse of Change," many Hoffer articles of this era anticipated a deep chasm in American life: between those who viewed the tumultuous Sixties as producing positive alterations to the status quo, and those who saw the Sixties as undermining the status quo. In "Thoughts on the Present," he identified the central mistake of those who thought well of the changes:

> We of the present have a more vivid awareness of the tragic paradox central to the human condition than had any [generation] before us. ... Our increased awareness has come from new revelations not about the nature of evil but about the nature of the good. No other generation has been made so poignantly conscious of the perils of doing good. We know that to set out to do good is to run the gauntlet of baffling, grotesque side effects. ... The ills and woes which beset our society at present and strain it to the breaking point were born of a concerted effort to right wrongs and do good: to give equality to the Negro, improve the lot of the poor and throw open all the gates of education and self-improvement.

Hoffer brought this hardening conservative stance to a post that changed his career trajectory: as an appointed member of the President's Commission on the Causes and Prevention of Violence, convened in the wake of the assassinations of Martin Luther King Jr. and Robert F. Kennedy. Since Hoffer's October 1967 chat with President Johnson in the Rose Garden, he and the White House had been in touch several times. At the president's behest, Hoffer met Vice-President Humphrey in his San Francisco Hotel room; Humphrey emerged to tell a reporter that the talk had been "invigorating ... like wholesale sunshine in the living room. If I didn't do anything else worthwhile on this trip, talking with Hoffer made it worth ten times what it otherwise would have been." Johnson similarly had Hoffer confer with Walter Heller, the former chairman of the Council of Economic Advisors, on Heller's visit to San Francisco.

After Johnson's surprise announcement on March 31, 1968 that he would not stand for re-election—a decision taken in reaction to the growing public anger over an increasingly unpopular war—Vice-President Humphrey began a campaign to become the Democratic candidate for president, and he solicited and won Hoffer's support. Previously, Hoffer had backed the mayoral campaign of Democrat Joseph Alioto, who after his election appointed Hoffer to San Francisco's Arts Commission.

Later in 1968 Johnson would name Hoffer to the advisory council for the Peace Corps; Hoffer would respond in a note that he was deeply honored but felt "a fraud" for going around "shooting my mouth off" and having no experience or learning that qualified him for the position. "If you are a fraud, then the country needs more frauds," Johnson replied. "And if more people could shoot their mouths off with your wit and wisdom, your concern and compassion, the world would be a better place."

Hoffer's presence in State Department seminars, in work for the USIA, and in his appointment to the Peace Corps advisory body drew no adverse reaction from the public, but his appointment to the Violence Commission was controversial. Following the assassinations of King and Kennedy, Hoffer had insisted to a television interviewer that Americans were not violent people, citing as evidence that Sirhan Sirhan, who had shot Senator Kennedy, was a Jordanian. Outraged by that opinion, and by Hoffer's newspaper columns, dozens of people complained to the White House that Hoffer was biased and should not be appointed; many letter-writers also objected to another commission member, Senator Roman Hruska, a conservative Republican from Nebraska. But Hoffer was no more conservative than Hruska or the majority of the eight-member commission, which included Milton Eisenhower, brother of the former president, Cardinal Terence Cook, and House Majority Leader Hale Boggs.

Hoffer was also importuned from the right for working with President Johnson. Georgie Anne Geyer, returning from the USSR, brought presents to Hoffer and Lili but told him she was disturbed that he would have anything to do with Johnson, whose liberal policies she believed that Hoffer decried as much as she did. CBS, in reaction to the Johnson appointments of Hoffer to various posts, decided not to air further interviews during the election year. As a White House wag had noted, in the Sevareid broadcast Hoffer had been so complimentary to the president that he was surprised the Republicans had not asked for equal time.

Hoffer signaled that he was not going to be a complaisant committee member of any organization. At a public meeting of the San Francisco Arts Commission, he at first listened so quietly to several speakers and to a discussion about art in the various city neighborhoods that a reporter for the *Examiner* thought he might be napping. Then Hoffer posed two questions to the panel: how do you delineate a neighborhood, and how do you decide what is art. He opined that all neighborhood boundaries were arbitrary, and that art was found in bars as well as in museums and on church walls. An impassioned discussion ensued. "The dull days of the Art Commission meetings were over. Hoffer's seeming siesta hadn't really been a siesta at all," the reporter concluded. Hoffer later recalled being thrilled at another meeting by speeches made by residents of Bernal Heights, "a workingman's neighborhood where people of different ethnic backgrounds live side by side." The commission's expert had rejected their application to paint their high school in red, white and blue, saying that the colors were too garish. But after the locals—most of them, immigrants—made an impassioned case for their patriotic scheme, the commission, to Hoffer's delight, voted unanimously to agree to it.

Over the summer of 1968, Hoffer continued to fulminate in columns about the need to "forcefully deal with those who mistake leniency for weakness," among them the director of the American Civil Liberties Union, who had chided the police for being unduly harsh in putting down riots. Minorities were bullying the majority, Hoffer believed, and, "You wonder when and how the majority will stand up against the minorities that smirch and torment it. Does the decent, hard-working majority ever lose patience?"

Hoffer did not attend the first public meeting of the President's Commission on the Causes and Prevention of Violence but did fly to Washington to attend the second, on October 23, in the Senate office building on Capitol Hill.

Assistant professor of sociology at Santa Cruz Herman Blake testified while wearing an African tribal shirt and dark glasses; he insisted on playing an audiotaped diatribe by Black Panther Huey Newton, in jail awaiting trial for killing a policeman. (Blake and Newton would later collaborate on a book, *Revolutionary Suicide*.) After playing the tape, Blake told the panel that to properly ascertain the causes of violence they must go out and see the "shacks and hovels" in which the poor lived.

"All my life I was poor," Hoffer erupted at Blake. "When I was picking cotton, Negroes were eating better and living better than I was. Your rhetoric went down fine with [the other commissioners]. It didn't go down fine with me. It wouldn't go down fine with the longshoremen." Silence descended on the hearing room.

Blake resumed his testimony: "I'm talking about communities where people live in poverty and die in poverty and they rage about it."

"Rage is something that doesn't come from frustration. Rage is a luxury and you can't afford it," Hoffer retorted, and began to shout at the professor. Blake responded in kind, and then walked away from the witness table.

"Mr. Hoffer's statements are indicative of the racist philosophy of this country," said Commissioner Leon A. Higginbotham, an African-American federal appeals court judge in Philadelphia, and called for Hoffer's expulsion from the Commission. The hearing went on.

Former student activist Tom Hayden, who had written a book about the recent race riots in Newark, next took the microphone. Hearing Hayden speak of anger at the war in Vietnam as the cause of ghetto and campus violence, Hoffer broke in to say that the campus demonstrators were "having the time of their lives" while behaving like "hoodlums." Student protest leader Henry Mayer then chimed in about "that arrogant exercise of official violence," the war in Vietnam, asserting that students were alienated. Hoffer interrupted again: "You people want power. You say you are alienated, but I haven't seen a single alienation that a little power can't cure." He then stalked out of the hearing himself. Returning for the afternoon session, he listened for a while to Sam Brown, a former divinity student who had led the presidential-nomination campaign of Senator Eugene McCarthy. But when Brown began to opine about the democratic process, charging that Humphrey had not won the nomination fairly, Hoffer retorted that he did not accept that Brown or any of the other witnesses believed in the democratic process— rather, he accused, they had resorted to violence. With that he left the hearings, intending never to return, but to avoid embarrassing Johnson he did not resign.

The episode was a disaster for Hoffer's public image. In no way contrite, he became increasingly acerbic about contemporary matters. Writing a column about "Negro Anti-Semitism," he shouted that blacks were dying in droves in Africa at the hands of Arabs, yet African-Americans ignored that and chose instead to make anti-Semitic attacks on American Jews and on Israel. He railed similarly in "The Cure of Lawlessness," "Who Is Sick?" and "Clichés About America," all of which condemned various assaults on America.

Like the Republican candidate for president, former Vice-President Richard M. Nixon, Hoffer embraced "law and order," lambasted the protesters and rioters, decried the intellectuals who had led Johnson to his Great Society programs, and, using get-tough rhetoric, sought to marshal a majority reaction against the protesters. Nonetheless, Hoffer was appalled by the prospect of a Nixon presidency, believing that Nixon lacked an understanding of the workingman. Before Nixon had won the Republican nomination, Hoffer had written to former New York Governor Nelson Rockefeller, urging him to stay in the race, and during the presidential campaign he openly supported Humphrey. However, when Hoffer sent a contribution to the Humphrey campaign, the money was returned with a request that Hoffer help the candidate only by making more public appearances on his behalf.

In early 1969, as the Johnson Administration left office, the president's family asked Hoffer to assist in the compilation of a volume on the administration's successes, to be edited by historian James McGregor Burns; Hoffer worked on this, to Burns's satisfaction, and contributed the book's epilogue, adapted from his 1967 interview with Sevareid. Also in early 1969, Governor Ronald Reagan's office asked Hoffer to come to Sacramento for a chat. In 1967, when Reagan had become governor, one of his first actions had been to force the California Board of Regents to fire Clark Kerr, whom Hoffer had supported; and the governor was quite aware that Hoffer had spoken scathingly of him in the Sevareid broadcast. Even so, both Reagan and Hoffer advocated toughness in regard to campus protesters, and Reagan later recalled his 1969 conversation with Hoffer on this subject as particularly frank and salty.

Reagan and Hoffer had already become more in tune than Hoffer had been with Johnson: both Reagan and Hoffer had come to mistrust and to desire the repeal of the Roosevelt-era social reforms; both were free market capitalists; both saw the need for more discipline in society; both were deeply anti-Communist; and both appealed to blue-collar workers whom they believed shared their values.

The California governor summoned Hoffer in January 1969—as Johnson had in 1967—because of his appearance on national television. CBS's second Sevareid-Hoffer interview had just aired.

Since the first broadcast, Hoffer had been through eighteen months of retirement and a year of celebrity. Important events in the interim, such as the assassinations of Robert F. Kennedy and Martin Luther King Jr., and the change in the character of the war in Vietnam, had more deeply affected Sevareid than Hoffer: Sevareid had eulogized King as "the most important American of his time, black or white," and was moving toward Cronkite's position of advocating the end of American participation in the war in Vietnam. However, Sevareid still shared Hoffer's opinion of the usurpations of campus rebels, and had expressed the hope that the assassinations would "herald the ultimate end of the age of permissiveness, of organized leniency, of the equation of freedom with personal and political license."

"The Savage Heart" featured Hoffer uttering more outspoken railings against campus protesters, "Negro" rioters, charlatan leaders, and the unwillingness of the majority to fight to defend its territory. Hoffer took on Black Panther Eldridge Cleaver for being so disrespectful of a convention of lawyers that he appeared before them wearing a necklace of animal teeth. He took on Arthur Schlesinger Jr. for labeling Americans the most frightening people on earth for being the aggressor in Vietnam. Schlesinger, he implied, was no more than a power-hungry intellectual whose opinions on current events were worthless simply because the historian had "lived with Schlesingers all his life" and had no understanding of the workingman majority of the American population.

The most emotionally moving part of the broadcast was on the subject of aging. Hoffer read a poem about dying that he had written, years earlier:

How far ahead my waiting end.
The road runs straight I see no bend.
But somewhere there, I know not where,
I'll meet my end, my waiting friend.

He knows I come, I know he waits.
There is no bend, there are no gates.
The road is endless, but my end
Is somewhere there to meet a friend.

"Audience Loves, Hates Thorny Critic," UPI headlined its report about the 1969 Sevareid interview. "[Hoffer's] presence virtually detonates the mild-mannered stuff of videos surrounding prime time as he hurls verbal thunderbolts about contemporary issues," reviewer Rick DuBrow wrote, adding that Hoffer was both loved and hated for the same reason: "He talks back passionately, angrily, to some of the most publicized and powerful forces in the nation—including rioters, youth, and intellectuals who regard themselves as a rather special elite." A more negative view came from David J. Goode in the *Hartford Courant*: "Eric Hoffer, leading American apologist and perennial extoller of the virtues of Boobus Americanus, proved more entertaining than enlightening." Those who "hated" Hoffer were vocal enough that CBS scheduled a rebuttal hour, a week later, during which a panel commented on Hoffer. CBS staffer Marion Goldin wrote to Lili,

> The so-called "discussion" on CBS ... hardly made a dent; the panel was stacked and in their undisguised desire to attack Mr. Hoffer personally they barely touched the meat of his thoughts. I, for one, was indignant at the choice of "discussants" and so expressed my obviously impotent outrage before the program was aired. So I was particularly delighted that it had so little impact.

It was a moment when the rhetoric of the protesters and of militant African-Americans had ramped up to the point of accusing white liberals of exploiting blacks and of being racists. One target was Saul Alinsky, who sent to Hoffer his editorial in response. Alinsky had spent many years mobilizing black communities; few Americans, white or black, had done more for blacks:

I am not going to have these hotheads cutting the race issue with me. ... I think it is time that someone tried to restore a sense of balance in this race business. ... Unless whites overcome their own hang-ups so that they can both listen and speak to blacks in the same way that they would be listening and speaking to whites, and vice versa, we are faced with an imminent period of a few years in which a combination of black charlatans and white neurotics will sow a scene of disillusionment and bitterness which will provide a comforting rationale for all racial bigots, both back and white.

These were Hoffer's sentiments, too.

In the spring of 1969, Al Kuettner, a former UPI reporter who had already written an article about Hoffer for *Pace* magazine, took Hoffer to the just-forming Lane College in Eugene, Oregon, where the professors were retired mechanics and military, and the subjects included trade skills along with the academics. Hoffer loved it, as this was near to the ideal that he had imagined. Afterwards, he frequently cited this college and its experience in his conversation and writings. On the trip, Kuettner was accompanied by a young associate, Malcolm Roberts, who became friendly with Hoffer. Shortly after the article appeared, Roberts was summoned to Washington to become an assistant to Secretary of the Interior Walter Hickel, about whom Roberts had written an article for *Pace*.

In 1969 Hoffer, as with many Americans above the age of forty, felt that his positions on what was of value, what was proper behavior, and how our democracy ought to function had not changed but that others nonetheless perceived his positions as more to the right, politically, than they had been a decade earlier. The Nixon administration, in tandem with this feeling, as 1969 wore on and anti-war protests and ghetto rioting continued, argued for the tougher laws to counter violence. Hoffer's appreciation of the president increased; he told *Time* that Nixon was "a total surprise," that "It's wonderful when a man who is so denigrated turns out to be so good. I glory in it."

This was also when Hoffer began to favor in his correspondence those whose opinions were conservative, and all but stopped communicating with those who seemed too liberal. Among his new correspondents in 1969 were two who became long-term friends, Pauline Phillips, whose "Dear Abby" column was a fixture in many newspapers, and William Loeb III, publisher of the Manchester *Union Leader*, one of the most conservative newspapers in the country. Pauline and husband Morton Phillips played host to Hoffer and Lili in Washington, and Hoffer and Lili reciprocated when the Phillipses returned to San Francisco, where they had resided for many years before moving to Washington; and Hoffer and Lili frequently visited with the Loebs in their winter home in Reno, Nevada. A third Hoffer correspondent was Warren Burger, then a judge on a federal court of appeal; when *Newsweek* reprinted as an article a speech that Burger had given in 1967, Hoffer located the original speech, read it, and wrote a fan letter:

> Dear Judge: Your "Paradox in the Administration of Criminal Justice" is the most lucid piece of writing I have laid eyes on in what seems a lifetime. I have no taste for legal writing. You crystallize in me the feeling I had but could not formulate; namely, that the social body is perhaps more vulnerable and fragile than the human body. A scratch on the social body easily becomes a festering sore. We have to defend society against reckless individuals—well-meaning, humane, reckless individuals.

They began a correspondence, Burger—who would later tell Hoffer that he was "familiar" with all of his books—sending a copy of another speech he had made, in 1964, in which he had argued, "The warmth and compassion of Americans for the underdog, the underprivileged, and the troubled" was part of the American way, but when that compassion "spills over on judges it produces the visceral jurisprudence which plagues this land at the moment." Hoffer heartily agreed. President Nixon also read the *Newsweek* reprint of Burger's

1967 speech and shortly nominated him as chief justice of the Supreme Court. Thereafter, on occasions, when some issue before the Supreme Court moved Hoffer, he would write Burger a note, and received one in return.

Unused to churning out material on a weekly schedule, Hoffer did not like the alterations to his thought processes that the recurrent deadline imposed. Hoffer believed that his judgments about history and human behavior should be reached coolly, rather than in the heat of the moment, yet Higgins of the Ledger Syndicate continually requested columns on specific current subjects, and Hoffer occasionally complied. The result was an increasing gulf between the high quality of thought in the columns that were based on his notebooks, and the lesser quality in those columns featuring his reactions to current events.

Harper & Row's need for a new Hoffer book to take advantage of public interest contributed to Hoffer's willingness to ask them to issue his 1958-1959 diary, in 1969, as *Working and Thinking on the Waterfront*. Looking for material, he had unearthed the diary, read it at a single sitting, and been entranced, as had Lili when she read it. Among the ancillary reasons for publishing it now was that Lili and Selden had divorced, so the diary's tough words about Selden would not produce the same repercussions they might have provoked earlier.

Since this would be the first Hoffer book after the Sevareid interview, a major book club was willing to feature it—a virtual guarantee of sales—but only if Hoffer excised the harsher judgments about African-Americans and added an admiring sentence or two about Martin Luther King Kr. Hoffer refused; the book was printed as written, with no book club sale.

A Hoffer column in March 1969 was quite blunt in its assessment:

> It should be obvious that you cannot stop the militant students by satisfying their demands. These would-be history makers have stumbled on a terrible secret. They have discovered that the men in power on the campus are too confused, too unsure, too humane, and probably too cowardly to hit back hard. So they are pushing and pushing to see how far they can go.

This rhetoric spurred his invitation to testify before Congress on May 1, 1969. Senator John L. McClellan, Democrat of Arkansas, had for years used the Permanent Subcommittee on Investigations, which he chaired, to harass organized labor and search out pockets of reputed Communist influence. McClelland's new investigation targeted groups that fostered riots on campuses and civil disorder in cities, in the hope of pinning such upheavals on the far left. On the first morning of hearings, Hoffer was the sole witness. He began by reiterating what he had charged in his columns and to Sevareid: that permissiveness had spawned the student rebellions, which were spreading and "contagious." As an example, he outlined the spring 1968, students takeover and defacing of the office of Columbia University President Grayson Kirk:

> They got into his room. They pissed on his carpet. They burglarized his files. They used his shaving kit. Grayson Kirk did not forget himself. Now I remember when the longshoremen were talking about that. I think it would have been a wonderful thing, although it is not civilized, I think it would have been a wonderful thing if Grayson Kirk got mad, grabbed a gun and gunned them down. I think maybe he would have gotten killed, maybe he would have killed two of them when they were jumping up, but I think he would have saved Columbia. You have to get angry; you have to have courage enough to lay your life on the line. I think what you need, Mr. Chairman, is not new strong laws. You need men of strong character ... chancellors of universities and mayors of cities who

have the muscle, who love a fight, who when they get up in the
morning, spit on their hands and ask, "Whom do I kill today?"
These are the people who will save you.

Hoffer segued to discussing Clark Kerr, whom he now viewed as
a victim of his own "innocence and trustfulness." "It took your breath
away when you saw a punk like [Mario] Savio run rings around Clark
Kerr. Clark Kerr has more wisdom in his little finger than all those
students put together. But he was no match for Savio, and it was
intoxicating for college students the world over." Laughter from the
crowd at the hearing seemed to spur Hoffer to greater rhetorical
excesses: "Imagine, senators, [the rebellious students] can make
history! They have power! It's intoxicating. They have a taste for
academic flesh. They want to kill them! They want to eat them!"

All committee members present, with the exception of Abraham
Ribicoff, the liberal Democratic senator from Connecticut, agreed
with Hoffer. Dixiecrat Senator Sam Ervin of North Carolina mused,
"When I went to college, when students went to the dean's office,
students were in trouble. Nowadays when students go to the dean's
office, the dean is in trouble. You have, I think, put the finger on the
trouble with America."

"I ought to bite out my tongue for saying it—you know, these
[student rebels], many of them, are going to be pushing around and
biting people in Wall Street by the time they are forty. But I would
have them do it with artificial teeth. I would love them really not to
have their real teeth to do it with."

The only senator to take on Hoffer was Ribicoff, a former
secretary of Health, Education, and Welfare under Kennedy. When
Hoffer asserted that the university was "not a political institution ...
not an instrument for solving the problems of society," Ribicoff
countered by asking whether the purpose of a university was to do
defense research for the federal government.

Hoffer caught Ribicoff's drift, agreed that universities should
probably not be in the defense research business, and used this to

segue into his idea of a university as a place to learn at leisure and for the young to "discover what an idea is" and develop into mature human beings.

"But the professors don't give this [instruction in ideas] any more, and neither do the administrators," Ribicoff responded. "Touché," Hoffer conceded, and for a few moments he and Ribicoff had a real discussion about the purposes of universities, during which Ribicoff reminded him that the labor movement had had violent episodes. Hoffer conceded this too, but pointed out, "We didn't want to destroy the establishment, we wanted a piece of the pie." Under Ribicoff's prodding, Hoffer made some less heated and more cogent points:

> The sociologists and academists in general have so many articles of faith, like 'poverty breeds crime,' just like in some Catholic dogma ... or that violent programs from the television breed violence. ... My idea is just the opposite: that what television induces is passivity in the majority, meekness, timidity, cowardice in the majority, and when the majority is meek and cowardly, then the violent minority becomes more violent.

On that evening's network news broadcasts, the reasonable parts of Hoffer's testimony were ignored and the inflammatory parts shown. His table-pounding dramatic style and his bleeped but obvious expletives heightened the impact of his deliberately exaggerated positions. Reaction from the other news media was quick and negative: editorials and cartoons decrying Hoffer's call to violence. Many charged that Hoffer had become a true believer himself, advocating violence against those who did not share his beliefs. "A reactive voice of doom for the American right," the Providence *Journal* called him, a "tragic casualty" of the system that had made him famous.

Negative judgments on Hoffer were given a patina of scholarly analysis by a review of several of his books, including *Working and Thinking on the Waterfront*, in the May 8, 1969 issue of the *New York*

Review of Books, one of the country's premier literary magazines. Reviewer Edgar Z. Friedenberg, an academic, was at that time in the forefront of the professors decrying American participation in the war in Vietnam. The author, most recently, of *Coming of Age in America: Growth and Acquiescence*, he held quite a different view of campus protesters than Hoffer. In the *NYRB*, Friedenberg reviewed the just-issued 1958-59 diary as well as *The Temper of Our Time* and Tomkins' *Eric Hoffer, An American Odyssey*. One of the negatives for Hoffer in publishing his decade-old diary was that his 1959 positions on issues such as student protesters, and his use of racial code words, had by 1969 become "politically incorrect" and a reason not to view the diary kindly. Friedenberg was more than unkind; he assiduously deprecated Hoffer as well as his writings. The review's hectoring tone began in the opening paragraphs, with Friedenberg slamming Tomkins' *American Odyssey* title as inappropriate because Hoffer, unlike Odysseus, had never set foot outside of his home country, and arguing that while Hoffer was indeed American, he was not representative of anything exemplary. Friedenberg went on to cherry-pick from the decade-old diary, fixing on Hoffer's initial dismissal of Saunders Redding's book as evidence of Hoffer's anti-black attitude. A reviewer committed to fairness would also have mentioned the parts of the diary in which Hoffer wrote of coming to admire Redding and even to taking revenge on Redding's behalf on some nasty Asian journalists, but Friedenberg did not. In his effort to refute Hoffer's blaming of intellectuals for America's ills, Friedenberg also deliberately ignored Hoffer's characterization of America as a mass civilization and his celebration of the accomplishments of the masses, a common thread in the Hoffer books, in the Tomkins book, and in Sevareid's introduction. Unlike Garry Wills' 1963 evaluation of Hoffer's work, Friedenberg's was overtly political and made no attempt to understand or account for Hoffer's continuing appeal to that still-sizable fraction of Americans who were not anti-war and who looked askance at the excesses of protesters and rioters. (A year after penning this review, Friedenberg permanently left the United

States and resettled in Canada, giving as a reason that he no longer wanted to pay taxes to a U.S. government he disliked.)

A Hoffer column distributed in early June 1969, entitled "The Meek Majority," contained the sentences, "The other day, at Berkeley, a class of 250 students was addressed by an intruding Negro student as mother ... and warned not to come to class next day or have their throats slit. The punk was not thrown out. The professor, a famous teacher, begged the intruder to leave the class." Hoffer's description was too much for the San Francisco *Examiner*, which removed from his column the word "Negro," making the story incomprehensible. Shortly, Hoffer walked into the newspaper office and told the editor he would no longer be submitting squibs for the Sunday paper.

The *Examiner* was not alone in wanting to filter Hoffer, though; a number of the column's newspaper-publishers were wondering whether having Hoffer in their pages was worth enduring reader aggravation and angry letters-to-the-editor.

Hoffer found safer though more esoteric ground in deriding the work of Herbert Marcuse, a German-born social theorist and Marxist known as "the father of the New Left." After a career at the Frankfurt School of Social Research, Columbia, and Brandeis, in 1965 Marcuse had come to the University of California at San Diego, and had continued to preach an anti-Western philosophy and to participate in many student protests. Hoffer charged that such Marxist intellectuals took joy from inciting the young to rebel, and from attempting to bring down democracy and capitalism. Later, he would expand the notion that Marcuse's communism was an elitist conception, not one that championed the workers, charging in an article for *The New York Times Magazine* that Marcuse had the attitude of a "shabby would-be aristocrat ... offended ... by the failure of egalitarian America to keep common people in their place." He quoted Marcuse to good effect; the professor had written that he was frightened by "the degree to which the population is allowed ... to be ugly and uglify things, to ooze familiarity and to offend against good form." Hoffer responded by writing that to Marcuse, "there is something fundamentally wrong with a society in which the master and the worker, the typist and the boss's daughter do not live totally disparate lives."

Such columns displayed flashes of analytic brilliance, but Higgins of the Ledger Syndicate wanted his star to write more about subjects at the top of the news, begging Hoffer for a response to Senator Ted Kennedy's accident at Chappaquiddick in July 1969. As often happened when Hoffer was pushed in one direction, he went in another, refusing this request and all but swearing off current events in favor of mining his previous books for columns on "God and the Machine Age," "Man and God," "The Passage from Boyhood to Manhood."

President Nixon gave a speech on the evening of November 3, 1969, in response to anti-war protests that had brought hundreds of thousands of marchers to Washington, D.C. In it, he argued that the war in Vietnam must be won, and castigated the "vocal minority" who wanted the war declared over; should that minority prevail, Nixon said, "this nation has no future as a free society," and so he appealed to "the silent majority" to back his and America's efforts on the battlefield and at the peace table. This speech galvanized public support for Nixon and against the protesters. Demonstrations by "hard hats" in New York, San Francisco, and other heavily unionized cities—by Hoffer's sort of workingmen—followed, as did a resolution passed by the Democratic-dominated House of Representatives, 334-55, backing the president's path.

Hoffer, perhaps emboldened by this support for positions that he also embraced, returned to the attack in his columns towards the end of 1969, "Who Makes History?" "Black Power," "The Perils of Affluence." These unleashed bundles of protest letters, which the newspapers and the syndicator forwarded to Hoffer, who did not answer them. For a while longer he pressed on, to the point of writing a column on the "Negrification" of white American youth:

> The effect of the Negro Revolution on the non-Negro is as unexpected as it is puzzling. Why have the young so wholeheartedly

adopted the Negro's style of life? The negrification of the young will have profound and durable effects on our language, sexual mores, the attitude toward work, and on tastes and manners in general. Even white young racists are negrified and do not realize it.

Norman Mailer's celebrated 1957 article, "The White Negro," had tackled this subject from a different point of view, positing white adoption of black attitudes as an outgrowth of increasing alienation. But Hoffer on "Negrification," though acutely observed, was less of a reasoned critique and evaluation than an angry screed against what he saw as a diminished moral sense among the young.

Though Hoffer professed not to care what other people thought of him, he was aware of his own "hunger for praise. It is a misfortune that confidence should depend so much on what other people think of you—that faith in oneself, like any other faith, needs a chorus of consent." Since that chorus no longer sang his praises, he was discomfited. Shortly after submitting the "Negrification" column, Hoffer abruptly announced to the public in February 1970 that he was ending the "Reflections" column and would completely retire from public life.

"No more columns, no more television, no more lectures, no more teaching," he stated. Labeling himself once again "a violent man with a savage heart," he explained that while in his longer-form writings he had always been able to "transmute my inner violence to cool and thoughtful analysis," in writing the columns, "I have not found that possible. They have corrupted and distorted my true nature." He added that the columns had turned him into a "pessimist," even though he had always held the firm belief that America was not a country for pessimists.

But he also insisted, "We have become a nation of cowards. ... I am worried about a country in which people will not speak out for what they believe." He had spoken out, repeatedly, for what he believed and thought that others believed, but "I don't want to die barking. I'm going to crawl back into my hole where I started."

Chapter Nine:
Voice of the Silent Majority

Of the letters Hoffer received in response to announcing his retirement from public life, the most unexpected may have been from FBI Director J. Edgar Hoover:

> Too few of us dedicate ourselves to the interests of the country and the welfare of the people. Consequently, we can ill-afford to lose a single individual who understands these problems and is, himself, an excellent example of the sound, responsible citizen who is fully aware of the fact that it takes intelligence and devotion to preserve and maintain our institutions of freedom. You are such a man. I have long valued your keen ability to analyze situations and conditions which are draining the Nation of its vitality and leadership in the world. ... I deeply regret your plan to retire, although I fully understand your reasons for this decision.

Hoover was correct in his presumption that Hoffer had undertaken the newspaper columns, in part, as an obligation to the public, a purpose that John Higgins had stressed when wooing Hoffer, and one that Hoffer took very seriously. But it is doubtful whether Hoover or anyone else, including Hoffer, fully understood his reasons for retirement.

Chronologically 72, the former longshoreman suffered from chronic health conditions that now and then flared, giving him cause for panic—stomach problems, worsening eyesight, legs becoming less able to walk six miles a day. In his writing he also slowed down, returning to the more methodical, unhurried pace that he had used before beginning the columns.

Exiting public life also enabled Hoffer to spend more time with Lili. They did not marry. Hoffer later said that Lili wanted to, but that he had demurred, afraid that sustained intimacy would make him uneasy and difficult to live with; Lili later said that Hoffer had asked her to marry him but that she had declined out of a concern that living together would negatively impact his writing—she believed he needed his freedom to do his best work, and saw her duty as optimizing the conditions for it. "Some persons must love and be loved in order to be intelligent," he would soon write in a notebook. Differing on many issues, Hoffer and Lili settled into a routine in which each would express an opinion, the other would counter it, and then, having long ago agreed to disagree on that subject, they would move on to another one. When Lili asserted to a visitor that Selden had gone to jail for his cause and had been willing to die for it, Hoffer responded, "Lili, I have told you a hundred times: it is easy to die for what you believe. What is hard is to live for what you believe." James Koerner noted "grand, noisy arguments between Hoffer and Lili about Hoffer's tendency to stereotype races, nations, and individuals;" Lili told Koerner that she saw "people" while Hoffer saw "types." "Constantly engaged in one argument or another," Koerner summed up, "it is evident to everyone that they love each other very much." "What we are looking for is not people who agree with us but people who think well of us and know how to express it," Hoffer would write.

In his declining years, Hoffer thought each book would be his last, but between his retirement from public life and his death he would publish *First Things, Last Things*; *Reflections on the Human Condition*; *In Our Time*; the long diary *Before the Sabbath*; and *Truth Imagined*, more than half of his entire output. And in those books he would go beyond being the voice of the silent majority to become even more of a teacher and philosopher.

Although retired from public positions, he continued in public service. The Nixon administration, as had the Johnson Administration, asked him to firm the backbones of new State Department employees about to go to overseas posts. He lectured regularly to the armed forces service academies and schools, and Secretary of Defense Melvin Laird invited him to the Pentagon for one of his informal, unpublicized lunches with opinion leaders. Secretary of Health Education and Welfare Elliot Richardson got him to join the National Advisory Council on Adult Education—a group concerned with one of Hoffer's pet subjects. He had already become a friend of former governor of Alaska and current Secretary of Energy Walter J. Hickel, through Malcolm Roberts, now a Hickel assistant. Hoffer awarded Hickel, a self-made millionaire, his ultimate accolade: that he, too, could walk into a strange town with no money in his pocket and find a way to make an honest living—as Hickel had done when he had first arrived in Alaska. In late 1970, Roberts and his fiancée were having dinner with Hoffer in a San Francisco waterfront restaurant when the announcement came through that Nixon had fired Hickel. Roberts was chagrined, but Hoffer said, "Now you have a wide open door in front of you. What an opportunity!"

Through Roberts, who then went with Hickel to Alaska and a new life, Hoffer and Hickel became closer. At a dinner at Lili's, Hickel and Hoffer discovered that they both had been impressed by visits to community colleges that featured retired tradesmen as instructors, and that they shared a vision of trades instruction as part of a better curriculum, and of the use of television for remote learning. Hickel took these ideas, and Hoffer's enthusiasm, to AFL-CIO leader George Meany, and they jointly pursued them for several years. Hoffer had hopes for Hickel as a political leader, the sort of middle-of-the-road pragmatist with vision who could lead America out of its morass. "We need men of boundless courage like you," he told Hickel in a note.

Denis P. Doyle, working in Sacramento to revise teacher certification rules, reported to Hoffer that fall that a bill recently passed by the California legislature "was shaped by many of your ideas, taken both from your books and conversations. The arbitrary and usually meaningless course requirements for teachers have been eliminated, and we propose that teachers learn to teach by teaching. In addition, the requirement that a superintendent hold a credential has also been eliminated." These changes, Doyle later recalled, emerged from a tenet that he and Hoffer shared and had discussed, "radical democracy," by which they meant letting the people govern, wherever possible, without intermediaries; in this instance, that mandated allowing talented people to teach even though they did not possess the correct pedagogical degrees, and to manage schools if they were experienced managers but did not have school-system credentials.

At around the same time, Mayor Willard Dyke of Madison, Wisconsin requested Hoffer's opinions on the degree to which he should tolerate attacks on the police, how to combat inner-city violence, and whether the "silent majority" could be mobilized. Madison was the state's second-largest city and capital, home to 175,000 people and to a notable university campus bastion of anti-authority and anti-war rioting. Hoffer's answer to Dyke:

> There can be nothing wrong in appealing to the majority ... to fight against those who are out to destroy us. A silent majority is a cowardly majority. ... The rioters, the bombers, the drug pushers and those who attack the police must know that in Madison they are going to be smashed and annihilated. We must harass them and their shyster lawyers, and make life miserable for them. ... Idealistic hoodlums are hoodlums first, and should be dealt with as such. I would not worry about the law and the constitution; just now the victims have no constitutional guarantees, and as long as we are afraid we have no freedom. Rouse the people! ... The rioters, the bombers, and the criminals ... do what they do because they know they can get away with it. The moment they discover that in Madison they can't get away with it they will stop dead.

Dyke used Hoffer's letter as the center of an address to the state legislature. Three years later, Hoffer repeated what he had written to Mayor Dyke in a speech to a conference of 700 mayors; his exhortations to "Get mad, America!" and to take back streets from criminals had the audience on its feet and applauding.

The letter to Mayor Dyke showed Hoffer becoming the voice of the "silent majority," a stance that he elucidated at greater length in *First Things, Last Things*, published in 1971 as "A Cass Canfield Book," an imprint of Harper & Row. Canfield, an upper class liberal, had openly championed liberal causes since the days of Adlai Stevenson; still, he celebrated Hoffer as a genuine conservative, the articulator of a "sustained attack on the errors of our ways as he sees them," as the book's dust jacket put it. The chapters, the jacket continued, "challenge the current romantic reverence for nature, the tendency to capitulate to the violence of the young and the militant ethnic minorities, the downgrading of the common man, his needs and his achievements, and the corresponding tendency to belittle the character and accomplishment of our nation."

First Things, Last Things brought Hoffer closer to being the modern Montaigne, in that it showed him continuing to revise and augment his already-established tenets, and to adopt an even more conservative political posture than he had earlier embraced. But while throughout the various editions of Montaigne's *Essays* the author's Catholicism remained unchanged, as did his belief in the eventual triumph of good over evil, Hoffer in his book demonstrated the evolution of his viewpoint. It had become what he labeled a tragic view, built on three linked beliefs: that good and evil coexisted and that neither would ever fully triumph over the other, that there was no existence after death and therefore no discernible meaning to anyone's life beyond what one made of it, and that these understandings freed individuals to enjoy themselves in the present.

First Things, Last Things also illustrated Hoffer's big turn, from deconstructing America's external enemies to analyzing its internal ones. Its chapters included articles published during the previous few years, "Man's Most Useful Occupation," "The Birth of Cities," and "The Madhouse of Change," and two based on a long article in *The New York Times Magazine* in answer to the question, "Whose Country Is America?" Those latter two chapters examined the groups currently vying for the social and moral leadership of the United States of America; Hoffer drew sharp battle lines between the group consisting of the rebellious youth, the minorities, and their allies and prodders among the leftist and elitist intellectuals—and the silent majority, which consisted of the middle-aged and middle-class (the parents of the rebellious adolescents), and the working class. For decades, he argued, the silent majority had run the country and had done well in conquering the Depression and winning World War II, but now the rebellious shouters were attempting to push them from power. The shouters, Hoffer charged, "reserve their wrath for institutions in which common people are most represented: unions, Congress, the police, and the army." Hoffer included in his diatribe a dig at his *New York Review of Books* tormentor, citing Edgar Z. Friedenberg as having buttressed the case that Hoffer was making when Friedenberg had written, "elitism is the great and distinctive contribution [that] students are making to American society."

In a note to Hickel accompanying a copy of *First Things, Last Things*, Hoffer called it "an old man's book" and expressed the hope that its "pessimism" would soon be "proven wrong," even though the problems dealt with were, he emphasized, very real and troubling. In this book, he did outline a solution to the problems facing the silent majority: "Learn how to contain anarchy, how to regulate and manipulate everyday life and, above all, how to concoct a faith, a philosophy, and a style of life to suit the needs of a noncreative horde hungering for meaningful, weighty lives." A decade later, Reagan would build on just these elements in the 1980 campaign that won him the presidency.

John Seelye in *The New Republic* turned up his nose at what he labeled the "articulate ignorance" of *First Things, Last Things*, and another reviewer, a former academic, faulted it for "appalling

amateurisms in archaeology, history, philosophy, and social thought."
The New York Times Book Review assigned *Village Voice* reporter Joe
Flaherty to review the book. While any regular contributor to the
Voice, an artsy, anti-establishment, leftist weekly paper, might have
been expected to denigrate Hoffer's work, Flaherty did not.
Confessing that Hoffer was "a hard philosophical cargo to handle,"
Flaherty admitted, "At a time when policemen are called pigs, when
everyday work and experience is being demeaned, Hoffer's common
earthiness and toughness are not only desirable but needed. ... He
calls up the silent majority of most of my life's experience."

Hoffer now wanted his voice to be unfiltered by others. His
experiences at the hands of the news media left him with the
conviction that his words were frequently twisted or excerpted in
ways contrary to what he had intended. CBS had backed away from
any future commitment to air long interviews with him. As far as
Tomkins' book, while the *New Yorker* writer had done a good job of
presenting Hoffer, Tomkins could not help but write from the point of
view of a sophisticated intellectual and art-oriented reporter. More
annoying to Hoffer were the academic efforts to parse his writing and
to attribute various theories to him. When University of Illinois
doctoral candidate Paul Wesley Batty had proposed doing a thesis,
Hoffer refused to correspond with him or to comment on a draft. In
Batty's thorough analysis, he compared passages in Montaigne,
Renan, Burckhardt, and De Tocqueville to Hoffer's paragraphs on the
same subjects, tracing what he labeled Hoffer's "theory of mass
persuasion." Hoffer did not think he held to any particular theory of
mass persuasion, and may also have bristled at Batty's conclusion:
"Hoffer's 45 years as a working man ... have made accomplishment
his chief value. ... His own success in the established social order has
changed the perspective of the migrant worker who saw the seeds of
progress in El Centro's federal camp."

To forestall future interpretation of his work, and to get his own thoughts out in conversational form, Hoffer decided to work with Al Kuettner on a book of conversations. Kuettner was a veteran UPI reporter whose coverage of the civil rights struggle in the 1950s and 1960s had been widely lauded; after leaving UPI, he wrote two articles about Hoffer for *Pace* magazine and Hoffer was comfortable with him as an interviewer. But during Hoffer's column-writing period, the conversations project did not gel, and shortly after Hoffer stopped writing for the columns, Kuettner moved to Cincinnati for a new job. Kuettner implored Cass Canfield for a commitment and an advance for the interview book (so that he could take a leave of absence from his job), but he received a nebulous answer and could not continue. It was then that Hoffer asked James D. Koerner, the program officer of the Alfred P. Sloan Foundation in New York who was also an author on education reform, to take over the book project.

Hoffer would later tell his former student, Stacey Cole—who had once thought of writing a book on Hoffer—that Koerner was a man without malice. Koerner also proved to be of assistance to Hoffer in many ways; his wide circle of acquaintances included Jacques Barzun, to whom he introduced Hoffer's work and facilitated an exchange between them, and Clifton Fadiman, an author, television personality, and executive of the Book-of-the-Month club. Fadiman was also an admirer of Hoffer's, and Koerner arranged their meeting, prior to it asking Fadiman to tutor Hoffer on publishing, because Hoffer "has never had a literary agent, and he needs good advice about royalty rates, publication contracts, and related matters. (He is quite innocent about all that)." Koerner also introduced Hoffer to Joel Hildebrand, the celebrated chemist whom Hoffer referred to as his hero; and referred him to such wealthy acquaintances as Bill and Tess Koch of Berkeley, when Hoffer was looking for a house to buy, having become uncomfortable in his Chinatown apartment.

On Koerner's visits to San Francisco, he and Hoffer began taped conversations. In them, Hoffer revealed more details about his past than ever before, offered more unbridled opinions than he had in his columns, and dealt with rarified subjects not well-covered by other interviewers, such as the burden of freedom, that mix of open horizons and heavy responsibilities that Hoffer saw as the autonomous individual's glory and challenge. In America that burden was particularly acute, he felt, because the individual's freedom was greater than anywhere else. *Hoffer's America* was published in 1973 by a small press.

Hoffer also decided to correspond, and perhaps to influence, the next person to try to parse him for an academic project, Henry Nash Carrier III, a doctoral candidate at the University of Mississippi. Carrier's thesis was Hoffer's "Conceptual Approach to the Development of American Democratic Leadership."

Although Hoffer received a fair amount of mail from fans or from those rebuking him for his opinions, he chose to correspond with relatively few people. He almost never undertook correspondence in the service of aiding his own career, for instance brushing off suggestions for book topics from publishers and requests to provide blurbs for other authors—the sort of mutual back-scratching that he decried as endemic to the intellectual elite. Nor would he ply the proffered connections with the literati; his meeting with Clifton Fadiman went well enough, but friendship did not result. Hoffer much preferred corresponding with Barney Brown, a plumber from Stillwater, Minnesota. In a series of notes he encouraged Brown to "express your intense feelings in cool, precise prose" and not to let anyone tell him how to write. When Brown had a letter-to-the-editor published in his local paper and forwarded a copy, Hoffer wrote back that he enjoyed "seeing you throw your weight around. You remind me of Truman." Shortly, Brown had a longer article published, on the demise of education, and thanked Hoffer profusely for pushing him.

In the spring of 1971, once again having difficulty identifying a new book subject, Hoffer decided to keep a diary, as he had in 1958-59. He began convinced that his eyes were failing, which he attributed to reading too much, although "It is a waste of time since I get very little from what I read," and worried about going lame. Surprised at his rapid deterioration, he dreaded a planned trip to Austin, Texas and Boston, Massachusetts, allowed that he was feeling more intolerant than he had in the past, and needed to guard against that attitude leaking into his writing, which must remain analytic. He decided to cancel the trip on the grounds of ill health.

Next evening at Lili's he had an interesting encounter with sixteen-year-old Eric. "When I happened to say that there is not much history can teach us, precisely at a time when every mother's son is making history," the teenager produced a quote from Thucydides about the ordeal of affluence, and Hoffer was "impressed by the ease with which he found the quotation." They talked about various things, including the generation gap.

Many years later, Eric Osborne would recall that and other conversations with Hoffer in his youth, and observe, "Because Hoffer had so few physical things, possessions, what were dear to him were his ideas, and if you challenged those, he fought hard to defend them."

"Eric's ideas were not lucid enough," Hoffer wrote in his diary after this encounter with the teenager. "But it is clear that his mind is working [and] he may evolve into a competent artist and original thinker. Lili was in a good mood and very loving. I enjoyed every minute of it. It is a blessing that I grow old among these people." In a later entry he wrote, "Putting up with me is quite a burden for Lili, yet she can't let go."

Excited by the discussion, Hoffer stayed up late that evening, writing a section influenced by it: "What stares me in the face is the question whether free societies are viable in a climate of affluence. ... It is also questionable whether we can cope with drastic, rapid change in a permissive climate." Shortly, he would transmute his ideas and Eric's contentions into a paragraph that found its way into his next book: "It is remarkable how little history can touch us at present. The past seems too remote and different to matter. We can obtain insights about the present not from books of history but from books dealing with the human condition."

Two evenings later he had another "lively discussion," this time with Stephen Osborne, twenty-two and recently returned from two years in the Peace Corps, "about the stagnating effect of Islam. Islam's lack of inner contradictions induced not only stability but inertness. It is infinitely easier to be a genuinely good Moslem than a good Christian. An Islamic society is almost without a sense of guilt. It is difficult to visualize an Islamic society in the grip of a Protestant Ethic." These thoughts, also, would end up in a book.

Still glum, he told a Berkeley seminar, "Americans don't want to fight and they don't want to work. A fun-loving, undisciplined, iresponsible mass with easy access to drugs, copulation, and history-making by demonstrations. I described the young as a generation of idealistic baboons mad to play, but needing no participation of older groups and no instruction from adults. I had fun being harsh and pessimistic."

He was similarly tough in a chat with former Vice-President Hubert Humphrey on May 18, to discuss a potential 1972 run for the presidency:

> I suggested that in the coming presidential campaign he should concentrate on the serious problems which face this country, should discuss lucidly the evils that beset us, and suggest cures. ...
> It was naive advice. But I feel that the evils at present so directly affect the individual that he should listen to those who have something sensible and practical to say about possible solutions. ... I doubt very much whether I made an impression.

He advised Humphrey not to attack Republicans but did not give his reason: a belief that Democrats, as much as Republicans, were responsible for the country's problems.

He could not help seeing a "dark" outlook for America, because youth rebellions and "Negro" demands were "going to turn America into a backward country. ... Hope cannot play a role in a spoiled generation that tasted everything and found nothing worthwhile." He applied himself to the task of copying out material from his notebooks for his next opus, *Reflections on the Human Condition*, a fitting title for a book that he thought would be a summation. He noticed his confidence ebbing and wondered whether he could "die gracefully" without "eating my heart out about not writing." He mused that many men who in childhood had troubles with their fathers, or were fatherless, had gone on to lives of importance and accomplishment—and could not resist a dig at sociologists who excused American blacks' lack of accomplishment by attributing it to the fatherlessness of so many ghetto children.

His health returned almost as rapidly as it had deserted him, and he reinstituted his trip with Lili to Austin and the inauguration ceremonies for the Lyndon B. Johnson Library, and to Boston, where he spoke at a small college. After the latter event, as he and Bishop Daniel Cronin were knocking back drinks, the bishop asked, "Eric, suppose you die and you find out there is a heaven, what are you going to do?"

"I'll have nothing to worry about," Hoffer responded, "because I, who don't believe in God, praise God more than anybody ever did, and I should get double credit for praising somebody I don't believe in." A thank-you letter to Hoffer from H. James Stone of Brockton, Hoffer's host for a dinner there, told of his impact on the laity: Stone wrote that the other dinner guests, "non-readers," all now wanted to delve into Hoffer's various books. Moreover,

> Meeting you and talking with you have served to reawaken my slumbering mind. In the past few years I have been enjoying myself, family, friends, hobbies, amusements, etc. Now, I am a little chagrined to discover that I had allowed a little rust to gather on the mainspring of my mind. You applied a little oil and the old clockwork is beginning to tick again with its former precision.

The trip also assisted Hoffer in regaining confidence. Earlier he had complained that the current rebellions were deep-sixing the elements of continuity in society, but had not explained how. Now he felt able to precisely identify those elements as order, routine, and respect for tradition, to name those undermining them, and to lay out the intellectual spadework to make his analysis into more than a whine:

> The people who see themselves as enlightened progressives and the like are automatically siding with the ... criminals against established authority. The intellectual Mafia in New York and San Francisco which includes the [ACLU, American Civil Liberties Union], would promote chaos if they could. The trouble is that I have no idea at all about the nature of spontaneous order. Is it possible to have order without coercion in cities packed with adolescents (10 to 30) and young blacks who are told that violence is revolutionary and idealistic? Secondly, I have no clear picture of what is going on in the minds of well-heeled liberals and radicals. Do they really hate the country which made it possible for them to live off the fat of the land?

A few days later, as a featured speaker at the second inaugural of Mayor Joseph Alioto, he gave an impassioned speech on behalf of the working population. It was the last time he was politically active on behalf of a Democrat. Later in 1972, outraged over the leftward turn of the Party and the selection of Senate dove George McGovern as its candidate for president, he sent a check to the Republican Party.

He stopped the diary just after pledging to make an entry every day, perhaps because he was writing regularly as he prepared *Reflections on the Human Condition*. Looking forward to the end of the era of the youth and minorities rebellion, he wrote to Carrier,

> "It is conceivable in the post-industrial era [that] practicality might have a new meaning—self-realization might become more vital than self-advancement. Things, including money, are likely to

become less attractive, and less potent to shape events. There will be a shift in preoccupation from natural to human resources. A hopeful vision of the future includes not only a cleansed and rehabilitated continent but also the possibility of some two hundred million people leading meaningful lives."

Reflections on the Human Condition, issued in 1973, reaped the benefit of Hoffer's earlier experience with a book of aphorisms, *The Passionate State of Mind*. He avoided that earlier volume's problems by not labeling *Reflections* as a book of aphorisms, and by providing guidance material for readers, dividing the book into five sections, each covering a single topic, and not over-condensing an idea into an aphorism if a full paragraph was required to properly explain it.

Reflections showcased Hoffer's deeper mining of shafts he had already sunk, and his willingness to replace earlier ideas with more nuanced ones. During the Violence Commission hearing he had shouted at "alienated" student leaders that they only wanted power; in *Reflections*, he advanced a more complete argument: "There is a spoiled-brat quality about the self-consciously alienated. Life must have a meaning, history must have a goal, and everything must be in apple-pie order if they are to cease being alienated. Actually, there is no alienation that a little power will not cure." While *Reflections* contained some classic Hoffer one-liners—"The savior who turns men into angels is as much a hater of human nature as the totalitarian despot who turns them into puppets"—its longer paragraphs were the seat of its wisdom.

The book's ideas were firmly rooted in Hoffer's tragic viewpoint. "We find it easier to believe in God than in the purposeful working of blind chance," he argued in the first section, about nature. He labeled man an "imperfect" creature whose "deficiencies" in physical abilities —when compared to those of animals—had nonetheless been the source of his creativity. Nature had left man unfinished, and "in the process of finishing himself man got out from underneath nature's inexorable laws, and became her most formidable adversary." If man created God in his own image, Hoffer asked, then in whose image did he make the devil? Tracing the devil's evolution from the earlier concept of a dragon—the amalgamation of various scare-inducing animal parts—Hoffer asserted that the continual tension between man and devil/dragon led to man's creativeness and to that mysterious "alchemy of the soul" in which malice and savagery became transmuted into love and charity. Montaigne, De La Rochefoucauld, Hume, Bacon, Pascal, and Renan, Hoffer asserted, also "derived an exquisite delight from tracing and identifying the questionable motives which shape human behavior."

Venturing to teach people how to live—something he had previously avoided—Hoffer stated, "It is not only more sensible but more humane to base social practice on the assumption that all motives are questionable and that in the long run social improvement is attained more readily by a concern with the quality of results than with the purity of motives." To assume otherwise was "romanticism."

In his second section, on "Troublemakers," Hoffer chastised those currently disrupting the world as "untrained quacks acting as obstetricians" whose only aim was to rip open the world's belly; as "dissenting minorities" who wanted to prevent the voices of the majority from being heard; as "untalented" pseudo-intellectuals unable to take advantage of a society that provided them ample opportunities for growth and accomplishment; as "a generation that demands instant satisfaction of all its needs;" and as "native-borns" who had resided in the U.S. for a generation or more yet did not appreciate the country's greatness in the ways that recent immigrants did. He chided all groups that insisted on having their members refer to themselves principally by occupation, origin, or beliefs—businessmen, religious followers, ethnics, or adherents to political parties—because, he wrote, such identifications prevented people from acting as human beings committed to freedom for themselves and for everyone else. The only "troublemakers" that

Hoffer liked were "proto-businessmen" trying to make their way in Communist countries, who were acting as the vanguard of revolution.

Section Three, "Creators," was deeply autobiographical, although the pronoun "I" did not appear in it. "Those who lack talent expect things to happen without effort," he asserted, while true creators understood that anything worthwhile took "persistence and patience." An affluent society meant problems for creators, who needed to make their own "scarcity" and produce their own, inner "economy of spirit" necessary to the creation of important ideas or works of art. "The unique and worthwhile in us makes itself felt only in flashes," Hoffer confessed, and added that it must be caught and savored, lest we be "without growth or exhilaration."

Hoffer's most important insight, in this section, was that true artists and thinkers were "preoccupied with the birth of the ordinary and the discovery of the known." To the true creator, "a common occurrence" could be "as revealing as an outstanding event," and he or she could also utilize the work of the middle-rank or mediocre artist as a trigger for the creator's better idea. In contrast, the non-creatives, a group that included not-very-good teachers and unin-spired managers who insisted on making themselves the center of the teaching and managing experiences, clung to the idea of an elite as the fount of all creativity. Insistent that "genius and talent" were "rare exceptions," this group refused to recognize, as Hoffer did, that the masses could collectively exhibit genius and talent—as when the "trash" of Europe, dumped in America, built its wealth.

"The contemporary explosion of avant-garde innovation in literature, art, and music" Hoffer charged, were the excrescences of a climate of "disintegrating" moral values. He similarly scoffed at the avant-garde's successes, attributing them to an audience willing to "admire what they cannot understand [and] which has no meaning or principle." The avant-garde also failed by embracing "total innova-tion," which he called "the refuge of the untalented and the innately clumsy" because it made ineptness seem natural and acceptable. "A true talent will make do with any technique." The ideal creator was the "stretched soul," torn by "opposite bents, tastes, yearnings, loyalties."

Section Four, a short discussion of "Prognosticators," seemed an interruption, a harking back to Hoffer's earlier work in its assertions that dictators such as Hitler and Stalin were able to forecast the future because they controlled the lives of their people.

Section Five, "The Individual," focused on the attitudes that the individual must avoid adopting, in order to assert and maintain individuality. It began in what must have seemed to readers an odd way, with a rumination on shame, which Hoffer identified as having become a personal and no longer a collective emotion. Such emotions that had once been the province of the group, Hoffer implied (though he did not state overtly), were now problems for individuals, and these included the emotions of resentment and revenge. "Retribution often means that we eventually do to ourselves what we have done to others," Hoffer wrote. But he also tackled the other side of this conundrum, our understanding of other people's problems. He insisted that we now habitually "exaggerate" other people's sins, such as "remorse, sensitivity, gratitude, attachment, hatred."

Conflating his two ideals, of the "individual" and the "creator," Hoffer recommended that individuals work hard to avoid incurring the sense of worthlessness that would often cut off individuals from their neighbors and friends, since, in Hoffer's view, connecting with other people was essential to recognizing "in the outside world [anything] that has a counterpart in us," an activity that he believed to be the basis of all original thought. But while in one paragraph he asserted that acknowledging our own unworthiness took "a leaden weight off our backs," in the next he seemed to contradict that sensation in asserting, "No matter what our achievements might be, we think well of ourselves only in rare moments." The goal was to reach a balanced view of one's self, and to do so, Hoffer recommended, "We need people to bear witness against our inner judge, who keeps book on our shortcomings and transgressions. We need

people to convince us that we are not as bad as we think we are. ...
The hardest arithmetic to master is that which enables us to count
our blessings."

What we all seek, Hoffer concluded, is to have others understand
us as individuals: "Societies, cultures, and civilizations—past and
present—are often incomprehensible ... but the individual's hungers,
anxieties, dreams, and preoccupations have remained unchanged
through the millennia. ... The individual who is more complex, unpre-
dictable, and mysterious than any communal entity is the one nearest
to our understanding."

Hoffer had been in his early 50s when *The True Believer* was
published, so it was the work of a mature man; *Reflections on the
Human Condition*, published when he was 75, benefitted from the
greater maturity and deeper insights he had won in the intervening
decades as he fully became "the longshoreman philosopher." But in
America in mid-1973 a display of maturity was not the surest path to
public acclaim. Moreover, as the book appeared at just the moment
when peace was declared in Vietnam, and when the Watergate Affair
was surfacing, *Reflections on the Human Condition* was ignored by
reviewers—it was neither timely nor did it contain the expected inflammatory and argumentative material that reviewers were familiar
with from Hoffer's newspaper columns.

By the summer, Hoffer himself was emotionally upset about the
Watergate Affair, then dominating the news with its almost daily
evidence of malfeasance at the Nixon White House. Lili explained in a
letter to Walter Hickel that the revelations had been "rough" on
Hoffer: "Even though he does not identify with the President it is as
though he had an inner commitment that [Nixon] be a great
president." Hoffer echoed this in his own letter to Hickel: "There is a
trend toward anarchy in every department of life, and the only way to
stop this trend is by activating the mute majority"—an action that

required "an exceptional leader" just when the country was effectively leaderless.

During this period Hoffer was cheered by private acclaim—Herman Kahn told Hickel, when the two met, at Hoffer's suggestion, that Hoffer was of high "importance to America at this time." Hoffer took some contentment from having friends like Hickel and Kahn, a loving relationship with Lili, enough money to pay for his material comfort, a book publisher and magazine editors still eager for his thoughts, the strength of mind to continue to write, and in those writings to be "preoccupied with the birth of the ordinary and the discovery of the known."

Retirement at Berkeley, mandatory at age 70, had been put off for him but at last this too was at hand. As Lili's teaching schedule permitted, she and Hoffer visited the Loebs in Nevada, and former student and Phillips Petroleum executive Charles Kittrell and his family in Oklahoma, and took other trips for his out-of-town engagements. At the urging of Lili and of younger friends, Hoffer moved from the Chinatown walk-up to a seventeenth-floor apartment in a new high-rise apartment on the water's edge that had replaced the union hall from which he had once been dispatched daily to dock work. The irony of the location was not lost on Hoffer. Enjoying the comfort and the view, he told his diary that he had earned it.

Chapter Ten:
"Old Age is Not a Rumor"

In his seventies, Eric Hoffer's attitude toward life reflected the softening of age and the fruits of his attempts to understand the upheavals of the Sixties and incorporate them into his thinking about human nature. Although defiantly claiming that his biases were still "the testicles" of his mind, this voice of the silent majority no longer wished to remain in a state of permanent anger at that majority's rebellious sons and daughters. Henceforth he would try to persuade both groups to do as he did, take the long view of America and its present predicaments. He observed in a notebook that it was no wonder so many people were currently "prey to doubts and fears about the future:"

> Consider what happened to us: An America that fought two wars simultaneously and was victorious in both in the Pacific and Europe; that gave billions to rebuild Europe and Japan; that pushed through the second industrial revolution and gave its people a taste of unimagined plenty; that plunged into an unprecedented attempt to right all social wrongs overnight—an America that has done all these things and also landed the first man on the moon, wakes up one morning and finds itself weirdly diminished and flawed. It finds its dollar devalued, its natural resources apparently depleted, its ethnic minorities climbing out of the melting pot, its youth alienated, its armed forces demoralized, its manufacturers shoddy, its workers negligent, its history besmirched by revisionist historians, its cities decayed and stewing in crime, its air and water polluted, and its leaders drained of confidence.

This analysis became part of a long speech that he gave several years later, in 1977.

The conclusions in that analysis were not those that the bulk of the general public agreed with; and Hoffer's view of the current state of affairs could easily be dismissed as the grumblings of an aging conservative who verged on the reactionary in his embrace of the past. But the two books that Hoffer composed in the next few years, *In Our Time*, a collection of 33 short chapters, published in 1976, and the 1974-75 diary later titled *Before the Sabbath*, published in 1979, reveal him as anything but doctrinaire and rigid, for in them he eagerly revised long-held opinions in the light of recent events, and became more positive and less cynical about the future.

In 1973-74 he still firmly believed that the mechanization and technological advances of the Sixties, by putting abundance within society's reach and by making certain kinds of work obsolete, had undermined the middle class's rationale for existence. But he now realized that what he had once dismissed as the naïve goal of rebellious youth, the pursuit of "meaningful" lives, had become critical to America's future. "Certain things have improved," he conceded. "The camaraderie of the young from all walks of life and their readiness to share what they have is beautiful to behold. ... Personal relations have become more gentle and kind, [giving] the hope of peace and amity between classes, nations and races. ... We now know ... that a sense of usefulness is more vital to the quality of life than abundance or even freedom." But he hastened to point out that the events of the Sixties had also demonstrated "that the adult's failure of nerve is more critical than the young's impulse toward anarchy [and] that righting wrong is a perilous undertaking which needs a tightening of social discipline."

Diagnosing among the young a "hostility to work on the assembly line"—something that since the 1920s he also had steadfastly refused to do—he proposed kibbutz-like communes whose residents would own as well as work in their factories, and who would do so gladly because they would share the toil among commune-mates and because they could offset that sort of toil by other "opportunities for meaningful work," including raising their own food and operating their own schools. Hoffer also lauded the eco-consciousness of the young, although he fretted that it might be counterproductive, since man's basic task was to subdue nature; and he embraced a cherished ecological goal, the elimination of America's over-reliance on fossil fuels, warning that "we shall somehow manage to hang on to the fossil-fuel tit for decades and go on wanting what we no longer really want. It is this lingering, debilitating crisis that we have most to fear."

He somewhat attenuated his bias against African-Americans; now recognizing that black adults were the most numerous and regular victims of urban crime, he placed them in the vanguard of a postulated "association of victims" who would come together to fight back against violence purveyors.

He became, if anything, more of an enthusiast for capitalism as he traced its roots to the Stone Age: "I can see the first trader, an outsider, approaching a strange human group, bearing a gift of something new and desirable, and then going from group to group, exchanging gifts." This analysis not only positioned capitalism as ancient and therefore essential to mankind, it also pilloried his favorite enemy, the scribe/intellectual, posited as capitalism's equally ancient opponent. History, he wrote, was an endless "tug of war" between the trader/capitalists and the "scribes," and such clashes of opposites were a primary way that humans interacted with their world. Earlier, he had not portrayed the clash of scribes/intellectuals and traders as having true benefits for humanity, but he now saw its "beneficent effects," the spreading of literacy beyond the monopoly of the scribe and the diffusing of riches beyond the monopoly of the trader.

Throughout the ages the best writers, artists, and composers had done what he did—studied, researched, interpreted the world, or created works of art or scientific breakthroughs—and had had no affinity for power or even for management. Only second-rate intellectuals sought to influence the organization and control of society. But in the modern era in the Western democracies they had become "adversary intellectuals" whose self-hatred led them to side "with the colored races against the white, with animals against man, and with the wilderness against the sown," and, if Jewish, to side "with the Arabs against Israel." In America, where this phenomenon existed at its worst, the adversary intellectuals' actions undermined the faith of the country's potential defenders, producing "a society that cannot meet, let alone anticipate, challenges and has no goal to strive for and hardly anything worth fighting for."

While writing such sections of *In Our Time*, in 1974-75, Hoffer also kept a diary with the objective of putting down something meaningful every day for six months, after which he would have earned a "blissful Sabbath" from writing.

The diary was composed during a period of significant transitions in American public life: Gerald Ford had recently succeeded the disgraced Richard Nixon as president, inflation was spinning out of control, the fall of Saigon was imminent, and the United States was approaching its 200th anniversary of independence. These facts influenced Hoffer, but in the diary his main intellectual inquiries were a comparison of the wisdom that came from the ancient Greeks with that passed down by the Hebrew prophets of the Old Testament, and an attempt to analyze the nineteenth century's industrial progress in the light of the twentieth century's chaos. Scattered among those entries were observations drawn from Hoffer's relationships with Lili and her sons.

Eric Osborne, then nineteen, was away working in Oregon, and regularly sent Hoffer letters. "The hard work of planting trees on the cold mountains justifies his existence, hardens his body, and seems to stimulate his mind," Hoffer reported approvingly to the diary on reading one such letter. Those letters also contained cash, a total of $1,400 by November 1974, Hoffer noted, sent because "Taking money [from me] apparently blemishes his independence." A few weeks later, picking up Eric from the train station, Hoffer noticed "an ascetic strain in him. He wants to live a clean, peaceful, strenuous life." After spending an entire day with Lili, Eric, Stephen, and Stephen's wife Beatrice, Hoffer noted how "preposterous" it was that he, who had spent so many years on Skid Row, "should worry about Eric going out into a cold world at the age of nineteen"—an instance of "the truth that we tend to see those we love as brittle and vulnerable."

Reading a history of Europe, Hoffer disagreed with its contention that no literature excelled that of Homer, Aeschylus, and the other Greek dramatists, because, he opined, those writers did not engage "the hearts and minds of people" as did the writers of the Old Testament. He saw the ancient Greeks as purveyors of the sort of ideas and art that mainly appealed to and influenced the intelligentsia, whereas through the ages the writers of the Old Testament had had much greater influence on ordinary people.

Hoffer's rejection of the wisdom of Plato tracked with that of Neitzsche and of Martin Heidegger, who had written that the Plato-Socrates search for truth and meaning had initiated skepticism and a cycle that led downward to nihilism instead of toward an appreciation of the wonders of the world. Hoffer had tried to read Heidegger but, as he had with Neitzsche, was deterred by wordiness and intellectual pretentiousness.

In comparing the social milieu of the nineteenth and twentieth centuries, Hoffer searched for explanations of what he viewed as the relative placidness of the former and of the latter's terrible upheavals and bloodletting. Here, too, he was in good company, Walter Bagehot in the nineteenth and Winston Churchill in the twentieth century having plowed this ground. He read and liked them both. Although Hoffer disdained Great Britain's class-conscious society, he admired its culture and was particularly upset by the drift in Great Britain, as the soft socialism of the post-war period seemed to reach an end point characterized by strikes, riots, shortages, and other civil disturbances. Great Britain needed a new Churchill, he wrote, but none were on the horizon. Hoffer would eventually decide that the calm of the nineteenth was an aberration, and that in the twentieth the world returned to its old savage ways, though in a post-industrial rather than a pre-industrial context:

> The nineteenth century despite its unprecedented changes was a century of law and order. In Britain, where the changes were most spectacular, the lower orders who early in the century had turned the cities into savage jungles became meek and law-abiding. The First World War was a watershed of effective authority. ... Was it the terrible slaughter of the war that shook authority? Hardly so. It was the loss of hope.

Hope—the belief that the future will be better and more benevolent—he similarly judged to be the most important casualty of the 1960s. This was quite an admission for Hoffer. In *The True Believer*, written a quarter-century earlier, he had portrayed hope as a false illusion, asserting that Nazism and Communism appealed to their true believers by offering them hope. In 1975 he still viewed hope as somewhat of an illusion, but as a necessary one. And he melodramatically asked, "Who slew America's hope?" His answer: "The murder weapon was forged in the radical-chic salons of Manhattan and Washington, and in the word factories of our foremost universities." He proceeded to trace "the mess we are now in" back to the "active" presidencies of Roosevelt, Truman, Kennedy and Johnson, arguing that when those Democrats tried to tackle problems, their solutions made things worse; therefore, he—and, he believed, the working class too—now in retrospect much preferred "Eisenhower's ability to keep things from happening."

Such Hoffer lines soon found echoes in candidate Ronald Reagan's speeches of the 1976 primary campaign, and later in Reagan's 1980 campaign, as did Hoffer's plaint, "Loss of nerve at the center and excessive safeguards of individual liberty have made of freedom an evil that robs us of personal security ... destroys schools [and] undermines morale in the armed forces. ... Libertarian legislators, judges, educators and doctrinaires [have been] the wreckers of free societies." Striking these same chords, Reagan appealed to Hoffer's audience, blue-collar men and women, and convinced them of the correctness of his cause.

Some revealing entries in Hoffer's 1974-75 diary did not make it into the published version but have survived in the archives. Among these were two early January 1975 observations. He first noted "an increased hostility towards the rich among common people," which he thought stemmed from believing, as he now did, that "come what may, the rich will grow richer while we grow poorer. The rich will never pay their full share of taxes, and will not reconcile themselves to diminished or fixed profits. No matter what laws are passed, the rich, with their battalions of shysters, will by-pass them." Drawing a separation line underneath that entry, he then confessed, "Of late I have been losing my way in dreams. Suddenly, I do not know where I am. Dreaming, with me, is not an escape from an untenable existence. Sometimes when I lay me down to sleep I am overcome at the thought of what's about me."

It is understandable that Hoffer would later not want to include these two thoughts in the published version, as the first contravened his long-held championing of capitalism and the second admitted that he was not always sure of himself. In a third, later diary entry that did not make it into the published version, he stated, "I shall not welcome death. But the passage into nothingness seems neither strange nor frightful. I shall be joining an endless and most ancient caravan." It was a sentiment that echoed Montaigne and the Stoics.

The unedited diary shows him continuing to hatch thoughts and to revise them, an enterprise that he always savored. "Right now anger is a precondition of courage," he wrote on February 19, "A way must be found to make anger stronger than fear." Later that day he crossed out those lines and substituted, "Freedom from malice has been an endearing quality of American life. Is there a change taking place? Cowardice breeds malice." One day he asserted that societies need a passion for excellence to remain vigorous; a few days later, labeling that conclusion "highfalutin," he instead wrote, "A society stays vigorous so long as it can educe dedication and craftsmanship from the people it pays well to do the world's work." He was still tough on himself. Reaching for a theory that would tie Great Britain's illustrious past to its physical isolation from Europe, he tried to contrast "insular" and "continental" societies, and toyed with what might be the characteristics of each. But he quickly abandoned the theory upon realizing that the example of France—a favorite of his—did not fit within the rubric.

The published version records his New Year's resolution to stop smoking, but not, as the unedited diary does, his April 27 "heroic gesture" of throwing away all of his tobacco and his noting the nasty effects of his nicotine withdrawal. Perhaps most importantly, his announcement to the diary, "Self-denial is self-assertion," never appeared in the published version, although the thought is central to Hoffer's view of himself and to his philosophy of how to exist in the world. It is likely that Hoffer himself eliminated the thought from the published version because it was such a naked statement of his core belief.

He was more comfortable in writing about larger themes. In May, he observed that the silent majority had no hopes, but that it did have fears:

> Fear of inflation, fear of violence in the streets, fear of having houses and cars ransacked, fear of losing its children to the drugs and drift culture. A party that aspires to become a part of the majority must address itself to these fears. ... The question is whether the Republicans can develop the sweep and drive to stir the majority and convince it that there are practical ways to curb its fears.

Hoffer expressed similar thoughts in a chapter of *In Our Time*: "Everything that has been said in the past about the anarchic propensity of the masses fits perfectly the activities of students, professors, writers, artists and their hangers-on during the 1960s, whereas the masses are now the protagonists of stability, of continuity and of law and order." The Sixties, he charged, had brought to the surface "the failure of nerve of those in command." In his view, that failure had created a vacuum and the consequent need for "a revitalization of traditional authority" as a "counterbalance … to the disruptive minorities if we are going to have the minimum of personal safety and social discipline required for civilized living."

Both Hoffer and would-be presidential candidate Ronald Reagan were construing the Sixties as a "terrible decade" in America that, in Hoffer's words, had brought "individual and communal tragedies" that were "still contaminating family life in the 1970s," in the sense of continuing to encourage "an escape from the discipline of family, school and job."

Although Hoffer had deliberately refused to take on the responsibilities of a family as a father or stepfather, he nonetheless believed in the need to reassert those values. Reagan and other cultural conservatives were stressing this, as well. Child psychologist James Dobson, later the leader of Focus on the Family, was just then using as the centerpiece of his best-selling books *Dare to Discipline* and *Hide and Seek*, the need for family- and school-based discipline as a counterbalance to the "permissive parenting" of the Sixties.

Hoffer's real prescription for countering the decline in morals had little to do with parental toughness and fiscal rigor. To insure a more mature view of life, he wrote, required making "the tragic sense … a permanent part of our inner landscape." He argued that only by doing so was it possible for people to be more compassionate towards their fellow human beings. Having compassion was more important to society now than it ever had been, Hoffer believed; but it was an achievable goal because compassion was rooted in what happened naturally in a family. He partially explicated this idea in a paragraph with strong autobiographical referents:

> We think of those we love as easily bruised, and our love is shot through with imaginings of hurts lying in wait for them. A loving wife cannot help imagining the wounds which a day's participation in the rat race may inflict on her husband, and he in turn senses the fears, born of unavoidable physical decline, which prey on his wife's mind. Their impulse is to protect, console, and reassure each other. Parents overflow with compassion as they see their children go out into a strange, cold world.

The children of the Sixties, he acknowledged, had shown themselves to be very good at the "creation of family ties between strangers," another obvious key to having compassion. In compassion was hope for the survival of mankind. We all must learn, Hoffer wrote, that we ride together on the planet, "an island of life in a dark immensity of nothingness." Then, mutually aware that all living things will eventually die, we will realize that "the survival of the [human] species may well depend on the ability to foster a boundless capacity for compassion." Only such compassion can counter what the "enormities of Lenin, Stalin, and Hitler" have taught us, "that man is the origin of all evil."

In 1977, the seventy-nine-year old Hoffer, who kept telling the world that he was four years younger, resided in the most luxurious apartment he had ever inhabited, had a companion who adored him but who made few demands, a publisher committed to continue to issue his books, and considerable mental health. Though he told his notebook, "old age is not a rumor," and though he regularly noted the steps in his physical decline and the evidence of loss of mental agility, he was still vital. That was the conclusion of George Will, then a columnist for the *National Review*, who had just won a Pulitzer Prize for his commentary in 1977 when he interviewed Hoffer. Opining that Hoffer had been one of the "most sensible voices" of the 1960s—though Will added that this was not saying much—the columnist judged him as "charismatic," and, adopting Hoffer's contention that talent was a species of vigor, contended that Hoffer had become more vigorous with age, and that he was, as the article's title put it, "A Young 75-Year-Old."

Will's celebrating of Hoffer in the pages of National Review certified that the longshoreman philosopher was now fully accepted as a conservative. That enshrinement was a principal reason why Hoffer was being all but ignored by the more mainstream news media, which were more liberal than they were willing to acknowledge, and which regularly dismissed the opinions of conservatives as unworthy of consideration. Hoffer did not fight against this pigeon-holing. He now mainly wrote for conservative publications, for instance, completing at Bill Loeb's request a front-page review in the Manchester Union Leader of an article by Aleksandr Solzhenitsyn. The speeches he gave and his appearances at the armed services colleges and at nuclear strategist Herman Kahn's Hudson Institute seminars did nothing to dispel the idea that he was a political, economic, and moral conservative.

In Hoffer's final decade he produced his most profound analysis of the basis of conservatism. It was a natural force, he wrote, the counterpoint to an "innate anarchy" that got loose at various points in history and wreaked havoc but that was usually kept in check by mankind's equally-innate striving to "wrest a living from grudging nature." Prior to the nineteenth century, chronic scarcity of food and housing had forced humans to work hard and continuously to earn their living, and to relegate the "innate anarchy" to short-lived episodes. But since then the industrial and technological revolutions that had allowed mankind to conquer nature also allowed us to banish scarcity. Quelling the need for the majority to work so hard then unleashed the current iteration of "innate anarchy," in the form of the "explosion of the young, the dominance of the intellectuals, the savaging of the cities, the revulsion from work." In Hoffer's view, social order was and should always be "the product of an equilibrium between a vigorous majority and violent minorities." Today's "violent minorities," he charged, were no different from those of the past; what had changed was the majority's willingness to take action—the current "meekness" of the majority was spurring the violent minorities to greater excesses. To counter those "violent minorities," order must be restored by force.

Using force to suppress an anarchy that he called innate seemed at odds with Hoffer's advocacy of more compassion as the basic cure for what ailed the world, but Hoffer construed majority action to restore order, tranquility, and progress as a precondition to the pursuit of compassion—threats to the survival of the peace-loving majority must first be met before anything else could be done. By the late 1970s, this, too, was the solution offered by conservatives in the U.S., Great Britain, France, and other Western countries—calls to the majority to defend social structures and their authority, to restrict social coddling, to emancipate business from governmental restraint, and to militarily limit the spreading influence of the Communist enemy.

Hoffer forcefully expressed such ideas in his 1977 speech in the small town of Bartlesville, Oklahoma, to an audience of 3,500. Phillips Petroleum executive Charles Kittrell arranged the event. Kittrell and Hoffer had met years earlier, when the former Marine took advanced management classes at Stanford. Their friendship continued because they largely agreed on economic and political matters, Kittrell in his own speeches advocating toughness against Communism combined with deregulation of industry, and because Kittrell was generous in supporting Hoffer's projects and things that celebrated Hoffer.

In addition to having Hoffer paid well for the Bartlesville speech and others in the ensuing two weeks in Oklahoma, Kittrell also purchased a bust of Hoffer from Jonathan Hirschfeld, the young sculptor who had created it, and he helped underwrite the publicity for a new documentary on Hoffer produced by entertainment journalist Jeanne Wolfe and directed by Canadian documentarian John McGreevy. *The Crowded Life* was seen on public broadcasting stations in January 1978. In it, Hoffer's increasingly conservative views came through in his interview sections and also in those in which actor Richard Basehart read from Hoffer's work, to appropriate visuals.

In connection with the program Hoffer sat for an interview with *People*. Asked about his former enthusiasm for President Johnson, Hoffer responded that Johnson had unfortunately become an activist president, and that America was best served by presidents who did as little as possible. Roosevelt had been a "disaster," starting the "welfare mess;" Eisenhower "sat on his ass and we were a thousand times better off." Hoffer railed against contemporary society's lack of discipline, a quality that he deemed essential to the maintenance of freedom, and called upon the authorities to act more aggressively against violence by punishing evil-doers, explaining that as a "savage" he continued to believe in "retaliation" even though the majority of Americans had been "bussed, bamboozled, brainwashed, and bullied" into not reacting with enough severity. Asked about his next book, he said it was a diary called *Before the Sabbath*.

He had wanted to publish that diary in 1975, right after writing it, but that plan had been upset by the concerns of Eric Osborne. In an undated letter to Hoffer in the archives, Eric wrote from Yellowknife, the capital of Canada's Northwest Territories, objecting to the manuscript's references to him. He recalled having asked Hoffer many times, during the diary's composition, whether it mentioned him, and that Hoffer had said no; but in Eric's reading of the manuscript he noted such passages. In the letter, he lambasted Hoffer for past hurts and injuries, not only to himself but to Tonia, even as he praised Hoffer for his ideas and theories, and for the honesty of the previous published diary, *Working and Thinking on the Waterfront*. Most passages about Eric Osborne in *Before the Sabbath* were removed prior to publication.

Even so, Hoffer could not prevent a break with Eric. Distraught, Hoffer sought assistance from his old friend Margaret Anderson. They had gotten in touch again through Koerner, who knew Anderson; for the book *Hoffer's America*, Koerner and Anderson had together looked over the early notebooks that Hoffer had given to the San

Francisco Pubic Library, and she had renewed her acquaintance with Hoffer. After receiving word from Hoffer of the break, Anderson wrote in 1977 that she had seen this breach coming, and had worried about it because until then Hoffer had "gone through life pretty much secure from loss because you had not really given your heart away anywhere." She had feared, and thought that perhaps Hoffer had, as well, that Eric might "make your hurt public;" therefore, she implied, keeping the breach private was good, and she expressed the hope that it would heal.

Her letter's main purpose was to dissuade Hoffer from making good on his threat to destroy the rest of his notes—"You might as well destroy your books"—and to offer the consoling thought that if Renan or Pascal's notebooks had survived, Hoffer would have read them with pleasure. She begged him to keep his notes, hoped that in time he would feel "less savage," and pledged, "Know that across the months and years, you have always had my love."

Yielding to this advice and to similar entreaties from other intimates, Hoffer allowed Lili to store his notebooks, correspondence, and papers in her home, pending his decision on their eventual disposition. He also agreed to have former student Stacey Cole, now a professor at Ohlone College, come in weekly to assist him with his correspondence.

On Hoffer's agenda was a best-of-Hoffer book, *Between the Devil and the Dragon*, a compilation whose contents were being chosen and condensed by Harper, rather than by Hoffer, and would contain the complete *The True Believer* and selections from the other books. In 1978 Hoffer wrote out his idea for the compilation's flap copy, a short paragraph that stands as his clearest statement on how he judged his own writings and hoped that the public would assess them:

> Here is a collection of lucid thoughts on every aspect of human existence and Western civilization. The uniqueness of man, the uniqueness of the Occident, and the uniqueness of America are the

central themes of Hoffer's thinking, and the reader will find them brilliantly expanded in this volume. It is a profound book yet as easy to read as a novel. It is a book for all tastes and occasions, and a most stimulating companion.

The text of *Between the Devil and the Dragon*, when published in 1982, confirmed by its omissions and condensations that the publisher felt the need to excise from the canon the most intemperate aspects of Hoffer, those of the "Reflections" newspaper columns and of the more vitriolic essays and diary entries, the Hoffer who railed against "Negroes," student rebels, and specific academics such as Marcuse. Even so, the compilation's 486 pages sparkle with ideas and present a lifetime's worth of the fruits of a mind making interesting inquiries into its own, and mankind's, place in the world.

In 1979, Hoffer's health began to fail markedly, and throughout his remaining years he was in and out of hospitals for stomach and bowel troubles, emphysema, and difficulties in walking. He told interviewer Dr. Eugene Griessman, an old friend, that ten days in intensive care had cost him $10,000 and he could not afford another ten, claimed that his publisher had made millions from his books but that he had not, and that there was "no purpose in life, only chance."

Nonetheless, he was in good form in August 1979, when Wally Hickel and Malcolm Roberts flew him up to Anchorage for a speech to Commonwealth North, a Alaska-oriented think tank begun by Hickel and another former governor of that state. Hoffer read from a prepared text to an audience of five hundred about the interrelationships of technology, the exhaustion of raw materials, the ubiquitous social anarchy, the difference between the nineteenth and twentieth centuries, and the need for strong governments, echoing many points made in his recent books. He drew laughter and applause with such lines as, "No one foresaw that the education explosion, made possible by advanced technology, would swamp societies with hordes of educated nobodies who want to be somebodies and end up being mischief-making busybodies." He quoted Burckhardt, Bagehot, Disraeli, and William Blake, blamed the current morass on the disjunctions caused by World War I and Franklin Roosevelt's reforms, and shook his head over the presidency of Jimmy Carter, drawing more laughs. He concluded his 45-minute address with a solution to current troubles that he told the audience it might find "far-fetched—a boundless capacity for compassion" that Hoffer believed must be the primary goal of all education.

Denis Doyle, now living in the east, came to see Hoffer in San Francisco. Doyle had been directing his thoughts toward the reform of public education, at the Brookings Institution, the Department of Health, Education and Welfare, and at the Hudson Institute. He was developing a program of "radical decentralization" that included school choice for parents, magnet schools, stricter assessment and evaluation of teacher performance, the use of class standards and testing, as well as instruction that featured the inculcating of the values of a democratic society. Hoffer was enthusiastic in his support for this agenda.

In his final years Hoffer worked on two further books, the series of recollections, drawn from early notebooks, that became the posthumously-published *Truth Imagined*, and a book of quotes and comments, culled from the note cards onto which Hoffer had copied out quotes from a wide range of authors, accompanied by his comments about the quotes. Since his eyesight and ability to write legibly were fading, Hoffer decided to work on the quotations book with Stacey Cole and typist Gemma Kabitzke, who would transcribe the comments that he dictated to Cole. Hoffer and Cole met weekly, on Wednesday afternoons. In January 1980, Cole wrote to Koerner, seeking funds to underwrite his and Gemma's work, and offered a portrait of the lion in winter:

Because of his deteriorating vision he is unable to dip into the cards, many of which he can still recall almost verbatim once I cite the author and begin to read them aloud. There are quotations there from sources both well-known and obscure that are timeless—some hilarious, some so startling and insightful that they take one's breath away, to use a Hofferism. I can't imagine anyone who could not be both entertained and informed by a volume that contained an edited version of these cards.

Two weeks later, Cole reported to Koerner that Hoffer was "attacking" the cards with "heartwarming" vigor and enthusiasm,

... plunging into the treasure trove of a lifetime of reading and rediscovering here, discovering anew there, and everywhere sifting, measuring, and taking stock of the thought on the card, testing it against the thought in his mind—the comparisons, contrasts, parallels and polarizations occupy him most of the day and part of the night. He has seemed wonderfully alive—and lively—the last two weeks. The task is a monumental one.

A typical quote was from Lord Acton, "There is no liberty where there is hunger. The theory of liberty demands strong efforts to help the poor, not merely for safety, for humanity, for religion, but for liberty." Hoffer's comment was not so much an interpretation of this statement as an answering one that emphasized his own take on liberty and its relationship to hunger: "Acton could not foresee that the end of hunger will mean the end of the invisible hand of scarcity which regulates and disciplines people, and creates the need for a new despotic power to contain anarchy. In other words, there is no liberty not only where there is hunger but also where there is widespread abundance. The zone of individual freedom is midway between the extremes of scarcity and plenty." This was an idea that could have sustained some greater elucidation, perhaps even a meditation on its relationship to capitalism—but Hoffer was no longer in shape to undertake such inquiries.

The range of Hoffer's reading was conveyed by some of the "A" authors; Hannah Arendt, Aristotle, French philosopher Raymond Aron, Marcus Aurelius, German chancellor Konrad Adenauer, Vice-President Spiro Agnew, and Max Ascoli. It was clear from his comments on their writings, that he felt at home among the intellectually celebrated authors, and in having, as it were, a dialogue with them—as he was seldom able to do in his daily life, except when a Sevareid or an Alinsky happened to visit.

Koerner could not find a reason to have the Sloan Foundation become involved in the Hoffer quotations project, but he did help to secure some assistance for it from a smaller private foundation, and Charles Kittrell also contributed some funds. Parts of the book were eventually typed—in large type, so Hoffer could read it—but the result was never published. One reason may have been a break between Hoffer and Cole, in February 1982 that left the younger man perplexed and unable to figure out what might have gone wrong after four years of close work together.

Sooner or later Hoffer broke with almost all of those who became close to him, perhaps because the obligations that usually accompanied such closeness frightened him. Cole idolized Hoffer, and after the break wrote to him that at his feet he had learned a great deal about life, including an appreciation for its "contradictoriness [which] at times you exemplify ... gloriously." The break may have been occasioned by Cole having loaned to a biographer, James T. Baker of Western Kentucky University, his notes of Hoffer's Berkeley lectures in 1964 and his tape recording of an address that Hoffer had given at Boston College. Hoffer had frequently objected to anyone tape-recording or even taking photographs of him during such lectures.

Baker's brief biography of Hoffer, a volume in the Twain American Authors series, was admiring, judicious, and illuminating, and made no untoward use of the Cole-recorded materials, which repeated observations that Hoffer had made in his published writings, although the recorded iterations were tougher. In any event, as

Hoffer had told Baker when they met, "You don't need to ask me any questions, really, because all I have to say, all I am, all I have said or will say, it's in the books." Baker agreed. "Hoffer and his nine original books," the biographer summed up, "form one of the richest veins a student of philosophy, history, or sociology could hope to mine."

Cole shortly returned to Hoffer's good graces, but the quotations-and-comment project was never completed.

At Lili's suggestion, Hoffer reached out to former editor Elizabeth Lawrence for assistance on *Truth Imagined*, especially in regard to his romantic episode in the 1930s. She encouraged him to tell it and asked only for minor clarifications. His major compositional strategy in the volume was to highly condense his early fiction. The 170 pages of "Four Years in Hank's Young Life" shrank to two-and-a-half of the twenty-seven episodes in *Truth Imagined*'s 97 pages, and the 83 pages of "Chance and Mr. Kunze" filled only two more sections.

According to Lili, Hoffer wrestled with the book and more than once wanted to abandon it, but she convinced him to continue the task. Wracked by pain, he found it difficult going, and Lili may have attempted to help get it finished by doing some editing of what many reviewers later found to be a choppy manuscript.

The most deeply felt and coherent parts of *Truth Imagined* were Hoffer's glimpses into his childhood. Not wanting to write a full memoir, Hoffer perhaps envisioned this book as a companion volume to *Between the Devil and the Dragon* in providing background for that compilation's non-fictional essays. The conversational tone of *Truth Imagined* conveys Hoffer the performer rather than Hoffer the formal essayist. It also shows him, in his final years, leaving behind the mantle of the modern Montaigne and attempting something that Montaigne never did, deliberately fictionalized storytelling, even as Hoffer used these stories in the same way as he had always used his essays, to understand and advance moral truths. At life's end, the master of stripping away illusions took to creating them.

Hoffer's handwriting had become spidery and less controlled as he began what would be his last notebook, in September 1981. His students, he reported, had given him a television set, since illnesses had forced him to spend more time in his apartment, and he found himself arguing with the TV. (He did not add that he also now had a telephone.) For years he had shopped at the Stragers' Flower Box on Jackson Street, weekly picking up roses for his room and for Lili's home; now, since he was less able to get out, the Stragers delivered the flowers to his apartment. He marveled at such kindnesses.

Afraid that he had run out of topics for *Truth Imagined*, he nonetheless chewed over the nature of obedience to authority, something that he believed had permanently changed during his lifetime: "Never again will millions march to slaughter at a word of command," or, for that matter, he added, march willingly into factories. President Reagan had recently broken a strike by the air controllers union when Hoffer wrote in the diary, at 12:30 on the morning of September 21, "Reagan's determination to repeal the New Deal is panicking unions and government bureaucrats. My impression is that the majority sides with Reagan. But there is no telling how the struggle will end."

He told journalist Tom Bethell, who had returned to San Francisco, that Reagan had been underestimated—just as the elites had always underestimated ordinary Americans—and that the silent majority had at last woken up. He acknowledged to Bethell not having foreseen the emergence of the religious right, which, to his approbation, was currently pushing morality issues.

Bethell was with Hoffer when Selden Osborne arrived, and Hoffer introduced Selden as a true believer, a "doctrinaire socialist." The discussion moved to Harry Bridges, the union's leader, a Communist whom Selden said was "afraid of educated longshoremen."

"No," Hoffer countered, "he was afraid of longshoremen he couldn't use."

Selden advised that he and Hoffer disagreed on everything. "I favored democracy in the union, Eric said it wasn't so important." "All his conclusions are wrong—every one of them. But he writes beautifully and he asks the right questions," Selden added.

Hoffer characterized the United States as the country of the common man, while Selden said it was "imperialistic," an epithet that had also been frequently used by linguist and social critic Noam Chomsky, a man Hoffer said he could not stand—he pulled out a note card, read to Bethell a Chomsky quote, and professed puzzlement over its anti-American, anti-Israel stance. Hoffer went on to tease Selden, in front of Bethell, as having been an "exclusivist," resentful that the government had not given him a larger role to play; but he also told the journalist that he had always learned from Selden.

After Selden left, Hoffer asked Bethell, "Do you think he likes me, deep down?"

Hoffer may have had doubts about his personal relationships, but had few if any regrets in regard to how he had spent the bulk of his life, believing that he had generally done what was necessary and possible for him so that he could survive, optimize his writing conditions, and continue to grow mentally. He had created books and uttered words that had influenced the thought of his times, a significant achievement, and he had done so largely on his own terms. From thirty years of having been exposed to the American academic and literary world, as well as to the many books that he had read, he understood that he was more unlike the usual inhabitants of the literary and academic worlds than any other contemporary writer who consistently addressed the large questions about human nature and purpose. Sevareid, who continued to visit Hoffer in San Francisco now and then, and other worldly-wise friends such as choreographer Jacques D'Amboise, cherished Hoffer for just this quality.

Perhaps knowing this would be his last notebook, Hoffer made a few summing-up entries, for instance, the contentions that he had never in his life "competed for fortune, for fame, or for a woman ... never belonged to a circle or clique ... never savored triumph, never won a race." Who was he kidding? He knew very well that he had competed with Selden for Lili, had taken pride in his union, and from time to time had savored particular triumphs—lecture appearances, battles with nasty journalists, and the meeting with President Johnson, to name a few. We never compete so hard as when we think we are just expressing our individuality.

On September 27, he confessed to the diary that he had endured "scores of desperate hours coping with gas pressure" that had prevented his sleep, and that two nights earlier he had vomited for the first time in his life. It all made him wonder, "How does a man die? Does he know when death approaches?" The illnesses gave to him "the feeling that I am entering the realm of the unknown."

Shortly he was taken to a hospital for emergency treatment. Returning to the apartment, he had a visit from Selden, and the very next day, October 10, 1981, Hoffer wrote out his unvarnished thoughts in what he may have believed to be a deathbed confession:

> The sin of my life has been to invade a neighbor's nest and take his wife. The people I sinned against were not the husband but two of the children, Tonia and Eric. Eric believes he is my son and has renounced both his mother and me. I am on terms of warm friendship with the husband. ... My influence on the family has not been all bad. I have been generous with myself and my money and the truth is that Selden did not love Lili and felt my invasion as a liberation. He told me yesterday that my intrusion enriched the children's life and whatever I have saved will be theirs when I am gone. My attachment to Lili after 33 years is undiminished.

Charles Kittrell and other friends, knowing of Hoffer's rapidly deteriorating health and of his affinity for the tenets of Ronald Reagan, campaigned to have the president honor him, enlisting Sevareid and other prominent people in that quest. The White House notified Hoffer that he would receive a Presidential Medal of Freedom in a ceremony in March 1983. Other honorees were to be conservative notables, preacher Billy Graham, *National Review* founder James Burnham, and playwright and ambassador Clare

Boothe Luce. Hoffer was too ill to attend, but Lili went; Reagan recalled to the crowd his 1969 meeting with Hoffer and the "salty" advice Hoffer had proffered.

Learning of the honor to Hoffer, Peter Worthington, editor-in-chief of the Toronto *Sun*, thanked Kittrell for having made it possible: "Too often greatness is overlooked until it is too late. I feel as if I had been honored by Eric Hoffer being honored, + I suspect many who appreciate the clarity of his thought + the integrity of his outlook feel as I do."

By then Hoffer was mostly confined to his bed, and seldom left the apartment, even with assistance. Everything ached. He hardly ate anything. His main solace was his view of the waterfront. Lili, Stephen, and Selden Osborne were his most frequent visitors; he had alienated or rejected many other people he had known, at Berkeley and on the docks, and he refused to tell his remaining friends how ill he was because he did not want them coming to visit him out of pity.

On the evening of Saturday, May 21, 1983, Hoffer told Stephen Osborne, in a telephone conversation, "I want to be able to go to sleep and that's it." A few hours later, he died in the apartment.

Later, when Lili went to clear out the apartment, she found it mostly empty, nearly as much so as his Clay Street tenement walkup had been.

Epilogue:
The Dedication

Eric Hoffer's funeral ceremonies drew mostly his intimates, a crowd that the San Francisco *Examiner and Observer* estimated at sixty. Lili characterized his death as "redemption," and opined that Hoffer had been a "rare" man though "of the common earth," a man who was "unique and considered everyone as unique as himself." Selden added that Hoffer's mind had been "clear to the very last," and that in his final days his thoughts had centered on the uniqueness of man: "You know, he had written about the unnaturalness of nature. Now, he felt that nature is predictable, but human nature is not; it was that notion that he wanted to explore." Stephen Osborne read three of Hoffer's poems, among them the haunting verse about "meeting my end, my waiting friend." Stacey Cole told the mourners that the true monument to Hoffer would be found "in the hearts and minds of hundreds of thousands of people not yet in this world" who in the future would read his books.

Georgie Anne Geyer's obituary column recalled that when she had visited San Francisco in the fall of 1982, she had tried to reach Hoffer but had not been able to, probably because he was in the hospital. She had wanted to tell him "that he was right," that American intellectuals had "become so theoretical that they are missing totally where freedom resides in the real world." She had also wanted to ask him some questions: how could intellectuals be so ignorant of reality, and what was the significance of America once again going through such a self-critical phase?

Another syndicated columnist, Paul Greenberg, in his obituary column dubbed Hoffer "an abbreviated DeTocqueville, turning out provocative snapshots instead of long discursive sketches," and contended that Hoffer had outraged the "conventionally liberal ... particularly when he defended conventional values." Hoffer's writings had fascinated ordinary people, Greenberg contended, but not the "deep thinkers," because "he was too rough-hewn, too simple." The Philadelphia *Inquirer* recalled Hoffer as "a one-man happening whose lively mind amazed millions who read his books and saw him on television." Similar respectful obituaries appeared in *The New York Times* and other newspapers.

William F. Buckley Jr. sent condolences to Lili and added that he and Milton Friedman had recently been discussing Hoffer's works, "which we both so profoundly admire." Less-well-known fans of Hoffer's work, and people who had encountered him over the years, also wrote to Lili. The dean of the John Burroughs School in St. Louis, where Hoffer had so memorably interacted with the students in 1967, told her that Hoffer's appearance there had been one of the top highlights of his twenty-four years in education: "Who can tell how many young minds took a turn that day—how many were stimulated into <u>thinking</u> and stepping into unknown terrain? This, for me, is the real immortality of men—that 'something' that flows from them into another generation and helps shape the core of those transformed beings."

Reviews of *Truth Imagined*, published six months after Hoffer's death, were decidedly mixed. The San Francisco *Chronicle* said that the book "must be read with affection, for it was certainly written with love for us all," and the Amarillo *Globe* characterized Hoffer as "a Jack Kerouac with a purpose, [whose] faith in, and understanding of the so-called common man sets him apart from formally educated philosophers of this century." The syndicated John Barkham review, calling it an "unsentimental" memoir, pointed out that its "meat" lay "not in a life so meagerly lived but in the thinking of a mind that forever hungered after knowledge and sometimes drew unorthodox conclusions from his reading and experience."

Negative reviewers were many, and seemed to use Hoffer's death as occasion to attack him more severely than they would, had he been alive to strike back. The Schenectady *Gazette* contended that Hoffer must have been pressured to write the memoir, because it had "the feel of a pulled tooth." The Los Angeles *Times'* book review editor wrote, "Modest he is. Also sometimes stiff, standoffish, and mysterious. The migrant Eric Hoffer had the hobo's reticence to revelation as well as routine. Hoffer turned into a learned man but not a loving one, more at ease with motion than emotion." *Book Week* labeled Hoffer "pretentious," Chilton Williamson Jr., in *National Review*, declared that as an intellect Hoffer had been "overrated," and *Kirkus Reviews*, which had a reputation for nastiness, pulled out all the stops:

> A fragmentary, desultory, and rather pathetic memoir. ... Why, after all his years of exhausting and underpaid labor, did he seem to have no sympathy for the oppressed? And then there are all those awful lectures on history-and-culture by a very half-baked autodidact. In his final lines Hoffer tells us he has no grievances and feels no remorse—perhaps because he was tone-deaf to the real music of human life. A sad but not moving farewell.

Lili Osborne, feeling that the family service had not provided an adequate opportunity to those who wished to remember Hoffer, and wanting some pubic memorial to him in the only city he had ever called home, pushed on various fronts to generate such a memorial. The project took her nearly two years. She asked Eric Sevareid to speak even before the details had been set in place. The commentator had retired from CBS in 1977, and had since turned down many requests for speeches; nonetheless, he promised to come, and asked Lili what he ought to say. She told him that the central theme should be that Eric Hoffer had been "everyman."

The dedication ceremony, held in March 1985, brought together several elements of Hoffer's life: it was held near Pier 39 of the San Francisco waterfront; it featured the unveiling of a sculpture by Robert Barr named "Skygate," an abstract, arch-like structure constructed from mirror-polished stainless steel, commissioned through the offices of the San Francisco Arts Commission, on which Hoffer had once served; and a plaque that honored Hoffer for his contributions to San Francisco and to American cultural life. Political dignitaries, Berkeley colleagues, Arts Commission members, a couple of reporters, and those who had liked Hoffer's work attended.

In Sevareid's keynote speech, he recalled that within minutes of meeting Eric Hoffer in 1967, he knew he had found what the French called "a friend of the heart," and had soon lost his heart to this "everyman." Ever since, Sevareid said, he had taken sustenance from Hoffer as a person and from his writing: "Questions that troubled me for years were suddenly answered in his brief words." Sevareid dubbed Hoffer a "classical humanist" who knew that "man is the glory and the problem and the terrible danger," and a native-born American who thought

> ... as if he had come as an immigrant in steerage, and saw the new land with the immigrant's fresh eye, in all its happy contrast with the rest of the world, and the world's past. ... Because he was saturated in the history of civilizations he knew politics, economics, history, military affairs. ... He knew that the ultimate mystery does not lie in outer space but in inner space, terra firma, inner man.

Sevareid asserted that Hoffer was the quintessential American, and that to him,

> America meant freedom. And what is freedom? To Hoffer it is the capacity to feel like oneself. ... He was the first important American writer, working class born, who *remained* working class in his habits, associations, environment ... a national resource, the only one of its kind in the nation's possession.

In the decades following Hoffer's death, his reputation and book
sales did not so much diminish as atrophy. They did so in tandem with
the fading of the America that he had known—the manufacturing
society whose workingmen were European immigrants and their sons
and grandsons—and with the prodigious growth of a service
economy and of a consumerist culture that inherently rejected the
toughness he advocated, and with the downfall of his particular
enemy, the Soviet Union and its Communism. Despite Lili's efforts to
keep alive Hoffer's work and the memory of his extraordinary
presence and personality, his books, with the exception of *The True
Believer*, went out of print. Every once in a while, a conservative social
critic such as P. J. O'Rourke would quote him, but Hoffer was mostly
absent from popular culture. By the turn of the twenty-first century,
the name Eric Hoffer and the label the longshoreman philosopher
were no longer recognized by the majority of Americans, those born
after 1951, the date of publication of *The True Believer*.

The September 11, 2001 terrorist attacks on the World Trade
Center towers and the Pentagon brought Eric Hoffer's name and his
works back into the public discourse. His delineation of the
motivations and characteristics of true believers, recalled for the
public by those who had read *The True Believer*, helped Americans to
understand what was nearly inexplicable, that Muslim fanatics in the
service of a holy cause would commit suicide to murder thousands of
people in America's financial and governmental capitals. As one post-
9/11 scholarly article put it, Hoffer "offers an integrated approach for
the psychological theories of terrorism. This approach weighs both
situational factors and people characteristics and tries to explain the
reasons of mass movements." In an issue of *Philosophy Now*, Tim
Madigan rediscovered Hoffer's writings as he searched to understand
the terrorists, and lauded Hoffer as "a modern-day Socratic figure, a
working-class hero and longshoreman/intellectual."

Renewed interest in Hoffer's insights also benefitted, after the
2001 terrorist attacks, from the coming of age of the Internet, with its
ability to disseminate information, making available dozens of Hoffer

quotations and references, and enabling a lively market for second-hand copies of Hoffer's books. Shortly, Hopewell Publications began to arrange with Lili to reprint many Hoffer titles that had gone out of print, and to sell them mostly through Internet retailers.

Around this time, as well, a fire in Lili's Clayton Street home did considerable damage but spared her attic, in which Hoffer's materials had been stored. Lili's realization that only chance had saved the Hoffer materials spurred her to transfer the archives to the Hoover Institution at Stanford, where over the next few years they were catalogued and indexed. Lili wrote notes on many of the documents, indicating their origin, or what Hoffer had said to her about them, or her assessment of the document's importance.

Today, in the midst of the greatest and broadest upheaval in a wide area of the world since the fall of Communism, the anti-authoritarian uprisings in the Arab Middle East, Hoffer's insights about the character and motivations of those who participate in mass movements and the chaos attendant on any social change have once again begun to be cited by columnists and editorial writers. The crowds in the streets of Cairo, Tripoli, Sana'a and other capitals are largely composed of those who had until recently been without hope and, as Hoffer had described, appear to be motivated principally by hope allied to the promises of a more equitable, less repressive society that their "revolutions" are projecting. Their expectations of democracy and economic prosperity after a change in governments may be unrealizable, but such ideals energize them.

Scarcely a day goes by without some blog, concerned mainly with personal matters, quoting one of Hoffer's pithy sayings, generally to add heft and insight to the blog author's topic of the moment. Such bloggers underscore Hoffer's relevance to today's personal problems as well as his timeless understanding of the difficulties that the autonomous man encounters in a conformist society. Lines like the following seem all the more relevant now:

> Free men are aware of the imperfection inherent in human affairs [and] know that basic human problems can have no final solutions, that our freedom, justice, equality, etc. are far from absolute, and that the good life is compounded of half measures, compromises, lesser evils, and gropings toward the perfect. The rejection of approximations and the insistence on absolutes are the manifestation of a nihilism that loathes freedom, tolerance, and equity.

Eric Hoffer's writings and his heroic, lifelong struggle to make the most of his untutored intellect and to devote himself to the study of mankind's place in the world while he remained a workingman, provide insight and inspiration for today and for future readers. Although his books were written decades ago, they contain cogent and relevant observations about many elements in human affairs that have only grown in importance, such as the prevalence of true believers in our midst and the chaotic nature of the social change that has become our constant companion. His tenets regarding the individual's need to choose a path in life rather than let it be chosen for him or her, on the character of humanity's relationships to nature, technology, and religion, on the need for compassion and for the individual and collective embrace of sustaining moral and ethical values, continue to resonate and, as have the insights of good writers through the ages, they help us evaluate the world around us and learn how to live.

Source Notes

General Note

The principal sources for this book are in the seventy-five linear feet of materials in the Eric Hoffer Archive at the Hoover Institution, and are cited in the notes below as EHHI, with specific file numbers. Generally, sources that are fully listed in the bibliography are referred to in the notes in shortened form, and I have not cited daily newspaper and weekly magazine reviews of Hoffer. Also, the notes are cumulative: books and materials cited in early chapters are not separately cited again when used for later chapters.

Prologue

Background: Shachtman, *Decade of Shocks*.

On Sevareid: *Not So Wild A Dream*; Schroth; Eulogy for Eric Hoffer, EHHI 7.3; Transcript of broadcast, September 19, 1967; CBS correspondence file, EHHI 27.16; introduction to Tomkins, *Eric Hoffer: American Odyssey*; Sevareid correspondence file, EHHI 38.10.

Articles: Fincher; Gordon; Terence O'Flaherty, interview with Eric Sevareid, San Francisco *Chronicle*, November 17, 1967.

Chapter One

Lili Fabilli: interviews, April 23 and July 28, 2010.

Letter, Eric Hoffer to Margaret Anderson of May 19, 1941, as typed by Anderson, EHHI 25.10.

Possible 1898 birth date: Bethell, "The Longshoreman Philosopher."

EHHI 94.15, a notebook from 1981-1982, contains material on Hoffer's family and his early days, some of which also appears in *Truth Imagined*.

Walter Galenson. *The United Brotherhood of Carpenters*. Cambridge: Harvard University Press, 1983.

Fyodor Dostoevsky. *The Idiot*. New York: Vintage Books, 2009. Translated by Richard Pevear and Larissa Volokhonsky.

Herman Hesse. "Thoughts on *The Idiot* by Dostoevsky," in Hesse, *My Belief: Essays in the Life and Art*. New York: Farrar, Straus & Giroux, 1974. At: www.gss.ucsb.edu/projects/hesse/works/idiot.pdf

A. S. Byatt. "Prince of Fools," *The Guardian*, June 26, 2004.

Hoffer, "Four Years in Young Hank's Life," novel, typescript in EHHI 43.23.

Hoffer, "From Town to Town," short fiction fragment, in notebook in EHHI 79.2.

Hoffer, 1959 diary, EHHI 63.4.

Chapter Two

Montaigne, Essays.

Charles H. Foster, "Montaigne Incarnate," *Virginia Quarterly*, spring, 1979 (contains Huxley quote); Bakewell, Sarah, *How To Live, or A Life of Montaigne*. New York: Other Press, 2010.

Notebooks containing fiction and readings, EHHI 79.1.

"Farm Labor in the 1930s," in *Rural Migration News*, October 2003, Volume 9, # 4. At: http://migration.ucdavis.edu/rmn/more.php?id=788_0_6_0.

"Tramps and Pioneers," holograph in notebook, EHHI 47.13. See also EHHI 79.2.

Draft of first EH letter to Margaret Anderson, n.d., EHHI 78.5.

T. S. Eliot, "Tradition and the Individual Talent," in *The Sacred Wood: Essays on Poetry and Criticism*, 1922. Gloucester, U.K.: Dodo Press, 2009.

"Four Years in Hank's Young Life," holograph and typescript, EHHI
    43.22 and 43.33.
"Chance and Mr. Kunze," EHHI 79.1, fragments of holograph; and
    43.12, typescript.
Draft letter to Margaret Anderson to accompany submission to her of
    "Four Years" typescript, EHHI 45.9.
Margaret Anderson's retyping of Hoffer's letters to her of May 14,
    1941 and December 24, 1949. EHHI 25.10, *op. cit.*
Peter Viereck, "But—I'm a Conservative!" *The Atlantic*, April 1940.

Chapter Three

Wellman; Weir; Pearce.
 "The ILWU Story" at
    http://www.ilwu19.com/history/the_ilwu_story/the_new_union.htm.
Herb Mills, "The Social Consequences of Industrial Modernization.
    Part One, The Good Old Days," at:
    http://www.ilwu19.com/history/frisco/page1.htm.
Robert Carson, ed., *The Waterfront Writers*. San Francisco: Harper &
    Row, 1979.
Materials in the San Francisco Public Library, Hoffer collection.
    Notebooks in PL 2.1,n.d. Also SFPL 1.2, 1946; SFPL 1.3, August 1947
    to January 1948; James Day interviews, 1964. Transcripts in EHHI
    56.2.
Notebook, November 1949 to January 1950, EHHI 82.2.
E. Thomas and J. Fischer memos, 1950, EHHI 49.5.
Margaret Anderson, letter to EH, December 19, 1977. EHHI 25.10.
Alfred North Whitehead. *Science and the Modern World*, 1925. New
    York: Free Press, 1997.
Hoffer re Anderson: Calvin Tomkins notes from interview with Hoffer,
    1966. Tomkins materials, Museum of Modern Art, File IIB.7.
Jacket copy: EHHI 49.2.

Selden L. Osborne, "Why I Am A Socialist—An Historical and Psychological Analysis," SLID Essays, Summer, 1935. In Joseph P. Lash Papers at the Franklin Delano Roosevelt Presidential Library. At: http://newdeal.feri.org/students/slid02.htm.

Lili Fabilli's Berkeley days: Lisa Jarnot, "Two: A Company of Women," at: http://www.angelfire.com/poetry/lisajarnot/freshman.htm.

Chapter Four

Miss America asked about Marx: William Manchester, *The Glory and the Dream*. Boston: Little, Brown, 1973.

Arthur Schlesinger Jr. "Not Right, Not Left, But a Vital Center," *The New York Times Magazine*, April 4, 1948.

Editors of *Time*, preface to *The True Believer*. New York: Time Reading Program, 1963.

Reviews and blurb materials of *The True Believer*, excerpted in Scrapbook, EHHI 5.2.

Richard Rovere. "A Few Inescapable Themes," *The New Yorker*, April 7, 1951.

Georgie Anne Geyer, obituary of EH, May 26, 1983.

Anonymous. "Literary Stevedore," *The New Yorker*, April 28, 1951.

Bertrand Russell. "How Fanatics Are Made," *The Observer*, London, March 23, 1952.

Richard Donovan, "Migrant with a Message," *The Reporter*, October 30, 1951.

Draft letter, EH to Elizabeth Lawrence, San Francisco Library Hoffer collection, PL 2.4.

Bill Dale correspondence file, EHHI 28.3.

O'Brien to Hoffer, July 4, 1951, in EHHI 36.8.

G. T. Lanham letter to Gruenther about Eisenhower and *The True Believer*, quoted by Anderson, EHHI 5.2, *op. cit.*

Anthony Leviero, "President Urging A Book To Friends," *The New York Times*, March 19, 1956, quotes Dr. Gabriel Hauge.

"What The President Reads," *Newsweek*, April 30, 1956, reproduces
   pages from Eisenhower's copy of *The True Believer*, with his
   handwriting in margins.

Chapter Five

O'Brien to Hoffer, *op. cit.*
EH to Margaret Anderson, in notebook of May-July 1951, EHHI 82.13.
SFPL PL 2.4, two notebooks, "Aphorisms I and II."
Notebook of November-December 1951, EHHI 82.17.
Selden Osborne to EH, n.d., EHHI 36.16.
"Nest" and "taken": notebook of 1981-82, entry of October 10, 1981.
   EHHI 94.15.
Lili Osborne to Calvin Tomkins, April 17, 1968. Tomkins Papers, IIA.20.
"We clash": Selden Osborne to EH, Jan. 20, 1964, EHHI 36.16.
Saul Alinsky to EH, April 14, 1958. EHHI 25.5.
Hannah Arendt to EH, March 13, 1955. EHHI 25.6.
Norman Jacobson to EH, December 27, 1957. EHHI 32.3.
Eugene Burdick, "Epigrammatist on the Waterfront," *The Reporter*,
   February 21, 1957.
Eisenhower speech, Public Papers, at:
http://www.presidency.ucsb.edu/ws/index.php?pid=10394.
Harry Bridges note, EHHI 55.8.
1958-59 diary, EHHI 63.3, handwritten original.

Chapter Six

Automation: Wellman; Weir; Chris Carlson, "Mechanization on the
   Waterfront," at:
   http://foundsf.org/index.php?title=Mechanization_on_the_Waterfront.
African independence: Tom Shachtman, *Airlift to America*. New York:
   St. Martin's Press, 2009.

Richard Hofstadter, *Anti-Intellectualism in American Life*. New York: Random House, 1963.

Reviews of *The Ordeal of Change*, EHHI 58.4.

Garry Wills, "Eric Hoffer's True Beliefs," *National Review*, June 18, 1963.

Norman Jacobson correspondence, EHHI 32.23.

Lewis & Clark student newspaper, in EHHI 1.3.

Jeanne Jacobson correspondence, EHHI 150 and 32.21. Box 150 contains notes to her from EH that Mrs. Jacobson returned for the archive.

Chapter Seven

Jeanne Jacobson correspondence, *op. cit.*

Diebold, bank manager, and Khrushchev statements, Charles Markham, ed., *Jobs, Men and Machines: Problems of Automation*. New York: Frederick A. Praeger, 1964.

Daniel Bell, The Coming of the Post-Industrial Society. New York: Basic Books, 1973.

Scalapino incident: Tom Lovell, "American Liberal Intellectuals and the Vietnam War," at: http://www.raleightavern.org/lovell2002.htm.

Ernest Zaugg, "Eric Hoffer's Great Debate on Vietnam," *People*, the California weekly, issue of July 25, 1965.

Polling data: Shachtman, *Decade of Shocks*.

Ascoli: Editorial in *The Reporter*, December 14, 1967, in Lovell, *op. cit.*

Comments on "Negroes," EH notebook #79, Spring 1964. Typescript, EHHI 93.6.

"Quotations and Comments" typescript, in EHHI 45.2.

Lauren Langman, "Dionysius—Child of Tomorrow," *Youth and Society*, vol. 3, #1, September 1971.

Hoffer at Sproul Hall: John Vanek, "Eric Hoffer Speaks Out on Student Politics," *The Daily Californian*, February 17, 1967.

Norman Cousins, in *Saturday Review* correspondence, EHHI 38.2.

James Day interview transcripts, *op. cit.*

Thomas J. Sugrue and John D. Skrentny, "The White Ethnic Strategy," in Bruce J. Schulman and Julian E. Zelizer, eds., *Rightward Bound*. Cambridge: Harvard University Press, 2008.

Tomkins note to editor: Tomkins Papers, Museum of Modern Art, file IIA, 21.

Hoffer, Lili Osborne, and Selden Osborne notes to Tomkins, *op. cit.*

Shawn note, EHHI 36.2.

Gloria Revilla Doyle, A Journey Not Chosen.

Tomkins thank-you. EHHI 122.26.

Georgie Anne Geyer, "He's every man's working man," Chicago *Daily News*, November 14, 1967; Hoffer obituary, May 26, 1983; EHHI 30.1.

John Burroughs speech. *"The John Burroughs World,"* issue of March 7, 1967, reprints Hoffer's note to the dean. EHHI 1.4.

E. C. Rowand correspondence file, EHHI 37.18

O'Flaherty interview with Sevareid, *op. cit.*

Visit to President Johnson. All materials pertaining to Hoffer, including letters from Freeman, Moyers, and Valenti, and Hoffer's notes to and from the president are in the Lyndon B. Johnson Library and Museum's Eric Hoffer file, WHCF—Name File, Box 250.

Eric F. Goldman. *The Tragedy of Lyndon Johnson*. New York: Knopf, 1969.

Chapter Eight

Leonard Earl Johnson, "Remembering KLJ, and Eric Hoffer," blog entry, at:
htttp://leonardearljohnson.blogspot.com/2010_01_01_archive.html.

Cass Canfield to EH, April 23, 1968. EHHI 30.14.

Higgins, EHHI 1.3, and 122.7.

"Savage heart." EHHI 95.2, publicity materials for syndicated column.

EH columns, EHHI 95.

Meeting with Humphrey, "People in the News," AP, October 11, 1967.

Meeting with Walter Heller, LBJ Files, *op. cit.*

Art commission meeting, San Francisco *Examiner*, April 2, 1968; and EHHI, Box 120.

Violence commission hearings. Newspaper reports, e.g., UPI, "Hoffer Walks Out at Violence Hearing," October 24, 1968, and EHHI Boxes 99-119.

Nelson Rockefeller to EH, EHHI 37.13.

Humphrey returns money, EHHI 32.13.

Reagan invitation, 1969. EHHI, 37.4. The president recalled the visit during the award of the Presidential Medal of Freedom, 1983, in EHHI 7.1.

Sevareid eulogized King: Schroth, *op. cit.*

Alinsky, correspondence, EHHI 25.5.

Malcolm Roberts, correspondence and telephone interviews, 2010-11.

Phillips, EHHI 122.13, and Loeb, 122.9.

Warren Burger, EHHI 26.20.

McClelland committee, newspaper reports; Weir.

Edgar Z. Friedenberg, "Only in America," *The New York Review of Books*, May 8, 1969.

Norman Mailer, "The White Negro," *Dissent*, Fall 1957 issue. At: http://www.learntoquestion.com/resources/database/archives/003327.html.

Chapter Nine

J. E. Hoover to EH, February 26, 1970. EHHI 32.7.

1971 diary notes, EHHI 66.6.

Walter J. Hickel: materials from Papers of Walter J. Hickel, Consortium Library, University of Alaska Anchorage.

Malcolm Roberts, correspondence and interview, *op. cit.*

Denis P. Doyle to EH, September 30, 1970. EHHI 28.12.

EH to Mayor Dyke, October 8, 1970. EHHI 28.18.

Joe Flaherty, *New York Times Book Review*, July 25, 1971.

Al Kuettner, EHHI 33.15.

James Koerner, EHHI 33.9, and 122.4.

Cole re Koerner, Stacey Cole to EH, n.d., EHHI 27.15 and 121.9.

Letter, Koerner to EH, Sep. 19, 1971, encloses Fadiman to EH,
September 12, 1971.

Koerner files, EHHI, *ops. cit.*

Henry Nash Carrier, III. EHHI Box 150.

Barney Brown, EHHI Box 153, contains copies of EH letters and
Brown's articles.

Dialogue with Eric Osborne: Eric Osborne telephone interview,
January 23, 2011.

Bishop Cronin story. EH, during Q and A session following a speech in
Anchorage, August 7, 1979. Hickel Papers, *op. cit.*

James Stone to EH, July 11, 1971, EHHI 39.6.

Check to Republican Party, 1972. EHHI 37.7.

EH to Carrier, September 6, 1972, EHHI Box 150, *op. cit.* ·

Hickel re Kahn; Lili Osborne to Hickel; EH to Hickel; and Malcolm
Roberts to EH: Hickel Papers, *op. cit.*

Chapter Ten

Speech notes: EHHI 43.3.

Handwritten diary 1974-75, EHHI 71.12. File 71.13 contains holograph
and typescript.

Ronald Reagan 1976 campaign: Craig Shirley, *Reagan's Revolution.*
Nashville: Nelson Current, 2005. Reagan 1980 campaign: Lou
Cannon, *President Reagan: The Role of a Lifetime.* New York: Simon
& Schuster, 1991.

George Will, "A Young 75-Year-Old," *National Review*, 1977.

Nancy Faber, "Eric Hoffer at 75 Is Still 'Just Shooting My Mouth Off.'"
People, January 16, 1978.

Eric Osborne to EH, n.d., EHHI 36.14.

Margaret Anderson to EH, December 19, 1977, EHHI 25.10.

"Collection of lucid thoughts," 1978 notebook, EHHI 94.14.

Eugene Griessman, "The Weariness of a True Believer," *Atlanta Weekly*, April 26, 1981.

Transcript of Commonwealth North speech and Q and A, Hickel papers, *op. cit.*

Working with Stacey Cole, EHHI 27.15.

Cole to James Koerner, January 1980 and February 21, 1980, EHHI 33.9.

Quotes and comments manuscript, EHHI 45.2.

Cole-Hoffer break, Cole to EH, n.d., EHHI 121.9 and 27.15, ops. cit.

"You don't need to ask me," EH to Baker, *Eric Hoffer, op. cit.*

Elizabeth Lawrence, EHHI 74.5.

1981-82 notebook, EHHI 94.15, *op. cit.*

Tom Bethell, EH obituary, *American Spectator*, August 1983.

Worthington to Kittrell, March 3, 1983, EHHI 33.6.

Epilogue

Funeral: EHHI File 4.8.

Obituaries: Geyer, May 26, 1983; Greenberg, June 1, 1983.

William F. Buckley Jr. to Lili Osborne, May 31, 1983, EHHI 121.7.

Reviews of *Truth Imagined*, EHHI 74.6.

Memorial, 1985. EHHI 7.5.

Tim Madigan, "The True Believer, Revisited," *Philosophy Now*, #34, 2001.

Lili Fabilli: interviews, *op. cit.*

Selected Bibliography

Papers and Archival Materials

The Eric Hoffer Archive at The Hoover Institution.
The Eric Hoffer Archive at The San Francisco Public Library.
Lyndon B. Johnson Presidential Library, Eric Hoffer File.
Calvin Tomkins Papers at the Museum of Modern Art, Eric Hoffer files.
Papers of Walter J. Hickel, Alaska State University, Anchorage.

Books

Baker, James T. *Eric Hoffer*. Boston: Twayne Publishers, 1982.
Batty, Paul Wesley. "Eric Hoffer's Theory of Mass Persuasion,"
    doctoral thesis submitted to University of Illinois, Urbana, 1970.
Doyle, Gloria Revilla. *A Journey Not Chosen*. Chevy Chase: Summerfield
    Press, 2004.
Hoffer, Eric. *Truth Imagined*. New York: Harper & Row, 1983.
– *Between the Devil and the Dragon*. New York: Harper & Row, 1982.
– *Before the Sabbath*. New York: Harper & Row, 1979.
– *In Our Time*. New York: Harper & Row, 1976.
– *Reflections on the Human Condition*. New York: Harper & Row, 1973.
– *First Things, Last Things*. New York: Harper & Row, 1971
– *Working and Thinking on the Waterfront*. New York: Harper & Row,
    1969.
– *The Temper of Our Time*. New York: Harper & Row, 1967.
– *The Ordeal of Change*. New York: Harper & Row, 1963.
– *The Passionate State of Mind*. New York: Harper & Row, 1955.
– *The True Believer*. New York: Harper & Brothers, 1951.
Hofstadter, Richard. *Anti-Intellectualism in American Life*. New York:
    Knopf, 1963.

Koerner, James D. *Hoffer's America*. LaSalle, Illinois: Open Court Publishing Company, 1973.

Montaigne, Michel de. *The Complete Essays*. Translated and annotated by M. A. Screech. New York: Penguin Books, 1987.

Schroth, Raymond A. *The American Journey of Eric Sevareid*. Royalton, Vermont: Steerforth Press, 1993.

Sevareid, Eric. *Not So Wild A Dream*. New York: Knopf, 1947.

Shachtman, Tom. *Decade of Shocks, 1963-1974*. Simon & Schuster, 1983.

Tomkins, Calvin. *Eric Hoffer: An American Odyssey*. New York: E. P. Dutton, 1967.

Weir, Stan. *Singlejack Solidarity*. Minneapolis: University of Minnesota Press, 2004.

Wellman, David. *The Union Makes Us Strong*. Cambridge, U.K.: Cambridge University Press, 1995.

Articles

Bethell, Tom. "The Longshoreman Philosopher," *The Hoover Digest*, 2003, No. 1.

– Obituary for Eric Hoffer, *American Spectator*, August 1983.

Burdick, Eugene. "Epigrammatist on the Waterfront," *The Reporter*, February 21, 1957.

Donovan, Richard. "Migrant with a Message," *The Reporter*, October 30, 1951.

Fincher, Jack. "San Francisco's Longshore Philosopher," *West* (*Los Angeles Times* magazine), June 11, 1967.

Faber, Nancy. "Eric Hoffer at 75 Is Still 'Just Shooting My Mouth Off.'" *People*, January 16, 1978.

Friedenberg, Edgar Z. "Only in America," *The New York Review of Books*, May 8, 1969.

Geyer, Georgie Anne, "He's every man's working man," Chicago *Daily News*, November 14, 1967.

Gordon, Mitchell. "Eric Hoffer, Aphorist From the Bronx," *Wall Street Journal*, September 13, 1967.

Griessman, Eugene. "The Weariness of a True Believer," *Atlanta Weekly*, April 26, 1981.

Pearce, Dick. "Longshoreman Writes Book About Philosophy," *San Francisco Examiner*, February 26, 1951.

Tomkins, Calvin. "Profiles: The Creative Situation." *The New Yorker*, January 7, 1967.

Will, George. "A Young 75-Year-Old," *National Review*, 1977.

Wills, Gary. "Eric Hoffer's True Beliefs," *National Review*, June 18, 1963.

Zaugg, Ernest. "Eric Hoffer's Great Debate on Vietnam," *People*, the California weekly, July 25, 1965.

Acknowledgements

My gratitude to the late Lili Fabilli Osborne, with whom I worked on this book prior to her death in the summer of 2010, goes well beyond my dedication of the book to her. I also thank Eric Osborne for his cooperation and assistance, as well as lawyer John McKay. My thanks, as well, to Malcolm Roberts and Denis Doyle for sharing their memories of Eric Hoffer with me, and for their enthusiasm for this biographical project.

At the archives of the Hoover Institution at Stanford University, I would like to thank Carol Leadenham, David Jacobs, and the entire staff, who were unfailingly helpful in my research among the Hoffer archives, as well as upholding the highest standards of professionalism in their care of Hoffer's papers. I also thank Andrea Grimes of the San Francisco Public Library for her assistance with Hoffer's early notebooks, stored in that institution.

At Hopewell Publications, Christopher Klim, the novelist who has overseen the publisher's decade-long drive to once more bring Hoffer's works to the public, was a most perceptive editor.

I should also like to thank relatives and friends who read parts or all of the manuscript and offered cogent suggestions, starting with my wife, Harriet Shelare, my cousin, Eugene Mills, and friends David Burke, Richard Hayes, Bruce McEver, Don Oresman, Herbert Parmet, and Walter Woodward. My gratitude, too, to my fellow directors of The Writers Room in New York, and to publisher Janet Manko of *The Lakeville Journal*, for their continued encouragement on this project.

All of their efforts notwithstanding, any errors remaining in the manuscript are mine.

– Tom Shachtman
Salisbury, Connecticut, June 2011

About the Author

Tom Shachtman is the author of two dozen books, the co-author of an additional ten, and the writer of documentaries broadcast on ABC, CBS, NBC, and PBS. His books about world history include *The Day America Crashed, The Phony War 1939-1940,* and *Decade of Shocks 1963-1974*. His books about American society include *Rumspringa, The Inarticulate Society, Skyscraper Dreams,* and *Around the Block*. Among other awards, he won the 2010 American Institute of Physics science writing prize for his script of the two-hour NOVA documentary based on his book, *Absolute Zero and the Conquest of Cold*.

RUMSPRINGA: TO BE OR NOT TO BE AMISH

"Shachtman is like a maestro, masterfully conducting an orchestra of history, anthropology, psychology, sociology, and journalism together in a harmonious and evocative symphony of all things Amish."
— *Christian Science Monitor*

AROUND THE BLOCK

"To answer such questions as whether small businesses create jobs and how they survive the competition with big business, Shachtman spent a year exploring the assorted enterprises in a square block of Manhattan's Chelsea. The book is crowded with real people speaking candidly about plans and problems as varied as their occupations, which range from dog grooming to wholesale plumbing supplies. A grand idea, splendidly executed."
— *The New Yorker*

ABSOLUTE ZERO AND THE CONQUEST OF COLD

"Analyzes the social impact of the chill factor, explains the science of cold and tells the curious tales behind inventions like the thermometer, the fridge and the thermos flask ... . Excellent use of analogies ... [an] astonishing observation ... a fascinating finale ... . Recounts the history of cold with passion and clarity."
— *The New York Times Book Review*

Lightning Source UK Ltd.
Milton Keynes UK
UKOW02f1511200317
297052UK00002B/574/P